telling writing

HAYDEN ENGLISH LANGUAGE SERIES

Robert W. Boynton — Consulting Editor

AN INTRODUCTION TO MODERN ENGLISH GRAMMAR
J. Malmstrom

LANGUAGE IN SOCIETY
J. Malmstrom

THE DICTIONARY AND THE LANGUAGE
R. Lodwig and E. Barrett

WRITING TO BE READ
K. Macrorie

TELLING WRITING
K. Macrorie

ENGLISH I and II: A Contemporary Approach
R. W. Boynton, R. Johnson, and R. Reeves

telling writing

KEN MACRORIE

Professor of English
Western Michigan University

HAYDEN BOOK COMPANY, INC.
Rochelle Park, New Jersey

The author would like to thank the proprietors for permission to quote from copyrighted works, as follows:

RAY BRADBURY: from "Seeds of Three Stories," written for *On Writing, By Writers,* William W. West, Editor; copyright 1966 by Ginn and Company. Reprinted by permission of the publisher.

SAMUEL BUTLER: from *The Complete Works of Samuel Butler* and *The Notebooks of Samuel Butler,* published by Jonathan Cape Ltd. Reprinted by permission of the Executors of the Samuel Butler Estate.

TRUMAN CAPOTE: from *Writers at Work, The Paris Review Interviews,* edited by Malcolm Cowley. Copyright © 1957, 1958, by The Paris Review, Inc. Reprinted by permission of The Viking Press, Inc.

STUART CHASE: from "Writing Nonfiction," writen for *On Writing, By Writers,* William W. West, Editor; copyright 1966 by Ginn and Company. Reprinted by permission of the publisher.

JOHN CIARDI: from "Work Habits of Writers," written for *On Writing, By Writers,* William W. West, Editor; copyright 1966 by Ginn and Company. Reprinted by permission of the publisher.

SIDNEY COX: from *Indirections for Those Who Want to Write.* Reprinted with permission of the publisher. Published by Alfred A. Knopf, Inc. Copyright © 1947 by Alfred A. Knopf, Inc.

T. S. ELIOT: from *Writers at Work, The Paris Review Interviews,* Second Series, Copyright © 1963 by The Paris Review, Inc. All rights reserved. Reprinted by permission of The Viking Press, Inc.

PAUL GOODMAN: from *Growing Up Absurd.* Reprinted by permission of the publisher. Copyright © 1956, 1957, 1958, 1959, 1960 by Paul Goodman. Published by Random House, Inc.

DONALD HALL: from "A Clear and Simple Style," © 1967 by The New York Times Company. Reprinted by permission.

MICHIHIKO HACHIYA: from *Hiroshima Diary,* published by the University of North Carolina Press, reprinted by permission of The University of North Carolina Press.

JAMES D. HART: from *Oxford Companion to American Literature,* Fourth Edition. Reprinted by permission of the publisher. Copyright 1965 by Oxford University Press.

ERNEST HEMINGWAY: from *Writers at Work, The Paris Review Interviews,* Second Series, Copyright © 1963 by The Paris Review, Inc. All rights reserved. Reprinted by permission of The Viking Press, Inc.

WALTER LIPPMANN: from *Public Opinion,* published by The Macmillan Company, copyright 1922 by Walter Lippmann. Reprinted by permission of The Macmillan Company.

ROBERT LIPSYTE: "Mets Beat Giants 8–6, on Swoboda's Homer in 9th," © 1966 by The New York Times Company. Reprinted by permission.

12 13 14 15 16 17 18   PRINTING

75 76 77 78   YEAR

preface

In boldface type in this book, along with the usual examples of bad student writing, appear dozens and dozens of striking, delightful, moving pieces of writing.

They were written in classes using the writing program presented here.

Incredible. How could they have been written in the courses where those deadly things called themes come from, and those affected sentimental stories that end up in the student literary magazine no one reads?

The answer is that a New English movement has begun. It is like the New Math in that it allows students to use their own powers, to make discoveries, to take alternative paths. It does not suggest that the world can best be examined by a set of rules. It does not utilize the Errors Approach. It constantly messes around in reality, and looks for strategies and tactics that work.

This movement in the New English gained part of its impetus from the revolution in language study; not from the brilliant analysis of grammar, but from the study of dialects—national, regional, and individual. Instead of fearing diversity in language, teachers began to respect it. For several decades linguists have been saying that at the age of six a child has mastered the major part of the grammar of his native language, and that he often speaks rhythmically and metaphorically. Now, in both writing and literature classes, teachers are freeing the student to use his natural powers of language and perception. They are giving up the notion that the student in the classroom should be allowed to use only a dehydrated academic tongue.

In the last five years the New English has been taking shape. A committee headed by Herbert J. Muller produced *The Uses of English* for the Modern Language Association, the National Association for the Teaching of English (United Kingdom), and the

National Council of Teachers of English. It brought together old questions and new ideas. At the same time, and since then, a number of teachers and writers in different parts of the world have been working out theories and strategies that all move in the same direction: for example, in Britain, David Holbrook and A. B. Clegg; in the United States, Jerome Bruner, Benjamin DeMott, Peter Elbow, John Holt, and Jonathan Kozol.

Telling Writing presents a New English writing program essentially the same as that in the author's *Writing To Be Read,* a text whose examples of writing were contributed mainly by high-school students. The program gives the student first, freedom, to find his voice and let his subjects find him; and second, discipline, to learn more professional craft to supplement his already considerable language skills.

And for both teacher and student, a constant reaching for truth, in writing and commenting on that writing. This is a hard requirement, for no one speaks truth consistently. A teacher must not insist that his students always write truths. As a human being he himself slips away from it frequently, and then his demand is hypocritical.

The means for setting loose truths in the classrooms are simple and undevious, but not naive. They escape the trap that so many non directive group leaders fall into—insisting that their clients or students bare their souls in frank confession and yet holding back most of the feelings they have as leaders about those they are leading. The New English teacher says to his students, "I want you to *try* for truths in writing and discussion. No one, however well intentioned, can succeed in telling truths all the time. I won't. But I will try, and I want you to try also."

In the New English the teacher does not correct papers but reads them, along with other members of the class. He urges students to rewrite those papers worth the effort and to polish those already successful. The habits of the professional writer are put into action.

Nothing is done to paralyze the natural urges of a writer to discover, to invent, to play with words. And nothing to let him avoid the public nature of writing. His words need to score with him and his peers. Therefore in this book the writing of beginners is presented authentically, with its individualities, its colloquial strengths, its convictions, its profanity, and sometimes its idiosyncratic grammar. In America today youth are confronting their elders in a new way. It is no time for falsity and pussy-footing.

viii

The commitment of the teacher to a New English is disturbing because it asks him to be honest about his requirements. I have tried for that honesty in this book. It contains no brilliant reports or objective scholarly papers by students because in its five years of operation the program has not yet produced exciting papers of these types. It has produced searching personal critical papers and deep and reflective narratives of experience. This is a good augury, for universities and colleges and schools need to move toward the personal and away from the dead scholarly paper and Ph.D. thesis. The subjective and the objective powers in all of us need to be faced and struggled with.

This text gives enough assignments to provide the student with a one-year course in writing. Teachers conducting one-semester courses are advised to omit some chapters and assignments and use them only as aids for students who need special help at a given moment. When the teacher springs students loose with free writing, he will be astonished by their command of language, but not all students will respond in the same way. For example, one student may write clearly and pointedly but in dull, child-like style. In order to stretch his vocabulary, he can be referred to the chapter on paraphrasing, which need not be assigned to the whole class.

The college students of this country already use language richly. It is time to hear their voices in the classroom. And their wit. Asked to practice word play, Julie Teitelbaum said, "I don't know what apathy means, and I don't care."

My thanks to my editors, S. William Cook, Jr. and Robert Boynton, who have encouraged me to write an untimid textbook and discouraged me from stuffing it with corn shucks.

K.M.

contents

telling writing

chapter 1
the
poison
fish

ONE DAY a college student stopped a professor in the hall and said, "I have this terrible instructor who says I can't write. Therefore I shouldn't teach English. He really grinds me. In another class I've been reading James Joyce, so I wrote this little comment on the instructor in Joyce's style. Do you think I should submit it to *The Review?*"

The professor looked at the lines she had written about her instructor:

> . . . the stridents in his glass lisdyke him immersely. Day each that we tumble into the glass he sez to mee, "Eets too badly that you someday fright preach Engfish."

and he knew the girl had found a name for the phony, pretentious language of the schools—Engfish.

Most English teachers have been trained to correct students' writing, not to read it; so they put down those bloody correction marks in the margins. When the students see them, they think they mean the teacher doesn't care what students write, only how they punctuate and spell. So they give him Engfish. He calls the assignments by their traditional name—*themes.* The students know theme writers seldom put down anything that counts for them. No one outside school ever writes anything called *themes.* Apparently they are teacher's exercises, not really a kind of communication. On the first assignment in a college class a student begins his theme like this:

> I went downtown today for the first time. When I got there I was completely astonished by the hustle and the bustle that was going on. My first impression of the downtown area was quite impressive.

Beautiful Engfish. The writer said not simply that he was astonished, but completely astonished, as if the word *astonished* had no force of its own. The student reported (*pretended* would be a truer word) to have observed hustle and bustle, and then explained in true Engfish that the hustle and bustle was going on. He managed to work in the academic word *area,* and finished by saying the impression was impressive.

> *But wise men pierce this rotten diction*
> *and fasten words again to visible things.*
> RALPH WALDO EMERSON

The teacher does not want Engfish, but gets it. Discouraged, he often tries a different tack. Asks the boys to write about sports, maybe. Then they will drop Engfish because they care about what they are saying. One boy starts his theme like this:

> The co-captains of the respective teams are going out to the middle of the field for the toss of the coin.

Engfish again. Only two teams play in a football game and there could be no reason in that sentence for using the word *respective.* But it was the sort of word the boy thought Engfish teachers wanted.

With all that fish smell permeating the room, the teacher feels queasy. He tries other ways of getting rid of Engfish. He asks the students to keep a personal journal. Maybe if they talk about themselves they will find their natural voices. The next day one of the girls turns in a journal containing this entry:

> It is hard to realize just how much you miss someone until you are away from this person. It seems that the time spent away from this person is wasted. You seem to wait and wait till you can see this person again. Then when the time comes, it passes far too quickly.

Another kind of Engfish—not fancy, academic language, but simple everyday words that say nothing because they keep all the girl's experience private. Anyone else reading that entry would forget it instantly because neither the writer nor the person written about come alive. A year later the sentence would mean almost nothing even to the writer.

A teacher becomes fed up with writing like that. He doesn't see that most of the signals in the school are telling students to write Engfish. Even the textbook begins with an Engfish sentence, and surely it should be a model of writing for students. Its first sentence is:

> If you are a student who desires assistance in order to write effectively and fluently, then this textbook is written for you.

Pure Engfish undefiled, a tongue never spoken outside the walls. No student would stop another on campus and say, "I desire assistance in locating Sangren Hall," or "Will you show me the most effective way to the bus stop?" Naturally the student thinks the textbook is a model of the language the teacher wants, so she gives that language to him.

Students thoroughly trained in Engfish are hard put to find their natural voices in the classroom. They have left them out in the hall. Much earlier in life, though, they occasionally have written sharply and truly, as this third-grader did:

> I can play huhawayun music on my gettar. It is like when grandma took a sick spell. Now she waz shut up tight as a jar with a lid on. She gave a scream. When she gave that scream it was high. But it got lower and lower. Huhwayun music sounds something like when she was getting lower.

From that passage a reader learns what "huhwayun" music sounds like.

> *Man's maturity: to have regained the seriousness that he had as a child at play.*
>
> FRIEDRICH NIETZSCHE

The difference between the college students' writing and the third-grade child's is simple: One is dead, the other alive. In the child's comments the words speak to each other—*high* speaks to *lower*. And the ideas and things speak to each other—the Hawaiian guitar is like grandmother, and when she was sick she was like a jar with a lid on. The whole passage speaks to the reader. It is not pretentious. It is not phony. It is not private. In the Engfish paragraphs of the student themes the words almost never speak to each other, and when they do, they say only "Blah."

College students were once third-graders and occasionally wrote like that. Where did they lose that skill? Why?

They spent too many hours in school mastering Engfish and reading cues from teacher and textbook that suggested it is the official language of the school. In it the student cannot express truths that count for him. He learns a language that prevents him from working toward truths, and then he tells lies.

In this empty circle teacher and student wander around boring each other. But there is a way out.

He told the truth in order to see.

GENE BARO

chapter 2
writing freely

TELLING TRUTHS

ALL GOOD writers speak in honest voices and tell the truth. For example, here is Eudora Welty in her novel *Delta Wedding* writing about India, a girl of nine, watching her Uncle George make up with his wife after a quarrel:

> Just now they kissed, with India coming up close on her toes to see if she could tell yet what there was about a kiss.

Asked what makes students write badly, Eudora Welty once said:

> The trouble with bad student writing is the trouble with all bad writing. It is not serious, and it does not tell the truth.

This is the first requirement for good writing: truth; not *the* truth (whoever knows surely what that is?), but some kind of truth—a connection between the things written about, the words used in the writing, and the author's real experience in the world he knows well—whether in fact or dream or imagination.

Part of growing up is learning to tell lies, big and little, sophisticated and crude, conscious and unconscious. The good writer differs from the bad one in that he constantly tries to shake the habit. He holds himself to the highest standard of truth telling. Often he

5

emulates children, who tell the truth so easily, partly because they do not sense how truth will shock their elders.

A seventh-grade boy once wrote:

> **I'd like to be a car. You get to go all over and get to go through mud puddles without getting yelled at . . . that's what I'd like to be.**

The style of this passage is not distinguished. *Get* is here not a key word and yet it is employed three times. The writer switches confusingly from *I* to *you*. The language of the passage is not exciting. No memorable pictures are projected. Yet the statement strikes with force because the boy speaks truly: his shoes and the tires of the car do become muddy. He gets yelled at by his parents and the car does not. The comparison surprises. Its candor draws a smile from the reader.

> *I never think I have hit it hard unless it rebounds.*
>
> SAMUEL JOHNSON

Any person trying to write honestly and accurately soon finds he has already learned a hundred ways of writing falsely. As a child he spoke and wrote honestly most of the time, but when he reaches fifteen, honesty and truth come harder. The pressures on his ego are greater. He reaches for impressive language; often it is pretentious and phony. He imitates the style of adults, who are often bad writers themselves. They ask questions. So he asks questions in his writing: "Did you ever think what might have happened to South Africa if the Boer War had not been fought?" A false question. The writer knows most—if not all—of his readers have not thought of this possibility. However well meant—a false question. In class this person is anxious to impress the teacher, so he begins his paper by saying:

> **The automobile is a mechanism fascinating to everyone in all its diverse manifestations and in every conceivable kind of situation or circumstance.**

His first remark is simply untrue. Cars do not fascinate everyone.

In this paper the writer has placed his vocabulary on exhibit (*mechanism, diverse, manifestations, conceivable, situation, circumstance*) rather than put it to work. An honest writer makes every word pull its weight. In this writer's opening sentence, the words *kind of* are not working at all. They could be dropped with no loss. What does he mean by "all the diverse manifestations" of a car? Cars don't occur in manifestations but in models. If the cars he is referring to are custom-made and not strictly speaking "models," then he should say he is writing about hybrid cars. At the opening of his paper, his reader has no inkling that he is talking about home-made cars. And nothing could be more untrue than the thought conveyed by the last phrase—that everyone finds cars fascinating "in every conceivable kind of situation or circumstance." When the valves need regrinding at 17,000 miles at a cost of $125.00, even the car lover finds his loved one repulsive.

Compare this writer's pretentious and untrue statement about cars with this account:

Thundering down a Northern Michigan highway at night I am separated from the rest of the world. The windows of the car are all rolled down and the wind makes a deep rumbling as the car rises and falls with the dips in the pavement. The white center lines come out of the darkness ahead into the beams of the headlights only to disappear again under the front edge of the hood. The lights also pick up trees, fenceposts, and an occasional deer or raccoon standing by the roadside, but like the white lines they come into view only for a few seconds and then are lost in the blackness behind me. The only signs I have that any world exists outside the range of the headlights are the continuous cheerping and buzzing of the crickets and the smells from farms and sulphur pits I pass. But the rushing wind soon clears out these odors, leaving me by myself again to listen to the quickly passing crickets I will never see. The faint green lights and the red bar on the dashboard tell me I'm plunging ahead at 90 m.p.h.; I put more pressure on the pedal under my foot; the bar moves up to 100 . . . 110. The lines flash by faster and the roar of the wind drowns out the noise of the crickets and the night. I am flying through. I can feel the vibrations of the road through the steering wheel. I turn the wheel slightly for the gradual curve ahead and then back again for the long straightaway. I press the pedal to the floor and at the same time reach down to touch the buttons on my left that will roll up the windows for more speed; the bar reads 115 . . . 120, buried. With the windows up, the only sound is the high-pitched moan from the engine as it labors to keep the rest of the machine hurtling blindly ahead like a runaway express

train. Only I have the power to control it. I flick on the
brights to advance my scope of vision and the white lines
come out of the black further up ahead, yet because of the
speed, they're out of sight even faster than before. I am
detached from the rest of the world as it blurs past. I am
alone.

HENRY HALL JAMES

This boy may have been driving at an immorally high speed—even
for a relatively uninhabited region—but he was writing morally,
because he was staying true to the feel of his experience. Writing this
way requires a quick jump in the car and a zooming away before one
remembers all the driving habits he has picked up watching bad
older drivers. Try writing for truth.

> *Never say that you feel a thing unless*
> *you feel it distinctly; and if you do not*
> *feel it distinctly, say at once that you do*
> *not as yet quite know your own mind.*

SAMUEL BUTLER

WRITING FREELY WITHOUT FOCUS

WRITING ONE: Write for ten minutes as fast as you can, never
stopping to ponder a thought. Put down whatever comes to your
mind. If nothing comes, write, "Nothing comes to my mind" until you
get started. Or look in front of you or out the window and begin
describing whatever you see. Let yourself wander to any subject,
feeling, or idea, but keep writing. When ten minutes is up, you
should have filled a large notebook-sized page. Remember you are
hitting practice shots. If what you write is bad or dull, no one will
object.

Save all the writing which you produce while reading this book.
Keep it in a manila filing folder so you can go back to it to revise
it or look for paragraphs or pages that may be combined or expanded
into stronger work. As time passes, you will see your words differently
and sometimes learn from them without doing further work.

Here's what one student wrote in ten minutes:

Electrical storm, the greatest show on earth and all for
free. It looks like arc welding, the helium arc on a torch.
Long day cooped up in dark, dirty factory welding gas
tanks, tanks for trucks, buses, tractors. Twenty-seven in
every hour day after day. Hot sparks, blinding flashes. Like

the time a tank had been cleaned with gasoline and the fumes not removed. Just one impression was the result, not heat or light or sound—all of them rolled into one impact when the torch set off the fumes. No real damage, just a lot of smoke and twisted metal. There was an electrical storm the night before I was to quit the job. It's strange how much more difficult it was to get up that morning dreading every hour of work. An interesting couple kissing with real passion in front of 23 people in a small room off the Union lounge. At any rate the electrical storm had knocked out the transformer and there wasn't any work that day. It didn't bother me, but what of the regular workers who the loss of a day's pay could mean the missing of a rent or car payment? Terror is a rare thing in American life, that is the fear of actual physical harm, but that last day at work I saw real fear in someone. All the workers were standing in the yard waiting to see if they were going to work that day and a truck driver brought in a load of steel. He thought we were on strike, and industrial workers are not well-known for the kindness they meet strike breakers with. And the driver had a lot to lose—his truck and perhaps a few teeth.

No Engfish in that writing. No phoniness or pretension. Apparently the writer put down words so fast he used his own natural language without thinking of his expression. He got a lot said in a short space, and at times wrote skillfully, as when he rendered exactly the effect of the explosion:

Just one impression was the result, not heat or light or sound—all of them rolled into one impact when the torch set off the fumes.

Like any human being who wants to communicate, he recorded facts that speak: a couple kissing in front of 23 people, a day without work might mean a worker missed a rent or car payment. Telling facts as true as those led him to a strong and surprising generalization: "Terror is a rare thing in American life."

But overall, the paper is a jerky piece of writing. The writer frequently changes subject without warning and hints that he realizes he's doing this by beginning one sentence with the phrase: "At any rate." He begins the paper talking about an unidentified storm, is reminded of welding, diverted by a couple kissing nearby, jogged by the memory of a storm that affected his work in a factory, and led to discuss the attitudes of industrial workers toward strike-breaking. He makes connections between some of these subjects and fails to do so with others. Apparently he does not develop the description of the storm that he begins with. He does not present a full picture of the kissing couple or the reaction or lack of reaction from the 23 people sitting nearby.

It is not a fully realized bit of writing, but it is honest and at moments strikes its own sparks and sounds its small explosions. The student who dashed off this paper can write, no doubt about that. And he got rid of his Engfish on the first try. He is on his way.

Another student in the same class turned in this paper for his first free writing:

> **Everyone wants to feel useful to someone, anyone. They want to feel they are doing something to help, even in a minor way. If you don't feel useful you become depressed. You feel without. No friends, nothing to look forward to. There seems a loss of ambition and concentration. The world seems against, you find unimportant matters to brood over.**
>
> **Whenever everything seems at its worst, you find a person who is worse off than you. Guilt runs through every pore, your petty worries become unimportant to you. The world seems much happier now.**

The writer of that passages was trying for Great Thoughts instead of for truth. His language comes out flabby and his great thoughts obvious and tired, with none of the surprise of the statement "Terror is a rare thing in American life." He doesn't really care what his words say, or he never would have written

> **Whenever everything seems at its worst, you find a person who is worse off than you.**

The fact is that when everything seems at its worst for some of us, we sometimes find a person better off than we are and we feel even worse.

In contrast, here's another person feeling badly about the world seeming against her, only she's trying to be true—to the world out there—the facts of it, to what someone actually said to her, and to her own feelings, not to what she thinks the teacher wants.

> **Everyone around here is having an awful time getting along with me. I'm being positively intolerable. Mom is**

trying really hard not to say anything in the wrong tone of voice, so that I feel kind of—what's that old-fashioned word, *ashamed* of myself. One day I'm in a great mood, and you could yell at me all you wanted without making me mad or hurt. The next day (or the next hour for that matter) you could say "Good morning," then yawn, and I'd burst into tears. I suppose that is not awfully abnormal (at least that's what Mom says—in her psychological tone, "It's just a phase. You'll grow out of it.") By the way, that makes me mad, too. I don't like to have my life summed up in a series of phases. It seems like she's saying, "You can't help acting like an idiot. It comes natural at this age. But don't worry, you'll outgrow it. It'll pass."

A good part of the time a person is writing, he must sense his reader out there. In a way he becomes his own reader while he writes. He talks to a reader and hears that talk himself. When you acquire that knack, readers will come along with you.

Behind that terrible piece of Engfish beginning "Everyone wants to feel useful to someone" may lie some good stories. But the writer never gave the reader a *Once*. He never began to describe the day on which he found a person worse off than him, much less showed the reader that person. The girl who said, "Everyone around here is having an awful time getting along with me," didn't get down to a *Once* either except when she quoted what Mom must have said once, or—more accurately—many times. If she had, she probably would have produced a long valuable story. The writer who thinks of a *Once* is almost sure to get going and say something that counts for him and his reader.

A professor received these paragraphs from identical twin girls in his class.

1

I have not had a bad day like that one for a long time. I guess this Christmas season was just too much. I feel like I have evolved from a cocoon now. I can see the light again. Things seem so funny when you see them, and it is like trying to look through cardboard. You are missing something.

2

The first day we got in the wrong math section. Wrong room—300 instead of 309. Then Tuesday we got stuck in the snow in the driveway, and we missed the math class.

Got there in time to say good-bye to the instructor. See you Thursday.

The first girl never got down to revealing the day, only the feelings she had as a result of it. Her metaphor about trying to look through cardboard is good, but the day is nothing at all because she refused to *once* it even once. The second girl let the reader know what happened, once, twice, and three times, and her paragraph swings a little.

When you write freely whatever comes into your mind, remember that memory or thought is now coming to you as a *once* and it probably is based on many *onces* you need to put down for yourself and your reader.

WRITING TWO: Write three or more of these absolutely free writings. Choose times when no one will disturb you, before breakfast or late at night perhaps. Go beyond ten minutes if the river keeps flowing. But don't expect anything. You're just warming up. Maybe none of your ten-minute writings will produce an interesting sentence. Don't worry. Write. And don't think about punctuation or grammar or style. Put down one word as a sentence if you wish. Maybe your writing will be completely uninteresting to others. As long as you are trying to write honestly and you are writing fast and steadily to fill up a page or two without stopping, you are practicing.

WRITING FREELY WITH FOCUS

Free, or "shotgun" writing (as teacher John Bennett at Central High School, Kalamazoo, Michigan calls it) involves no pressure. If the writer goofs he has not failed, but simply filled a page that can be thrown away.

WRITING THREE: Now try free writing with more purpose. Stay on one subject for fifteen or twenty minutes as the writer did when she said that everyone thought she was being positively intolerable. But if you find that subject takes your mind off to another related subject, let yourself go to that. The one necessity in such shotgunning is that you keep writing freely and quickly.

> *Thought is an infection. In the case of certain thoughts it becomes an epidemic.*
>
> WALLACE STEVENS

Here is a focused free writing:

> I was walking down the hill to the valley. Then all of a sudden, the girl in front of me took a flip. Ha! Ha! If I didn't know better, I would have thought that she was on the gymnastic team. I took no more than two steps. Wham! There I lay. Ha! Ha!
>
> Reminds me of a time back home when my friends and I went to Garbage Hill. A great place to go tobogganing. It was our first time there and we didn't know what the hill was like. Dark out, the sky was clear, and the night cold. At the bottom and about 150 feet out were the woods. We couldn't understand why people avoided them.
>
> We started at the top of the hill, an almost straight drop. I didn't think that we would be able to make it. Have you ever been on a vibrating machine? What a way to lose weight, or a few other things. Hit a mound toward the bottom of the hill. The toboggan flew through the air, along with a couple of my friends. There were just two of us left. We landed and shot. Everything became blurry. The woods came up fast. Whizzing past trees. Splash! There we sat, up to our heads in water.

This writing is so honest it reveals the writer twice making a fool of himself. He puts the reader there by *once-ing* both incidents.

Not every strong communication employs the secret of once. If a man is faithful to his feelings and true to the world he has experienced or imagined, he sometimes can write generalizations that carry the punch of particular facts, as did this student in a free writing:

> When I was a kid I was fat. It's no fun to be fat. I used to try to be jolly, but that's hard to do when you don't have a damn thing to be jolly about. How can you laugh after you spill your lunch tray all over the cafeteria floor? Or, even worse, score the winning point in a tense intramural game at the wrong basket. I couldn't run fast, which left out sports, and wasn't jolly enough to raise myself in the social strata, so I became—I guess it was inevitable—a nothing.
>
> But really, it's kind of fun to be nothing. You sit around with your nothing friends and laugh at the cool kids as they try to keep up their image. I didn't have to try, which relieved a lot of pressure, and was content in my nothing

world, a never-never land between social life and death. It's
easier my way, since I can think about other things that
are important to a kid—like grades. Every little kid has to
get good grades if he's a nothing, since there's little else
to do.

This peace was short-lived, because I started to emerge
from my ugly duckling shell, and the cool ones recognized
that I had potential. So I became one of the cool kids being
laughed at by the nothings. But at least now they applaud
when I spill my lunch tray all over the cafeteria floor—the
applause makes it cool.

When you write shotgun, don't fool yourself into believing that the
little papers printed here were written by persons trying to sound
impressive. They were writing as fast they could for truth, and these
papers represent only the moments when they hit the target. Often
they missed. When you sit down to write freely you must write as fast as
you can. You're being asked to move far away from Engfish and all that
fearful nervous act of trying to say what the teacher said or what he
wants you to say. Speak for yourself here. If what you say is too
personal or confessional, don't turn it in to the instructor, or ask him
to keep your name secret.

Consider this free writing.

The black row shifted again. Not all together like an
"about face," but one after another, in a chain reaction.
Without raising his hand, one black boy addressed the
white girl, "Listen baby, you just don't know what happened. We know. It wasn't no blind pig that set off them
riots." Chorus—"Yeah, we know."

The girl's fat face had two almost completely round red
blotches on it, but she continued, "Well, if you all know,
then why don't you tell us—tell me?"

He slouched down in his chair, half closed his eyes and
flicked his hanging wrist. "You don't wanna know. That's
all."

This paper reports an uncomfortable truth. It's not pleasant to
think that some black and white persons feel such hostility toward
each other, but the writer puts down her truth. It is more apt to move
men to action than Engfishy pleas for kindness and love.

> *There must be no gap between expression and meaning, between real and declared aims . . . It means not saying or thinking, "I didn't* mean *to hurt your feelings," when there really existed a desire to hurt. It means not saying "luncheon" or "home" for the purpose of appearing upper-class or well-educated. It means not using the passive mood to contribute to no one in particular opinions that one is unwilling to call one's own.*
>
> DONALD HALL

Telling our truths is hard. We all slip easily into deception—both of ourselves and others. But a continuing effort to tell truth when writing can become an exciting habit, and often one truth breeds another. On both the lowest and highest plane, try to be honest. For example, one girl wrote,

> **I just wish the city would plow the sidewalks. They do where I—well, where my folks live . . .**

She remembered she no longer lived at home but in an apartment and couldn't validly say the city plowed the snow at her place. The point she made is small and perhaps trivial, but the habit she was developing was large and valuable. If she had occasion to rewrite the account in which those sentences occurred, she would restate the fact and not call attention to the correction:

> I just wish the city would plow the sidewalks outside our apartment. They do where my folks live.

In the next focused free writing, the effort to tell truth paid off more significantly.

> **In a few minutes Mom and Dad are going out to eat. She's got on a long-sleeved yellow dress, black fish-net nylons and black heels. When she doesn't notice, Dad looks at her. Then he rests his head on the back of the red chair and closes his eyes.**
>
> **Last night Bob brought me home at twelve o'clock. We had been wrestling and playing tag on the grass in back of Sangren. We were still laughing when he let me out of the**

car. I pinched his buns and then he messed up my hair. We gave each other a noisy kiss under our five-watt porch light, and he left.

Mom and Dad were still up. I was relieved because I thought we might have wakened them. I started to go upstairs when Dad asked me to wait. I put my books down and sat at the desk. Mom's face was tight and her freckles were little red spots. Dad kept puffing on his pipe. He began. "Your mother and I have decided to get a divorce. But even though I'm leaving, remember you're still my daughter and you always will be."

Then he started to cry. Mom and I were crying too. I ran over and put my arms around him. His tears felt hot on my neck. Then he said, "Go to your mother, she feels bad, too."

He left tonight—to his little apartment on Copper Street. Mom helped him move, and she cried when she saw it. The bedroom is lavender with a purple bedspread. The furniture looks like Antique Barn. A big crack runs up and down the door. When he left, he took a lamp, four glasses, and an ash tray.

> . . . what is always provocative in a work of art: roughness of surface. While . . . [these writings] pass under our eyes they are full of dents and grooves and lumps and spikes which draw from us little cries of approval and disapproval.
>
> E. M. FORSTER

You may wonder how these students could produce such complete writings in a quick rush. Actually several of the accounts ran longer, and their wasted words and irrelevant parts were dropped. One or two papers came off the writer's pen just as they are presented here, but that is a rare happening even for professional writers.

> . . . I sometimes begin a drawing with no preconceived problem to solve, with only the desire to use pencil on paper and make lines, tones and shapes with no conscious aim; but as my mind takes in

*what is so produced a point arrives
where some idea becomes conscious and
crystallizes, and then a control and ordering begins to take place.*

HENRY MOORE, SCULPTOR

WRITING FOUR: Write freely for twenty or thirty minutes about something or somebody you knew. Let yourself record the lumps and grooves, the dents and spikes.

The vital difference between a writer and someone who merely is published is that the writer seems always to be saying to himself, as Stendhal actually did, "If I am not clear, the world around me collapses."

ALFRED KAZIN

chapter 3
what
is
good
writing?

HERE is a poem written by a college girl.

Around the driveway
and down our side of the block
my father's hand was on the back fender
and he was running behind and beside
giving me safe speed
so I could concentrate on steering.
Just coasting
I avoided the big trees,
maneuvered around people on the sidewalk
and began to see the cracks in pavement ahead.
He said
I was doing fine.
But the pedals came up from behind
reminding my legs they were long enough
and nudged my heels to cooperate
to push my own weight
down and around

unmercifully faster
laughingly
leaving him behind.
I turned a corner
and for a moment looked back
at him on the front porch
wearing an undershirt and uncertainty.
Too soon
way on the far side of some block
I try to keep my balance.

                              LOIS BERG

The poem speaks the girl's affection for her father without hearts and
flowers. It puts the reader on a real bicycle that is moving over a real
street with father's hand on the rear fender. It does not take the
reader down the road of life guided by some mysterious spirit. The
narrator does not kid herself about father. He encouraged her, but
was no shining knight, rather a man wearing an undershirt and
uncertainty. She will have a hard time keeping her balance without
him, but she knows she will have to ride on her own someday—everyday. This is good writing: it does not waste words, it shows that the
writer knows what she is talking about—the pedals come up from
behind—its facts speak more than their literal significance.

                    There is no wing like meaning.
                              WALLACE STEVENS

Any kind of writing improves as it approaches the skills with which
Miss Berg wrote her poem. For example, economy. The man who
must write directions for opening and storing a jar of peanut butter
improves as a writer as he learns to say more with fewer words. The
writer for the Sears Roebuck catalog improves as he learns to drama-
tize more fully the product in use—to put the reader there, seeing
and feeling what he will buy. Here is a good piece of writing from the
Sears Spring Through Summer Catalog, 1966:

> Dropped in mid-summer from a helicopter when loaded
> with 25 pounds of sand . . . also dropped when frozen at
> 20° below zero . . . IT BOUNCED." But Sears new ex-
> clusive Trash Can simply wouldn't break! (and because
> it's all heavy-weight plastic, there was *no noisy metallic
> clang*).
> Sears Best . . . because of these important reasons:

> Because Handy Bottom Grips plus side handles and lid handle for easy portability. No hand-cutting bail handle here.
>
> Because friction-fit Top stays on without twisting, fits snugly without getting stuck.
>
> Because No Seams. Holds water, won't leak. The utility area stays cleaner . . . won't be as likely to attract pests.
>
> Because Stands Boiling Water, "boiling" hot sun . . . "boiling" hot concrete. Made to withstand the weather.
>
> Treated with SANI-GARD to retard odor and bacteria . . . Won't "pick up" odors . . . resists the growth of fungi, mildew and bacteria that cause them.

In some senses, Lois Berg's bicycle poem cannot be compared with an advertisement for a trash can; its intention is different, its achievement greater. But the Sears writer comes closer to creating good literature than many admen. He does not shoot off a roman candle of unsupported adjectives—Magnificent! Unheard-of! Stupendous! Instead he tells clearly how the can was tested for durability. Like Lois Berg he makes the reader believe, because the details he presents suggest that he knows what he is talking about.

Writing a sports report, "Orioles' 16 Hits Rout Yanks, 9-4," for *The New York Times*, August 11, 1966, Joseph Durso shows that like a poet he knows how to make his words speak to each other as well as to the reader:

> The barrage consisted of these consecutive elements: a triple to left by Russ Snyder (leading the Yankees to draw their infield in), a single past the infield by Frank Robinson, a single past the infield by Brooks Robinson and a home run past everybody by Powell.

"Past the infield . . . past the infield . . . past everybody." The Sears writer said "Because friction-fit Top stays on . . . Because No Seams . . . Because Stands Boiling Water . . ."

Steve Smith begins his column "Sport" in *Car and Driver*, September, 1966, with this paragraph:

> After completing our six-car comparison road test (elsewhere in this issue), we started back to the city on the Long Island Expressway, known variously as the L.I. Distressway, and the world's longest parking lot. It was a quiet Tuesday afternoon, so we weren't expecting much traffic. Soon, however, the three westbound lanes reached the saturation point, slowed to a crawl and then to a stop.

Temperatures and tempers rose. Some of the traffic bled off onto the two-lane parallel service road, allowing about half-a-mile of progress before clotting. Somebody had the bright idea of trying three abreast, and traffic telescoped another few hundred yards. In desperation, drivers veered off the roadway onto the center mall and the outside verge, becoming trapped by cars that had pulled off to let radiators cool. Finally, those that were able inched north and south the width of the island, then turned east. Within three hours, every major artery into the city was hopelessly snarled. Nothing moved. The System had broken down once again.

Mr. Smith cites two humorous names for the Long Island Expressway, employs sound beautifully in ending his sentence "slowed to a crawl and then to a stop" and makes the words *bled* and *clot* speak to each other in a metaphor. Like Miss Berg he seldom uses dull and empty verbs like *have, make, is,* and *come.* Instead he says *telescoped, veered, trapped, pulled off, inched, snarled,* and *broken down.*

In *The Field Book of Ponds and Streams* (G. P. Putnam's Sons, 1930), Anne Haven Morgan writes:

> Mayfly nymphs are of many shapes and sizes; some have flattened heads and bodies and their sprawling legs are held akimbo as in *Heptagenia.* Active runners, like *Calliboetis,* are set high on spindling legs, while the little creeper, *Leptophlebia,* almost drags its low slung body.

Like Miss Berg, Dr. Morgan employs adjectives that are not vague and inert, but precise and active: *flattened, sprawling, spindling, low slung.*

Guidebooks are usually crammed with fact but written without flavor. *The New York Guidebook* edited by John A. Kouwenhoven (Dell Publishing Company, 1964), includes a chapter by Jean Shepherd, who writes:

> After midnight you can fuel up for your stroll at Riker's Corner House on the northeast corner of Sixth and 57th. By day it is filled with quick-lunch office types, but after midnight (it's an all-night, seven-day-a-week operation) there's as motley a crew as you can find this side of an average painting by Hieronymus Bosch. Good guys and bad guys, reverends and chicks, all assembled for a plate of scrambled eggs with onions, or a slab of chocolate cream pie. There are no tables, only a horseshoe-shaped counter,

which is served from somewhere in the kitchen by an endless belt on a high podium in the center. At Christmas-
time the podium is covered with elves, brownies, and a tiny
electric train that I once saw derail and crash into seven
banana splits. The applause was deafening. In the spring,
this same treadmill is decorated with plastic daffodils and
rubber tulips, and so each succeeding season is celebrated
amid the hamburgers. It's the only way some of the cus-
tomers can tell what time of year it is. Many of them have
not seen the sun since they were kids.

Before you start east on 57th, look up Sixth Avenue. Two
blocks north you will see the dark mass of Central Park,
unfortunately an excellent place to stay out of after dark.
There are romantics who will disagree with this. But there
are equally large numbers of experienced patrolmen and
unfortunates who have been mugged, who will tell you the
truth.

Like all good writers Mr. Shepherd chooses from his experience
what surprises him and will surprise his reader, and he delivers it in
sentences that hammer the surprise: ". . . a tiny electric train that I
once saw derail and crash into seven banana splits." He knows the
strategy of using unexpected words together: "each succeeding season
is celebrated amid the hamburgers." And he is not willing to gloss
over truth to make Central Park at night seem romantic to tourists.

Writing is good not because of who writes it or where it appears.
Shakespeare and William Faulkner have written badly at times, and
good publishers have marketed bad work. Writing is good because
of what it says, how it opens up a world of ideas or fact for readers.
And how accurately and memorably it speaks, a voice issuing from
a human being who is fascinating, surprising, illuminating. But still
a man and a writer who does not always strike sparks.

> . . . failure . . . is the poet's only real
> business. The one hope is for a better
> and better failure . . .
>
> JOHN CIARDI

Most good writing is clear, vigorous, honest, alive, sensuous, appropriate, unsentimental, rhythmic, without pretension, fresh, metaphorical, evocative in sound, economical, authoritative, surprising,
memorable and light. If you set out to collect examples of good

writing you will be surprised to find how many writers you admire are humorous or light. *Hamlet,* a story of decadence and tragedy, is at the same time one of the lightest plays ever written. Mark Van Doren, a professor at Columbia University who encouraged many young persons in America to keep writing until they became successful authors, used to say in his literature classes that a great work of art possesses a quality of lightness. It is never like a ponderous public building that looks as if it is going to sink into the ground. Lightness can be achieved in many ways—by varying style; by continually lifting the reader with genuine, rather than trick, surprises; by not taking oneself too seriously for the circumstances. For example, directions for cooking need not be boring and deadly: Irma S. Rombauer and Marion Rombauer Becker take space in *The Joy of Cooking* to put some joy into their opening discussion of salads:

> I remember the final scene of a medieval Maeterlinck play. The stage is strewed with those dead or dying. The sweet young heroine whimpers, "I am not happy here." Then the head of the house, or what remains of it, an ancient noble, asks quaveringly, "Will there be a salad for supper?"

This in a cookbook. Here is a college teacher's dittoed instructions for her students:

> Trippers will meet at 7:15 (Kalamazoo time) in front of the Union. The bus will leave promptly at 7:30 a.m. There will be no watering stops between Kalamazoo and Chicago, so I strongly recommend that you all eat something vaguely resembling breakfast before we start—something substantial and comforting like a Hershey bar.
>
> At 11:15 (Chicago time) we will go en masse to the Berghoff for lunch. The Berghoff is a marvelous old German place where the food is good and the prices are low. I think that the $1.50 lunch will make you all feel genial and broad-minded about Chicago, the museum, and modern art.
>
> After lunch everyone is on his own in the museum. Museum fatigue is a very real phenomenon and I caution you to use some restraint in your viewing, taking the 20th century first and whatever else you can manage after that.

The teacher who wrote these directions did not strain to be funny; she simply let her own voice take over instead of the voice of doom we often take on when we feel ourselves in a position of authority.

If you feel you can never write as well as John Steinbeck, Charles Dickens, or the writers quoted in this chapter, you may be right. But you can write as well as you spoke at your brilliant best when you were five years old, and you can write as well as some of the catalog or guide book writers presented in this chapter—if you find a voice that rings true to you and you learn to record the surprises of the world faithfully. The free writing by beginning writers quoted in the preceding chapters displays many of the characteristics of good writing discussed here; for example:

Opposition between facts that creates tension: . . . his little apartment . . . The bedroom is lavender with a purple bedspread.

Surprising happening, told with appropriate sound effect: We landed and shot. Everything became blurry. The woods came up fast. Whizzing past trees. Splash! There we sat, up to our heads in water.

Author speaking in authentic voice: I used to try to be jolly, but that's hard to do when you don't have a damn thing to be jolly about.

Character speaking in authentic voice: "Well, if you all know, then why don't you tell us—tell me?"

Economical use of words: The next day (or the next hour for that matter) you could say "Good morning," then yawn, and I'd burst into tears.

Apt metaphor: Electrical storm . . . like arc welding, the helium arc on a torch.

Surprising expression: And the driver had a lot to lose—his truck and perhaps a few teeth.

Strong verbs: He slouched down in his chair, half closed his eyes and flicked his hanging wrist.

Strong repetition: But really it's kind of fun to be nothing. You sit around with your nothing friends . . . content in my nothing world . . . .

The persons who produced these free writings may need to master additional skills, but they have already written many sentences that ring true and stay in the reader's ear.

The best writing, both prose and poetry, as Shakespeare pre-eminently shows, makes use, with condensation and selection, of playful, impassioned, imaginative talk.

SIDNEY COX

chapter 4

tightening

*— Don't use
categorizing words
unnecessarily.*

GOOD WRITERS meet their readers only at
their best. If you should read the sentences in their wastebaskets, you
would find them full of bad starts and complete misses. When you
write, you can discard your bad tries and forget them.

Benjamin Franklin, who helped Thomas Jefferson write the
Declaration of Independence—a skillfully revised document—once told
this anecdote to Mr. Jefferson:

> When I was a journeyman printer, one of my companions,
> an apprentice Hatter, having served out his time, was about
> to open a shop for himself. His first concern was to have a
> handsome signboard, with a proper inscription. He com-
> posed it in these words: "John Thompson, Hatter, makes
> and sells hats for ready money." with a figure of a hat
> subjoined. But he thought he would submit it to his friends
> for their amendments. The first he shewed it to thought the
> word "hatter" tautologous, because followed by the words
> "makes hats" which shew he was a hatter. It was struck out.
> The next observed that the word "makes" might as well be
> omitted, because his customers would not care who made
> the hats. If good and to their mind, they would buy, by
> whomsoever made. He struck it out. A third said he thought
> the words "for ready money" were useless as it was not the
> custom of the place to sell on credit. Every one who pur-
> chased expected to pay. They were parted with, and the
> inscription now stood "John Thompson sells hats." "*Sells*

hats" says his next friend? Why nobody will expect you to
give them away. What then is the use of that word? It was
stricken out and "hats" followed it, the rather, as there was
one painted on the board. So his inscription was reduced
ultimately to "John Thompson" with the figure of a hat
subjoined.

You can cut out the unnecessary words in your writing in this
way. The principle is simple: don't repeat words or ideas unless they
strengthen what you want to say. "Hatter . . . makes hats" repeats *hat*
to no avail. Don't tell your writer that "Mr. Smith is a man who—."
The words *Mr. Smith* reveal that Smith is a man. Don't say "Lincoln
School is a *school* that I really like." Look at what happens when a
writer cuts out weak repetitions:

Original. He looked at Mike. Mike was his brother.

Tightened. He looked at his brother Mike.

Original. The beginning of the play shows Richard as a confident and
strong man while the end shows him as a desolate and weak man.

Tightened. The beginning of the play shows Richard confident and
strong; the end shows him desolate and weak.

Before you get carried away with cutting out weak repetition,
remember that strong repetition is the heart of all good writing, in
fact the heart of all good music making, hurdle racing, hammering,
walking, or courting. Repetitions set up pattern. Only with pattern
can you achieve emphasis and variety. Da-da-da, da-da-da, da-da-dum.
That *dum* is smart because it comes after all those *da's*. It picks up
its power as you wait through all those *da's* for something to happen.
Repeat and vary. That is the secret of achieving significant form in
all art and communication.

This book will demonstrate how the repeat-and-vary pattern
strengthens writing in many ways, but for the present, consider only
how to omit those repetitions in your writing which are not working
powerfully, which get in the reader's way rather than drive them
down your road. If you can learn to say in a few words all you want
to say, with precision and fullness, you will delight yourself and your
reader. We all love a man who says a great deal in a few words. Most
of us feel that life will be too short; so we praise the man who can
hammer the nail with only three blows. We don't want to hear:

In order that the ruling organization of a country that is
committed to a democratic organization organized to give

the people a voice in its procedures, and thinks of their well-being, shall not become disorganized and come to an end in these times . . .

And we don't want to hear:

That government of the people and government by the people and government for the people shall not perish from the earth.

That's so much government that we can't hear the people. We want to hear

. . . that government of the people, by the people, for the people, shall not perish from the earth.

That statement repeats *people,* not *government.* The man who wrote those words respected people and knew his *repeat-and-vary* principle. Further examples of how to repeat words powerfully will be presented in Chapter 11.

REVISING ONE: In your WRITING ONE and WRITING TWO papers, lightly circle all repeated words. Then consider each one. Do you want to retain it? If you want to omit it, draw brackets in pencil around it so that after you show the revision to others and give it time to cool off, you can restore an omitted word easily if you choose. Thomas Jefferson used brackets to recommend omissions to others, and most editors today follow him.

> *Life is the elimination of what is dead.*
> WALLACE STEVENS

The words *which, who,* and *that* often clutter up sentences. Good writers remove excessive Whooery, Whichery, or Thatery.

1. Mr. Rendew, Alice's father, [was a man who] actually liked to have his lawnmower go wrong so he could tinker with its motor.
2. George [is the type of man who] always shines his shoes before going downtown.
3. [The people that] I would like to tell you about [are] Father and Mother.

Other words, for example *all* and *what,* often fail to add meaning to a sentence and need cutting.

1. [All] I wish [is that] he would admit that passion has a respectable place in our lives.

2. [What I mean to say is that] no child should eat his grandmother.

The careless use of the word *thing* is more serious and damaging.

Original. The thing that enrages me is mosquitoes inside my open shirt collar.

Revision. Mosquitoes inside my open shirt collar enrage me.

3. [The] first [thing] I'd like to say [is] . . .

Original. Of all the things in the world I can't stand, boiled hot dogs are the worst.

Revision. I can't stand boiled hot dogs.

Why do schools turn out students so masterly in word wastery? Simple. Knowledge consists to some extent in naming and ordering things. So schools teach categorizing—how to place things in classes, species, etc. (Note that the word *things* is used twice in the two preceding sentences, but meaningfully, not emptily. These two uses of *things* are necessary and justifiable.)

Thus educated persons become addicted to such categorizing words as:

type	situation	phase	factor
kind	area	aspect	one

Often the words are not pulling their weight in a sentence.

Original. The first level of the poem gives the situation of a dull sergeant speaking to a group of new recruits.

Revision. The first level of the poem presents a dull sergeant speaking to a group of recruits.

1. The Queen realized that her life was not [a] carefree and spotless [one].
2. He was a typical [type of] fraternity man.

When a writer must categorize and generalize, these words are valuable, but often they are abominations.

Namery, another sickness, is the habit of naming things which do not need naming. Consider this passage:

Juliet and Rosalind are women who fall in love. This is one of the few similarities between these two characters. They are different in age, with Juliet being an impetuous adolescent and Rosalind being a mature adult. This difference is illustrated by the manner in which each character falls

in love. Juliet rushes into romance and gets married as quickly as possible while Rosalind makes sure of her love for Orlando—a much more rational and logical choice than Juliet's.

This paragraph is devastated by Namery. The author says that Juliet and Rosalind fall in love and then unnecessarily says these acts are similar. He says the two are different in age and then later says one is an adolescent and the other an adult. He wastes completely the sentence:

This difference is illustrated by the manner in which each character falls in love.

because the next sentence shows the difference specifically. The paragraph could be cut in half without losing essential meaning:

One of the few similarities between Juliet and Rosalind is that they both fall in love; but Juliet rushes into romance while Rosalind makes sure of her love for Orlando. Juliet is an impetuous adolescent, Rosalind a mature adult.

Essentially Namery is a failure to recognize that one's audience may possess brains. The writer says:

George came in with a new idea. It was a thought that had never struck his boss.

The reader doesn't need to be told that an idea is a thought. All he needs is

George came in with an idea that had never struck his boss.

In schools, Namery usually involves a special vocabulary.

The causes of the basic difficulties in the area of mathematics are manifold. Fractions present the student with an entirely new set of assumptions.

The introductory sentence stupefies the reader with its dull buzzing. The writer should have said:

Fractions are hard to learn because they present students with new assumptions.

Too often writers introduce everything to their audience: "Now we are going to look at large cities and then we are going to compare them with small towns," they say, when all they mean to do is compare Chicago, Illinois, with Bad Axe, Michigan.

REVISING TWO: Take one of your free writings you like best and tighten it by removing all Whooery, Whichery, Thatery, and Namery.

When you examine your own writing for weak repetition, you may not be able to see it. You need a way of looking for it. Ask yourself where you have said something twice without meaning to. The following passage from a student paper shows weak repetition of both words and ideas. Try cutting it in about half.

> **Hands, did you ever notice how many different kinds of men's hands there are? I first began to notice hands when I found that all men's hands were not as large as my Dad's hands. They were large, strong, and forceful, yet always gentle like the man. His hand encompasses mine even now when he takes it gently yet firmly, as though providing it with a cover of protection against the outside world. But he has always been like that, strong and protective, yet gentle. When those hands hold a baby, the baby stops crying and is quiet as though calmed by their strength and gentleness. When those hands take a pencil and draw an idea, the lines are firm and confident. Other men seem to respond when they shake his hand to the friendliness and strength behind the handshake.**

The assertions in that passage are simple and unsurprising. They do not need a lot of repetition to be clear to the reader.

REVISING THREE: Look over two of your past writings for meanings unnecessarily repeated. For example:

Valerie scrutinized my face [carefully].

The word *scrutinize* means to examine carefully.

Original. Richard has a consistently bad habit of not listening to what people are saying to him unless he is sure it will please him.

Revision. Richard consistently fails to listen to people unless he is sure they will please him.

The word *habit* means a consistent or frequent action. Because *consistently* is used, *habit* can be eliminated.

The ground felt [peculiar. It was] soft as clouds.

If the ground was soft as clouds, it must have felt peculiar, and the writer need not make the opening comment. In the revision he hits the reader with his surprise. He does not waste a word telling him a surprise is coming. Note how the following verbose statement is brought alive by simple tightening:

Original. I see a man whose face is hidden by shadow except where the sun reveals it.

Revision. I see the sun-lit half of a man's face.

You may properly think of wasting words as a form of dishonesty. No one means to do it; but when he does, he risks losing both the reader's attention and trust.

> *A young author is tempted to leave any-*
> *thing he has written through fear of not*
> *having enough to say if he goes cutting*
> *out too freely. But it is easier to be long*
> *than short.*
>
> SAMUEL BUTLER

If you stand right fronting and face to face to a fact, you will see the sun glimmer on both its surfaces, as if it were a cimeter [scimitar], and feel its sweet edge dividing you through the heart and marrow.

HENRY THOREAU

chapter 5
telling
facts

TELLING FACTS are lying all around you every minute of your life. Through free writing you've already seen they are available to you without asking. So let them come to you. If occasionally they won't, look for them, run them down.

Instead of saying,

> I found my trip to see my fiancé was marvelous. Being with him was even more thrilling than I thought it would be. I think it's real love.

give the reader the fact that drove you to that generalization,

> **He had a two-week leave after Basic, so I flew to Jersey and we stayed with his parents on the Shore. It was great being with him—even when his whole family watched us watch television.**

Instead of trying to express how great, how small, how wonderful, how sad something is, establish its size or intensity with facts. This is the natural way to write. A college junior living on a large campus one day realized something about her home town. Instead of saying,

> I had never realized how awfully small my home town is— really small!

she gave the facts that led her to that realization.

I hadn't realized how small my home town actually is until
I received my absentee voter application from the township
clerk today. He enclosed a note with the proper forms:

> Theo—Fill in balance of form & return in envelope
> provided.
> > Be seeing you—
> > > (signed) Graydon

Now the meaning in *awfully small* is precisely established. The writer
did not have to organize a treasure hunt to find these telling facts.
They had come to her in an envelope and all she had to do was open
them to her reader.

Not all facts speak powerfully. Some add up only to boredom. In
that bad textbook you studied all the provisions of the treaties and
all the principal rivers, but the facts never bunched together and spoke
to you.

> *"It's something very like learning geogra-*
> *phy," thought Alice, as she stood on*
> *tiptoe in hopes of being able to see a*
> *little farther. "Principal rivers—there are*
> *none. Principal mountains—I'm on the*
> *only one, but I don't think it's got any*
> *name."*
> > LEWIS CARROLL

As a writer you can't help feel that all your facts belong together in
some way because they all belong to you, but your reader has no such
glue working for him. He may not know you at all, and he doesn't
know why one of your facts should appear beside another unless you
make its relationship apparent. The world of things and ideas out
there is no file drawer. It makes sense for us, reduces itself to something
comprehensible, only as we look at it with an idea or feeling that sorts
and selects. So the writer is under a fierce obligation to choose for his
writing those facts that seem to him and will seem to his reader to belong on the same page.

> *. . . only what fits is allowed.*
> NORMAN PODHORETZ

Professional writers make three or four drafts of their work to get
rid of the facts that don't belong. In going through the program of

this book, if you do not rewrite almost every paper that seems valuable to you and others, you will not give your thoughts and feelings the
presentation they deserve. Few good pieces of writing have been published that were not cut and revised and added to.

Consider what might be cut from this story to assure that everything that remains is fitting.

FIRST DRAFT

> Sitting in the Student Union watching the bus boys do their
> work brought to my mind memories of when Sandy and I
> were on Mackinaw Island last summer. The bus boy went
> around dumping ashtrays into his bucket, picking up trays
> with large assortments of trash, and stashing them under
> his cart.
>
> On the island the only mode of transportation is man's
> greatest invention, the horse. What caught my eye were the
> similar facial expressions on the bus boy in the Student
> Union and the boy who toted the wheelbarrow and shovel
> behind the horse carriages on the island.
>
> Sandy and I stopped and talked with that unfortunate
> fellow. We were quite lost, and needed directions, but who
> would ever think of asking a manure gatherer how to get to
> a certain fort on the other side of the island? Embarrassing,
> but we were lost. It was his expression which jolted me,
> though. An unsure expression, his mouth and eyes ab-
> stractly forming a question mark. Imagine. A job shoveling
> horse dung. Tourists with their Brownie Instamatic cam-
> eras and their insolent children asking about the boy with
> the wheelbarrow would be this young boy's biggest enemy.
> He was in view of the whole world. He's no different from
> anyone else, yet his job sets him apart.
>
> He was embarrassed as I, at first; but after bulling
> around for a few minutes, I knew that he was just like me,
> except he knew where he was. My embarrassment was like
> that of someone foreign to a large city asking a bum on
> Skid Row to get to such and such a street. Not quite as
> drastic, but on the same psychological level. But his expres-
> sion—so lost, so uneasy, and I was the one who was lost.

That paper was written freely in fifteen minutes. When the writer and
an editor worked it over until only the facts that spoke to each other
and to the writer's main intention remained, it was considerably

shorter. First, they decided that mentioning Sandy was unnecessary and confusing. She may have been fascinating and have said or done things that bore upon the author's relationship to the manure gatherer; but as she was presented, she didn't fit. She had not been made a working part of the story, and unless she were, she would have to depart. Second, they found many little facts and expressions in the story which were repetitive or weak, including the forced, unnecessary statement that the horse is "man's greatest invention." Here's the result of their revising:

SECOND DRAFT

The busboy in the Union went around dumping ashtrays into his bucket and stashing huge assortments of dishes and trays under his cart. His expression reminded me of a boy I saw on Mackinaw Island last summer, who toted a wheelbarrow and shovel behind the horse carriages.

I was lost and asked him, a manure gatherer, directions to a fort on the other side of the island. His expression jolted me: an unsure look, his mouth and eyes abstractly forming a question mark.

Imagine. A job shoveling horse dung! Tourists with their Kodak Instamatics and insolent children asking about the guy with the wheelbarrow.

We were both embarrassed. I felt like someone foreign to a large city asking directions of a bum on Skid Row; he expected me to be like the Instamatic People.

He was no different from me, except he knew where he was.

A fundamental in writing is to reach for a fact instead of trying to be lucky with a Great Idea. When you have to mention anything in order to tell a story or make a point, force yourself to put down the name of that thing if it has a name, or to show it in its particular setting or doing its thing particularly. Don't say you pushed the throttle and the motorbike did its thing. Give the name of that thing and the sound and feel or smell, or whatever you can.

Once a writer finds a telling fact and puts it down, it often pulls from the depths other telling facts. Once a university senior admitted that what she had written about her father was vague and unsatis-factory. Her professor told her to get some facts down, so they would begin suggesting other facts. She did. Here's the result:

Everytime I try to speak of my father I find words like *gentle, sweet, funny,* or *shy* popping up, and they are useless, meaningless. "Tell what your father *did*, what he *said*," you say, and I am stuck. How do I make a story from the things my father did?

I will tell you what he did.

My father walked to the far side of our pasture, found a cow with her newborn calf, and carried the calf home in his arms.

My father was rarely seen without at least two small children on or around him. He gave them horseback rides, told them funny stories, and lifted them atop a cow named Blackie, who didn't mind being used for a horse—his own children—until one by one all six of them grew too old for that sort of nonsense, then the young nieces and nephews, and next, last, the neighbor's children.

My dad followed me upstairs after he punished me once and said he was sorry and rubbed my back until I didn't cry anymore.

He raised and cared for twenty-five pure-bred Jersey cows, and he sang while he worked away his life and was poorer than any other farmer in the county.

My dad made a huge bowl of popcorn and spent countless hours reading Agatha Christie murder mysteries in bed as he munched.

Because he was an incurable dreamer, he straightened out the family's financial crises only on paper, by selling cows which in reality he could not bear to lose because he loved them.

When he was forty-seven years old my dad found out that he had a very serious heart condition, and he never went across the road to the barn again, but sat silent before the pot-bellied stove in our kitchen and puffed on a pipe. Every day he made tea and dry jokes for his wife and children and visitors.

When he felt stronger, he was sent to be rehabilitated in Waterloo, Iowa. On a bitter, cold day in January, 1959, he died in his sleep. He did not live to see his cows taken away that morning by the man who had bought them.

WRITING FIVE: Put down a telling fact about something that counts for you—an experience, idea, or feeling. Then wait to see if other facts are coming along behind it. If they are, start writing a story or extended comment without explaining or discussing anything except through telling facts. If you find the flow of facts has stopped, quit writing sentences and wait for a fact to arise. When it appears, write it down quickly as on a grocery list, then jot down others if they appear. After you have a sizeable list, begin writing again.

Shams and delusions are esteemed for soundest truth, while reality is fabulous. If men would steadily observe realities only, and not allow themselves to be deluded, life, to compare it with such things as we know, would be like a fairy tale and the Arabian Nights' Entertainments.

HENRY THOREAU

chapter 6
fabulous realities

MOST OF US go through each day looking for what we saw yesterday and we find it, to our half-realized disappointment. But the man who daily expects to encounter fabulous realities runs smack into them again and again. He keeps his mind open for his eyes.

Asked to expect surprise, a number of students explored their nearby worlds for fabulous realities. Here are some they found:

1. I was speeding along the highway when I saw a small yellow sign.

   SLOW
   MEN
   WORKING

   It was followed by a larger one in black and white, reading

   YOUR HIGHWAY DOLLARS
   AT WORK

2. At a football game yesterday at Waldo Stadium a blind man sat next to me listening to his radio.

3. I stood in the checkout lane behind a boy who looked about sixteen. He waited for the clerk to begin ringing up his package

of Pall Malls, then reached out and added five packs of bubble gum.

4. Ever since Rennie found out that Jane, his co-worker, doesn't like him, he tries to upset her when they are together. I asked him why he did this. He said, "I hate intolerant people."

5. At the Allegan County Fair I approached the cotton candy stand and told the girl I wanted pink. After she gave it to me she turned to get my change and I noticed a piece of cotton in her ear.

6. Today I found a dead bird in the gutter with its mangled wing held in place by "Magic Transparent Tape."

7. A drunk teenager trying to cross West Main at Michigan assisted by a little old lady.

8. I excitedly opened my only two valentines from males. They were just alike.

9. A girl with a deep V in her blouse holding her books over it.

10. A man returned to his parked car to find its hood and fenders gashed and crumpled. On the dashboard he found a piece of folded paper. Written in a neat feminine hand, the note said: "I have just run into your car. There are people watching me. They think I am writing down my name and address. They are wrong."

11. A small boy, obviously lost, walked up to a security guard at Hudson's department stores, and asked, "Did you see a lady walk by here without me?"

12. A pregnant woman carrying a globe of the world in front of her up a steep sidewalk in the city.

13. In the middle of a heated argument with me, my wife goes to the refrigerator, gets a bottle of ginger ale, fills two glasses, gives me one, and continues the argument.

Each statement surprises. It is not fairly surprising, but absolutely surprising, because it is unique. A robin sitting in the April snow in Illinois or Massachusetts would not qualify as a fabulous reality. In those states a late short snow often occurs after robins have arrived.

Tension is necessary to make a fabulous reality. Two things that do not belong together touch in some way. And their touching creates waves of further suggestion that are not stated. In the middle of the young man's argument, his wife interrupts him, but not to put him down, rather to make him more comfortable. The argument is heated; she gives him a cold drink.

> *When I went to those great cities I saw*
> *wonders I had never seen in Ireland. But*
> *when I came back to Ireland I found all*

*the wonders there waiting for me. You
see they had been there all the time;
but my eyes had never been opened to
them. I did not know what my own
house was like, because I had never been
outside it.*

BERNARD SHAW [*Keegan speaking*]

COLLECTING ONE: This weekend keep a piece of paper or note-
book in your pocket or pocketbook and jot down five fabulous realities you see. When you have a chance, write them in sentences. Keep
revising them until you have built up to the surprise rather than given
it away weakly. Note that most of the above fabulous realities (1) place
the happening in a particular setting, (2) put the reader there through
telling details, (3) make the action happen for the reader as it happened for the writer, (4) do not waste words, (5) do not explain, but
present facts and force the reader to find the surprise, (6) put the
kicker at the end.

The following passage suffers because of Explainery:

> **Last week I saw two guys walking down Western Avenue
> carrying on a conversation ten feet apart. I even walked
> between them. Interpersonal relationships are growing less
> personal, but this was too much almost to believe. One of
> them, I suppose, had determined to assert himself, keep his
> pace, and have the other come up to him. The other prob-
> ably determined the opposite, so they walked along making
> fools of themselves.**

That's a beautiful comment on life and contains all the elements
necessary to a fabulous reality, but it needs better telling. Here's a
possible rewriting:

> Last week I saw two guys walking down Western Avenue
> carrying on a conversation ten feet apart. As one quickened
> his pace, so did the other. Even when I walked between
> them, they kept up their conversation. Interpersonal rela-
> tionships are growing less personal.

In that passage the last sentence violates the rule for fabulous realities
of not explaining the point. But an editor might urge the writer to use
it there because its sociological language contrasts with the ridiculous
but down-to-earth behavior of the two boys and so creates another kind

of tension and surprise. You may find one of your fabulous realities gains by such a plain and outright judgment at the end, but usually these short charged statements lose too much of their electricity when judgments or explanations are given.

Note how the facts in this fabulous reality do all the telling by themselves.

> **A pimply-faced, dirty, barefooted, greasy, string-haired girl smoking a cigarette and eating a peanut butter and jelly sandwich riding a crowded elevator at the University of Michigan while reading How to Win Friends and Influence People.**

COLLECTING TWO: Collect five or more additional fabulous realities. Do not be easily satisfied. Tension. Punch at the end. Uniqueness. Implications or suggestions that spread beyond the statement.

The looking and discovering involved in producing fabulous realities is not a trick and not an exercise. It is the way good writers see. Because their eyes are not tired, their readers turn their pages with surprise. In *People of the Abyss,* a book about the city of London, Jack London wrote:

> From the slimy spittle-drenched sidewalk, they were picking up bits of orange peel, apple skin, and grape stems, and they were eating them. The pits of green gage plums they cracked between their teeth for the kernels inside. They picked up stray crumbs of bread the size of peas, apple cores so black and dirty one would not take them to be apple cores, and these things these two men took into their mouths, and chewed them, and swallowed them; and this, between six and seven o'clock in the evening of August 20, year of our Lord 1902, in the heart of the greatest, weathiest, and most powerful empire the world has ever seen.

Note that Jack London is here not just telling an unusual incident but is writing toward an idea—that the great English capital city did not save its citizens from degrading poverty. Surprising realities suffuse good essays and articles as they do good stories. One of the reasons students in schools seldom write powerful themes or essays is that they mistakenly think good nonfiction writing is abstract and dull. Actually, the best writers of nonfiction (articles, essays, autobiography, history, etc.) continually surprise their readers with fabulous realities.

When you read accounts others have written of surprising realities, like Jack London's, you may feel they were lucky but you were never blessed. But reality is often fabulous for the man who remains awake.

> *He [Thoreau] knew how to sit immovable, a part of the rock he rested on, until the bird, the reptile, the fish, which had retired from him, should come back and resume its habits, nay, moved by curiosity, should come to him and watch him.*
>
> RALPH WALDO EMERSON

The unfamiliar frequently appears amazing, as does the familiar when it is scrutinized more closely than usual.

WRITING SIX: Write a fabulous reality that is a page or more in length. You may already have found one that you can expand. Or you may have done a free writing that you can work up into a fabulous reality.

Here is such a free writing done by a college student:

> Fred came back into my existence yesterday like a forgotten pressed leaf falling out of a textbook. And for two hours I was eighteen again—how strange to speak from twenty-one as if decades had passed—and afraid of most of life and silly and laughing and anxious and oh so frightened of missing something. We sat in a plastic-coffee-spoon diner, the closest shelter to our clumsy accidental sidewalk meeting, and relived and laughed. Was it only three years ago and were those people Fred and Bob? Didn't someone put salt in this sugar dispenser by mistake, or on purpose? How many dreams had gone thud in the interim? Thank God for Simon and Garfunkel. Had there really been a time when both of us were afraid to go try out for a play? Then suddenly we were back there; no longer laughing at those boys of three years ago, but being them. We were caught in the performance of familiar scenes. Our course was set and—after two hours we ran out of material. And we sat and stared silently. The hamburger grill hissed, and the coffee was too cold to drink, even without the salt or

whatever. Didn't we have anything to say? Maybe next time. Yes. We agreed to get together but left the date uncertain. That was safer. It was good to be outside again, walking in a different direction from my friend, being twenty-one.

The material is there for a strong expanded fabulous reality. Part of it, that is. The two "relived and laughed," but the reader cannot reconstruct enough of that living and the quality of the laughter it evoked. The ending has the punch of a fabulous reality—might be made still stronger if the last words were "a different direction from my friend," and "being twenty-one" came earlier. Perhaps just a memory or two would fill out the story and make the account fabulous throughout.

Here's a passage from a student's journal that carrries all the elements. A fabulous reality is stated in the first seven words.

Privacy up here means taking a shower or pretending you're asleep. And even then you're still vulnerable to clumsy-but-well-meaning mouths full of teeth, and also to those (Thank God) infrequent asses called practical jokers equipped with ice water which every floor of every dorm seems blessed with.

There's always the cube of air I was assigned to. But there's always my roommate, too. And my suite-mates and my wall-mates and the girls across the hall and down the hall and everywhere, including the think room.

When I go out with Frank we have to talk to the whole lobby about how I'm sorry I argued with him and would he please forgive me for being so silly. (Frank doesn't have a four-speed, 327 H.P. apartment on wheels.) And I kiss him goodnight in front of my housemother, the assistant director, at least two staffs, and a major portion of my friends and enemies. One night I told him I loved him over the phone. Then I turned around. Carole was smiling with warm understanding as she dropped two nickels into the Coke machine.

If I spend one single night in any other bed but my own, I should legally have written permission from its assigned owner. And if I'm actually out of the red brick walls of Britton Hall between the hours of 11:00 P.M. and 7:00 A.M., eight different people must have on file not only the name, address, and telephone number of my haven; but

also the hours I will be in exile and the method of transportation I flee in—all to be filled out in the space previ-
ously allotted for said purpose on a white sign-out slip
which can be obtained only between the hours of 7:00
P.M. and 10:30 P.M. Monday through Saturday.

So I sit and sneak a look out my curtains (which are supposed to be closed from 7:00 P.M. to 7:00 A.M.) and dream
of taking a walk in the wind and the rain—by myself.

This girl made this entry in her journal in 1965. When it was published in the campus newspaper it was appreciated by students and it
may have had something to do with the considerable liberalizing of
dormitory rules since that date.

Thinking of the form of a fabulous reality, the writer could trans-
pose some of the paragraphs in the account so the paragraph ending
"Carole was smiling with warm understanding as she dropped two
nickles into the Coke machine" would end the whole story. The
present ending makes sense, but is too obvious. It pats the reader instead of socks him.

Life is routine more than it is fabulous. Without the steadiness of
the expected, newness is impossible or chaotic. But most of us would
gain from confronting a great deal more newness than we do.

chapter 7
through
facts
to realities

HERE is a passage that might be called Bad Edgar Allen Poe:

> Perhaps the most unusual incident of my childhood occurred in the living room of my own suburban home. The mantelpiece in that room was an eight-by-one-foot block of solid sandstone which protruded substantially out from the formation of lesser blocks which supported it. I was seated on the floor directly under the mantelpiece moderately absorbed in a book, when a harsh crack and a heavy grating sound tore my gaze upward. The mantelpiece was falling. Falling on me . . . I lunged. The movement was probably born more of instinct than logic, but it saved me certain injury. The huge sandstone mass missed me completely, but one of the smaller blocks dragged down with it fell with painful impact on my left forearm. I was quite lucky, or so I was told.

In that passage, the writer keeps nudging the reader and saying between the lines, "Isn't this a horrifying experience? Right now you're supposed to be thrilled and frozen in fear." The nudges are in the adjectives and adverbs: *most unusual* incident, protruded *substantially* (are most protrusions unsubstantial?), *moderately* absorbed (please man, look up the word *absorbed*), *harsh* crack (do cracks sound soft and sweet ever?), *painful* impact. The writer won't let the facts speak.

He's like a mother telling you her little boy is a great story teller and interrupting him to improve upon his story.

This account of the falling of a mantelpiece, like most poor writing, is heavy in style where it should be heavy in fact. The falling of a mantelpiece upon a child is a weighty matter, but here the writing is ponderous, not the blow from the mantelpiece. It's dishonest writing. Note the last sentence:

I was quite lucky, or so I was told.

You're not sure? You had to be told? Probably the writer began writing the account with the same dishonest attitude. He was going to impress people with a near tragedy. When a writer messes around with little truths in this way, he cannot go through the facts to larger truths. But if he keeps faith with himself and what he is writing about, he makes a small experience illuminate the nature of similar or parallel experiences the reader has had. For example:

> With one foot rested on a bag of cement and his chin leaning on the back of his hand, which was cupped over the end of a long-handled shovel, Steve watched me while I filled the cement mixer with shovelful after shovelful of gravel. As his blue eyes followed every movement I made, he twitched his bicep and kept saying, "I sure hope you can wheel cement. You said you could."
>
> Without answering, I began the mixer, and turned on the water. The drum inside rotated slowly, throwing the dry gravel and powdery cement together with a stream of water. Within minutes the solution had been thoroughly mixed and small, wet globs of cement were being spit out of the mixer as the cement inside slapped back and forth.
>
> Steve relaxed his bicep and motioned for me to position the wheelbarrow in closer to the mixer. After I was ready, he poured the cement into the wheelbarrow. Cement is thick but very loose, and moving it in a wheelbarrow is difficult. The momentum of the solution is in the direction it goes.
>
> I crouched down, picking up the handles, and eased forward. I felt every pound shift as half the mass of mud sloshed forward, the other half to the right. I took about five steps, moving each foot deliberately from one position to the next, as if a weighted yoke was balancing on my shoulders. After the fifth step I found myself struggling

with 400 pounds of cement and the next moment there lay an unplotted sidewalk and an overturned wheelbarrow in front of me. Steve, trying to control the twitch in his bicep, jeered, "I thought you said you could run a wheelbarrow!"

MICHAEL PARRISH

In that piece of writing, the cement moves and the writer gets to the wet facts and the feeling of things going out of control in the hands of a novice. The writer put down such telling facts that they said more than he expected them to. He wrote essentials and produced essences.

WRITING SEVEN: Choose an experience that affected you strongly and write down its telling facts as truthfully as you can. Try to go right through those facts until you feel inside the experience as physically as you feel the sweaty warmth of your body inside a thick unbreathing raincoat on a hot summer day.

Here's a girl doing that in what might be called a little case-history:

At 10:30 Wednesday morning—a few trucks every once in a while on I94 and one or two cars. Joe made me put my seatbelt on before he went to sleep in the back seat. My stomach was a little tense. I was constantly aware that I was driving someone else's car at an unwavering 65. It was like flying.

As I approached a slower-moving blue Galaxie, I put my turn signal on, glided over into the left lane before I came too close to him, never losing or gaining speed. I put my turn signal on after checking in my rearview mirror and glided back into the right hand lane still going 65. I was coming up to a cream colored Plymouth trailing a semi. I glanced in my side view mirror, turned my head slightly to check my blind spot—it was clear—and pulled into the left lane again. As I was practically alongside the old lady in the Plymouth, she started to move in my direction.

I was going to give her the horn and reached for the chrome half-circle. It wasn't there. Of course not, this wasn't my car. I didn't want to use the power brakes because I wasn't used to them and at 65 I was afraid I'd put both Joe in the back seat, and me, through the windshield. I was sure she wouldn't hit me. And she'd see me before she got much closer. I heard a small clank and the highway, trees, hills, and cars were spinning like a rotating

moving picture was being played around the windshield. I
felt a lurch and the picture had abruptly changed. I was
looking straight down the hood of Joe's car onto the
ground, think I was going to die. Only the words existed in
my head—"I'm going to die." The car bounced back down,
not turning over, and stopped. I turned around to see what
happened to Joe. He wasn't sleeping any more, but sitting
straight up. Leaning forward, clutching the back of my
seat, he was all right. The numbness left my body and was
replaced by a sense of people milling around the car and
opening the door next to me. I looked at Joe and started
to cry.

NANCY HUNTER

In that account the writer did not give the old line about a car
accident: "everything happened so fast it was a blur, and when I began
to understand what had occurred . . ." but let facts, recounted one after
another, show the instantaneousness and yet the clarity of the action
for her. That paradoxical combination is one of the essences of most
accidents.

The factual narratives in this chapter all tell what the writer did
and felt. They are written about him and from his viewpoint. Here's
a short account telling facts about *someone else's* experience and going
through the facts to the essence:

Two men are moving sod with a wheelbarrow on the lawn
outside Waldo Library. They take turns hauling the dirt
from the truck to the area for the new seedlings. When it's
one man's turn, the other walks behind a respectful distance, but doesn't touch the wheelbarrow even when it
stalls on a rock on the steep grade. He stands off a few
paces while the hauler dumps the load awkwardly, scrap-
ing with a shovel in one hand while tipping the wheelbarrow with the other hand and his knee. After all the dirt
is out, the second man steps forward and rakes the sod into
place. They then reverse jobs and repeat the operation.

What the observer of that little charade found by going through the
facts were the essentials of not working very hard.

The beginning writer should simply tell us what he knows. A case-
history of how he carried his papers on the route one morning, of how
he prepares for school in a family of seven in a house with one bathroom, of how he got ready to play his first game of varsity basketball.

A day, a week, an hour—some interval of his life through which he takes us as he carries out one connected action or watches someone else or something else go through a process.

WRITING CASE-HISTORIES

A person does not have to be a professional writer to tell a case-history with authority and power. He has only to know his journey intimately and carry some attitude toward it which enables him to select details that keep the history alive and significant— something more than a bad list of names and dates. Michihiko Hachiya, a medical doctor in Japan, was wounded on August 6, 1945, by the first nuclear explosion directed against human beings. The next morning he awoke to groans of patients and a new Hiroshima. He told the story of his experiences, a simple case-history of what happened to him then.

> Dr. Katsube looked me over and after feeling my pulse, said: "You received many wounds, but they all missed vital spots."
> He then described them and told me how they had been treated. I was surprised to learn that my shoulder had been severely cut but relieved at his optimism for my recovery.
> "How many patients are in the hospital?" I asked Dr. Koyama.
> "About a hundred and fifty," he replied. "Quite a few have died, but there are still so many that there is no place to put one's foot down. They are packed in everywhere, even the toilets."
>
> •   •   •
>
> Downstairs, I ran into Mr. Hirohata sitting on a bench and sat down beside him. Mr. Hirohata had been employed in the Telephone Bureau and was at work in the building when the explosion occurred. Despite the fact that he was less than four hundred meters from the hypocenter, Mr. Hirohata escaped injury.
> "How did you avoid injury when nearly everyone around you was killed or hurt?" I asked.
> "The thick concrete wall of the building protected me," answered Mr. Hirohata, "but people standing near the windows were killed instantly or died later from burns or cuts. The night shift was just leaving and the day shift coming

on when the explosion occurred. Forty or more were killed near the entrance. About fifteen employees in the construction department, stripped to the waist, were outside taking gymnastics. They died instantly."

"Doctor, a human being who has been roasted becomes quite small, doesn't he? Those people all looked like little boys after the explosion. Is there any reason why my hair should be falling out and I feel so weak? I'm worried, doctor, because I have been told that I would die and this has already happened to some people I know who didn't seem to be hurt at all by the *pika*."

"Mr. Hirohata, I don't believe you need worry about yourself," I answered, trying to be reassuring, "Like so many others, you've been through a dreadful experience, and on top of that have tried to work night and day here at the Bureau. What else could one expect? You must go home, stay absolutely quiet in bed, and get all the good nourishing food you can."

This excerpt from a 233-page book shows that Dr. Hachiya wrote down his experience in incidents and conversations as they came to him. He called the book *Hiroshima Diary: The Journal of a Japanese Physician, August 6—September 30, 1945.* He told what he did, what others did, whom he saw, what they said to each other. The writer of a case-history tries to put the reader there, right in the process, the place, the action. If he sees a man riding a bicycle with a broken red reflector on its rear bumper, he does not write: "I saw a man riding a damaged bicycle," but "I saw a man riding a bicycle with a broken red reflector on its rear bumper."

If you record the details of a process or experience and then write them into a case-history, in one sense you are an authority. You may not know more about that process or experience than some others, but your written record commands respect by its truth to particular fact. Here is a case-history written by a student:

THROUGH THE GATES

When I walked through the gates of McLean Steel everybody from the afternoon shift was watching me. They stared as if they could sense I was a new worker. As I walked I glanced to my left and saw a short fat man looking at me. He was clean and chewing a cigar between his crummy smile. I looked to the right and saw a kid about my age sitting on the curb. His clothes and face were dirty and he looked worn out. He wasn't smiling. I seemed to be on a long endless walk, but finally I reached the labor hut. This was the second initiation point, but the workers' stares didn't bother me because I had already seen the kinds of looks they were giving me. I wasn't surprised to find a lot of laborers were college kids working for the summer.

At exactly midnight our foreman for the week came into the hut with a job list. It didn't take long to find out how important seniority was in bidding for jobs. As it turned out, the lowest workers on the list, eight other college kids and I, had to work in the rust-furnace basement—a job no one else wanted. The basement was full of leaking hot water pipes which had rusted, and together with the heat gave the basement its name.

I went outside, grabbed a shovel, and followed the others. We went down flights of stairs to a basement full of many rooms. The heat was tremendous and soon everyone was in their T-shirts. It felt like we were being pushed into a large oven. The rooms were filled with mud, sand, slime, and bricks, as well as rocks which had hardened into large piles. Covering the basement floor were about six inches of muddy water.

Our foreman showed up and told us our job was to clean out about three-fourths of the rooms in the basement. We were supposed to place the debris on a conveyor. We all looked around and then at each other, and no one moved until the foreman yelled, "Are you guys waiting for an invitation? Get the hell to work!"

We divided the jobs so that two men worked with picks on the piles, four men shoveled, two men rolled the wheelbarrows, and the last man worked the conveyor. We switched jobs periodically so as to make the work even. I was sweating just standing still. The stagnant odor of the water made me sick. The rooms were small, so we worked under cramped conditions. Mike was swinging a pick and had to lean against a wall to get at the pile he was supposed to work. Hot water was leaking down the wall from the pipes above and hitting him. Leaning against the wall was the only way to get the job done. Somebody had to do it and since it was his turn, he didn't complain. Everybody else was doing their job. Bruce wore out his gloves, so everyone took turns going without gloves. The blisters came easier, but unnoticed after a while.

We worked at a good pace for three hours, until lunch time, which was at three in the morning. When I walked outside, a cool breeze gave me the chills. I just stood there, taking deep breaths, letting the air soak through all the bones in my body. Everybody sat on a curb looking out through a fence onto a street. It felt like being in prison. Nobody said much, and if they did, nobody listened. I took off my helmet and lay on some grass looking up at the stars. It was funny how good the calm night and stars made me feel. After twenty minutes I started back to the basement. I looked up and felt I was heading from heaven to purgatory.

When everybody reached the basement we decided to finish the job early. For two hours we strained and shoveled as fast as we could to get the job done. The heat soaked up what energy everyone had left and we were all exhausted. We found a long bench and sat down, waiting for quitting time. After a few minutes the foreman came back and told us to finish the rest of the basement, and left. No one moved: half of the guys didn't hear him because they were sleeping. When he came back, he kicked everyone awake and gave us a speech which was supposed to make us jump to our feet.

"Do you want your jobs?" he brightly asked. No one answered. "Then get up and start working and if I see anyone sitting down again, you're fired."

We started cleaning the rest of the rooms. The piles seemed larger, shovels were heavier, and wheelbarrows harder to push. Blisters didn't go unnoticed and backs started aching like hundreds of needles were sticking to our skins. When I was rolling one of the wheelbarrows to the conveyor, it tipped over. I bent to pick up some rocks and noticed him standing above the basement making sure the work got done, waiting for someone to relax. His smile made me feel like he was Satan laughing at all the suckers he had working for him in Hell.

Well, we got the job done and I got out of that hole and sat on a curb waiting to check out. Morning workers would glance at me when they walked by. I didn't smile.

> At eight in the morning I finally checked out and walking
> to my car wasn't surprised to hear, "Hey Joe, I'll meet you
> at the bar in ten minutes."
>
> I think I could have gone for a drink then.
>
> MARIO ROVEDA

Writing case-histories is one of the best means of learning the secret
of once. You can begin at a natural beginning—when you punched the
time clock and started work or when the first act in a process was
carried out. Then you can keep on telling the incident through time,
as it happened. To give your reader the full experience, you may have
to take facts from several different days' experience and put them together so they appear to belong to only one day. That's not necessarily
presenting the case falsely, if you're trying to show what the whole
experience has meant to you. Only if you distort the truth of fact and
feeling are you lying as a writer; for example, if you tell of working at
a Dairy Queen stand in a small town where business was almost always
slow and you collect facts from only the unusually busy days, like the
town's Centennial celebration, you would be misrepresenting the on-
going fact of your work. But if the Centennial day impressed you, you
might make your story a case-history of what a busy day was like in an
ordinarily unbusy town. Whatever your decision, it will be a liberating
one if you swing at some truths that counted for you.

Here's a case-history of a girl's love affair with a car.

FIRST CAR

> I had driven my first car somewhere between 1,000 and
> 1,500 miles, and a little slip of white paper in the glove
> compartment told me it was time for an oil change and
> grease job. So I pulled into a Shell station and asked if
> I could make an appointment. I was told to come back
> two days later at 5:00 and they would have time to do it.
> On that day I drove in and hauled out that piece of paper
> that told me what I was supposed to know about keeping
> my car running.
>
> "How many cans of oil does this car hold?" I asked, say-
> ing *cans* instead of *quarts, pints,* or *gallons,* so I wouldn't
> seem like I was totally ignorant.
>
> "It depends on what size can you use." He blew it, but
> saved me by adding, "It'll hold four of those over there in
> the window."

I smiled as if to say, "Of course," then like my dad had told me (and written on the piece of paper) I told him how to add the oil.

"OK," I said, "put in one quart less than it will hold and add a can of CD_2."

"I never heard of CD_2," he retorted. This made me feel superior because here I, just a car-stupid girl, knew about something he didn't.

"How about a can of STP?" he asked. He had to explain that it was an "additive" (which left a big question in my mind, but I kept my mouth shut).

"All right, if you're sure it's the same thing," I answered, knowing he couldn't possibly say it was if he didn't know what CD_2 was. "Put in one quart less than it will hold," I repeated, "and add a can of STP."

"Look, little Miss Wisconsin," he boomed—I guess he noticed my license plates—"STP *mixes* with the oil. It doesn't increase the oil level."

"But my dad said—" (I pouted, looking at my little white sheet of salvation). He didn't let me finish.

"That may be true if it's with that other stuff, not with this," he said, shoving a can of STP through the window of the car.

So I relented, figuring he must know more than I did, even if he hadn't ever heard of CD_2.

A few days later, I pulled in and a new guy came over to the car.

"Oh, so you're the girl from Wisconsin! What did your dad tell you to do now, put gas in it?"

Right then it became clear that I never could get excited about that car. It never would be mine. It belonged to the garage mechanic, the fuel pump, the oil can, and to the one thing that made it possible to get these—the credit card, which was in my dad's name. Even the charge card belongs to the oil company, really, so I'm just taking that car into its owners to care for, and who am I to tell someone what to do with what belongs to them?

DARCY CUDLIP

WRITING EIGHT: Write a case-history. Put the reader there through telling facts and try to go through them to some essentials of what you are writing about.

To do this you must know intimately and deeply what you are writing about. Either choose an experience or process you have gone through many times, or sit down before a happening and take notes on it as it happens.

REVISING FOUR: When you have finished your first draft of the case-history, put it aside for a day. Then read it aloud to see whether any leading idea or feeling emerges. If you find one stirring a little, consider cutting out those parts that do not touch this idea or feeling, and adding more details that strengthen it.

If you care about what you write, and know or observe it closely, you will reveal to your reader things he doesn't know. Stay awake when you observe. If you or other human beings are in action, the chances are high that you will be recording some fabulous realities.

One professional caution: Change any real names in your case-history to fictional names. What if your work becomes published, or passed around locally? What you consider an unbiased report of how Mrs. Smithweather, the science teacher, swore at John Saunders in lab may not strike Mrs. Smithweather in that way. If you had money, she might properly sue you for libel. Some real names you must keep in your writing or its point may be lost, but inspect all names and weigh the need to change them. Samuel Butler wrote a long book which became the classical English story of a sensitive son and a tyrannical, self-righteous father. Butler's real father was a sadist to him, but he refused to publish this book until after his father had died. And then it came out as a novel, with Butler's father carrying a fictional name. Butler himself died before *The Way of All Flesh* was published and he never knew that he had written one of the finest novels in the English language. The least you can do is protect Mrs. Smithweather and yourself by changing names.

But to have a full kit of auditory patterns curved to real emotions we do need to listen. We need to listen, with inside matching on our own part, to those whose phrases fit their inner state. We are lucky if we listen less to lecturers and experts, more to farmers, mechanics, truck drivers . . . laundresses, and children out of school.

SIDNEY COX

chapter 8
people
talking

"What?" said John.
"What'd you say?" said Mary.
"I said *what.*"

A pretty nothing conversation, but it probably caught you, held you, and perhaps brought a slight smile to your face. The moment a writer presents a person saying something and the reader realizes another person is around to hear it, a small tension builds in the reader until he finds out what the response is.

Think of using conversation in your writing. It's a way of adding opposition and suspense. Most persons who haven't written much dialogue think it's difficult to produce. On the contrary, it's easy for most beginning writers. They've heard conversation all their lives—listened to more words than they've read.

Conversation gives force to writing and cuts down on Explainery. In a dialogue the writer doesn't constantly say how the speakers feel as they respond to each other. Frequently they say the opposite of what they feel. The reader has to figure out whether one man's words are striking sparks with the others' or cooling them or making no contact at all.

When you write conversation, try for truth to the feeling and ideas expressed by persons in real situations. Try also for the true sound of each speaker's language–languages. Every person speaks a native language that belongs to his country. He also speaks a dialect, which belongs to part of the country. He speaks jargons or argots which belong to a group of persons he associates with at play or work—the gang from 14th Street or the guys at the Aerospace Company. And he speaks an idiolect, or personal language, which is his alone. It is spiced by a word or two he made up himself, or an original grammatical construction he fell into at age four and never climbed out of.

You can tell quickly when a written conversation is phony. Engfish conversation, for example. The supermarket cashier is saying "Oh, it's been delightful to have you as our customer today, Miss Watkins," or the bank manager is saying, "OK, Watkins. You write the check properly, we give you the bread."

Here's a college dialogue:

1

(Women's residence hall. Girl sitting at study desk. Enter Jean, friend from down the hall.)

Jean: Hi, Lin!

Lin: Hi, Jean: (Phone rings.) Just a minute. (She rises and walks to phone and picks up receiver.) Hello.

Tom: Hi, Lin. Whatcha doin'?

Lin: Oh, hi, Tom! I'm writing a paper for Teaching and Learning.

Tom: Huh?

Jean (turns and starts to leave room): Talk ta ya later, Lin. Tell Tom I said hi.

Lin (nodding to Jean): Writing a paper for Teaching and Learning. Jean said hi.

Tom: What's it about?

Lin: Just a paper on teaching.

Tom: Who's there with ya?

Lin: Nobody:

Tom: What the hell'd I hear then?

Lin: Jean just left.

Tom: Thought ya said nobody was there!

Lin (sarcastically): Huh?

Tom: Forget it! (Pause.) How many guys in your classes this semester?

Lin: Two.

Tom: Two? Come on, how many are there?

Lin: Two!

Tom: O.K. How many in your other class?

Lin: One.

Tom: Huh?

Lin: Yeh! Not many guys in elementary ed.

Tom: God, quit lyin' ta me!

Lin: I'm not lying, Tom!

Tom: Hell, come on, I know ya.

Lin: After three and a half years, you sure don't act like you do!

Tom: God, don't start preachin', this is costin' me money! (Pause.)

Lin: Okay. Goodbye! (Pause.)

Tom: Yeh. Bye.

Lin: Tom? I love you.

Tom: Can't hear ya, the damn fans are runnin'.

Lin: Tom, come on!

Tom (quickly): Yeh, I lub ya. Bye. (Click)

Lin: Sonofabitch!

That's a conversation. Two persons exchanging words, listening to each other, responding. Like most good writers, the author of that dialogue wrote out of close knowledge. If she were writing of diplomats or plumbers—making them talk—she might have made a mess of their conversation because she could not use her ear.

In the following dialogue, a mother uses her ear to remember how she and her boy talk to each other. The responses are quick and frank. You can tell that this mother knows her child but that he is not her peer.

2

(3:30 and my 7-year-old was arriving home from school.)

Hi, David, how are you?

OK, I guess. Didn't have a good day at school, though.

Oh? What happened?

Nobody likes me. Dave wouldn't let me play on his football team at recess.

Um, wonder why. You always have before. Did you say or do something to make him mad?

(Taking off his jacket and dropping it on the floor), Nope. He just said, "Brown, you can't play today."

Didn't you ask why?

If I had, he would have said, " 'Cause you're too stupid."
Nobody likes me.

David, you know that isn't true.

Yes it is. Mrs. Strand wouldn't ask me a question either.

Well David, I know everyone in the class can't be asked a
question every day. There just isn't enough time.

(Looking up at me in a disgusted way), Mom, there are
32 kids in my class. Everyone else was asked a question.

Oh good grief, David, everyone?

Well, almost. She doesn't like me, either. You don't even
like me, do you, Mom? You just yelled at me.

David, why don't you go in your room and play awhile?
(He gives me a big grin.) OK, Mom.

In informal conversation, persons seldom give speeches to each
other, or lectures. Part of the truth of Dialogue 1 comes from the
short answers given by the speakers. But sometimes a speech will erupt
into a little sermon. The writer presenting it must be sure it is lively
or that its dullness sharpens the whole dialogue or he will bore his
reader as the speechifier often bores his listeners. In the following dialogue, a girl suddenly gives a lecture to her roomates.

3

Barbie: Why don't you think he came?

Ann: I dunno.

Barbie: Maybe because we didn't really seem to click last
time we were together. Remember, I told you about it? He
was in a super good mood, and I was kind of depressed
because of all that work I had to do. Do you think that
could be it?

Ann: Maybe.

Barbie: I wish I just knew for sure. I hate guessing. I'm
sure I'd feel a whole lot better if I knew the reason.

Ann: What difference would it make?

Barbie: Well, at least I'd know. I wouldn't have to go
through all these tortuous guessing games, would I? It
would either be a good reason that I would accept and
forgive him for, and everything would be all right. Or else
it would be just an excuse and everything would be over.
But I'd know one way or the other. Don't you see that at
all?

Ann: He still didn't come, did he?

Barbie: God, Ann, aren't you the least bit sensitive? Or even curious? After all, Ben is a pretty big part of my life. He's the only boy I'm dating now and I see him practically every weekend. You know it's pretty hard to just meet boys anywhere. It's so much easier if you're at a party with a date. You meet a thousand guys that way. And they think you must have something to be there in the first place. They sure feel different about asking a girl out that they've met at a party before, and just picking someone up in the Union. I really don't understand you. Sometimes you don't seem to know anything about the way things are. You didn't even seem to care when Michael started living with some other girl all of a sudden. You never said a word to me about it. I thought you would feel something after a year and a half. I wish I knew what to do. At least you're usually sensible. Do you think I should call him?

Ann: I don't know if you'll understand this or not, Barbie, but *I don't care what you do!*

Because conversations are inherently dramatic they are often more persuasive than lectures or sermons or editorials. Here is a conversation that makes a point about the writer's attitude toward a patriotic ritual in a school. The reader is expected to recognize the point from what is said in the dialogue.

4

(Fifth-grade class, 9:00 A.M.)

Mike: Will you please stand to say the pledge.

Class: I pledge allegiance to the flag of the United States of America, and to the republic for which it stands, one nation, under God——

Teacher: Excuse me, class. Mike, why aren't you saying the pledge with us? You're the pledge leader. That's an important job.

Mike (hesitating): It doesn't make sense. Our nation isn't run by God.

Teacher: Now, Mike, we all know that we say the pledge so that we can feel we all belong to one nation, and we're working to make that nation great. Now you wouldn't want us to think you aren't proud of our country, would you?

Mike: No—I guess not.

Teacher: Let's start again.

(The pledge is said the second time.)

Teacher: All right, let's all get our handwriting books and beginning working on page 9. (Pause.) Mike, did you hear me? You're going to have to shape up. That's twice I've had to speak to you today, and in only ten minutes!

(Mike looks down at his feet as everyone stares at him, and mutters): See, God's not running my nation.

In the following dialogue a subtle tension is built without any stage directions or explanations by the writer.

5

(Open house on Sunday in the dorm.)

How do you like my room?

Who are those guys on the wall?

Just some friends. One of them is Jack. Guess which?

That.

Nope. That. I'll take him away. I'll replace them all when I get your picture.

You don't have to.

I know, but I want to. Do you want to see my photo album?

Sure.

Sit down. Oh, thanks for the roses again, see.

I see, they were long, that's good. Is that the card? What did it say?

Tom.

Let me see. Hey, I said to write more.

Here's a pen, write some more.

"To Renée with love." I don't sign my name that way.

Do it again there.

When was this taken? I don't like you with short hair. Don't cut it.

Why not?

Because I don't want you to.

O.K.

Who's that guy?

Jack.

Where was it?

In our back yard.

With a flower in hand.

I like it, it was our senior party. Let me take your pic-
ture. Don't get up! Come on.
Come on where? I don't like it.
Well, I do. Take that rose and hold it.
Do you always ask guys to hold flowers?
No, just special people.
How about Jack? Special people, eh?
That's all over. Take it now. Not in your mouth. Tom,
stay still.
I hate this.
You gave it to me.

In the above small drama you probably sensed the tight, nervous,
half-joking sound of a conversation between persons testing each
other's romantic feeling. A delicate probing, yet revealed in the
sparest dialogue.

> *I notice particularly the cadence of
> their voices, the sort of phrases they'll
> use, and that's what I'm all the time try-
> ing to hear in my head, how people
> word things—because everybody speaks
> an entirely different language . . .*
>
> FRANK O'CONNOR

WRITING NINE: Write two short dialogues that carry truth that
counts for you and voices that you believe speak truly and individually.

WRITING TEN: Now write down an experience or a person and
use dialogue to inject life and tension into the paper. Maybe you
already have done a free writing that can be extended and strengthened with conversation. Note how the dialogue in the following
paper gives validity to its happenings. The children have their way
of talking, the bus driver has his, and neither talking sounds like
the writer writing.

6

I do not enjoy riding in cars. My somewhat sane mind
becomes lost, and instinct takes over. Every driver on the
road, including the one driving me, must be a maniac.
Buses are different, however. On the campus route, it
doesn't matter where I sit. It's always so crowded you can't
see where you're going. The bus driver reigns supreme.
You put yourself in his hands and suddenly Linus's blanket

envelops you. Perhaps I should have said buses *were* different, though.

Yesterday my last class ended. I was wary. All of a sudden here comes the bus. Calling up some unknown energy reserve, I dashed to the corner; hair, purse, and earrings flapping. The all-knowing bus driver stopped. He was taking some grade schoolers home and said he had to go to the trailer parks behind Wayside before going to the East Campus. "Do you mind?" God, no. I just wanted to sit down.

The kids were running up and down and sticking their heads out the windows. In general, doing all the cute tricks that kids do to drive you nuts. I graciously bestowed my benevolent adult smile upon them. After making the stops at the trailer courts, there were still six kids left on the bus. The all-knowing bus driver said, "Where you kids go? You should have gotten off already."

Kid: Well, the bus picked us up this morning.

Bus Driver: Not my bus. Where do you live?

Kid: In those new apartments.

Bus Driver: What ones?

Kid: Those new ones by the old ones.

Bus Driver: What old ones?

Kid: By the railroad tracks.

Bus Driver: My bus isn't supposed to go to any new ones.

Kid: The bus picked us up this morning.

Bus Driver: Not my bus.

Meanwhile, we're going down Stadium Drive. The oldest girl, about eight or nine, starts directing the bus driver and we realize that the new ones are the new married apartments.

Girl: Turn in this driveway.

Bus Driver: My bus isn't supposed to go here. Nobody told me.

Kid: This is where the bus picked us up this morning.

Bus Driver: Not my bus. Is there a place to turn around?

Kid: Stop here. That's where we live.

Bus Driver: Where am I supposed to turn around?

Girl: Go around that curve, and there's a place.

The kids are disposed of. Soon now I'll be home. Around the curve we go. It looks like this road goes back to the main one. Uh, oh. Here comes a pickup, telling us to stop.

And there ahead, the road stops. It's not complete. Out stomps the pickup man.

Pickup: You can't get through there.

Bus Driver: Where can I turn around? Those kids said I could turn around.

Pickup: You can't bring that bus in here.

Bus Driver: Where the — am I supposed to turn around?

The pickup man stomps off, having preserved law and order. Now it's only the bus driver and me against this narrow road, perhaps wide enough for a car to turn around. But a bus? The bus driver is doing the things you do to a bus to make it go in reverse. And I realize I'm the only passenger. There are windows and more windows and I have a perfect view. In front is the unfinished road, to the right, a steep ditch, to the left, cliffs of apartments, and they're all panting. I'm sitting in the front, on one of those sideways seats that hold four people. *Reverse,* grrrind, I slam to the left. *Forward,* grrrind. I slam to the right. *Brakes,* pow! I fibrillate. Back and forth. Stop, go. Grrrind, pow! We almost go over into the ditch. We just miss colliding with a cliff. Then—ahhh—we've done it. We've turned around. The bus driver says he hopes it didn't disturb me. I stutter and gag on the tongue in my throat and just titter nervously. But I'm almost home. He stops, I grab onto the pole by the door and try to remember how to make my feet move. As I get down, he says, "If you hadn't been in the bus, I would have driven it in the ditch and let them bastards worry about it. Nobody told me I was supposed to take those kids there."

I watched the bus drive away on wheels of clay.

KATHLEEN BOLINGER

From now on when you write anything, consider whether dialogue may help your cause.

*Think of and look at your work as
though it were done by your enemy.
If you look at it to admire it you are
lost . . . If we look at it to see where
it is wrong, we shall see this and make
it righter. If we look at it to see where
it is right, we shall see this and shall not
make it righter. We cannot see it both
wrong and right at the same time.*

SAMUEL BUTLER

chapter 9
criticizing

CRITICIZING WRITING is painful and valu-
able. One cannot say "good" or "bad" unless he has developed standards. One of the best ways to build standards is to sit with five to
ten persons who discuss each other's writing, which they read aloud.
Then the novice critic can judge his responses against those of his
companions. In their faces he can see which writing holds or loses
them, makes them laugh or smile. In weeks and months of such
sessions, he develops bases for judgment, and all the while his own
writing stands in his mind, receiving a silent, secret criticism.

When his turn comes to read his writing aloud, he hears his words
as if detached from him. He instantly notes slips he failed to see
when he read over his work in his room. While he is reading before
critics, he finds himself saying "oops" and reaching for a pencil
with which to change a word or line. At first the experience of
reading to the group may be so frightening that he does not learn
from the responses (or lack of responses) because he does not fully
perceive them. But after a few readings, he comes to this awareness,
and the silence of the group at a moment when he thought his writing
funny or stirring shows him that he needs to take the writing home
and put it on the workbench, or perhaps throw it in the wastebasket.

> *I learnt to speak as men learn to skate*
> *or to cycle—by doggedly making a fool*
> *of myself until I got used to it. Then I*
> *practised it in the open air—at the street*
> *corner, in the market square, in the park*
> *—the best school.*
>
> GEORGE BERNARD SHAW

If the group responds positively in the right places, the writer will go home anxious to write more. Encouragement is the battery that motivates the car. Once the motor is running, the car can go for hundreds of miles on a small charge of praise.

Every writer needs encouragement, whether beginner or prize-winning novelist. Loren Eiseley, the naturalist and anthropologist who wrote *The Immense Journey* and other books which are the envy of professional writers for their style, said of his learning experience:

> My greatest fortune was in having understanding teachers
> . . . I shall always be grateful for the interest they took in
> my work, for their encouragement expressed or silently
> affirmed.

Here, briefly, is the history of a beginning writer learning to revise, to criticize, to take criticism, and thus to write more professionally:

Having finished his first draft, he reads it aloud to himself. He writes a second draft, cutting, adding, rearranging. He puts the writing away for several hours—or if he has time, a month, three months. He then reads it aloud and sharpens it. The next morning he polishes it.

> *. . . the mere act of reading aloud put*
> *his work before him in a new light and,*
> *by constraining his attention to every*
> *line, made him judge it more rigorously.*
> *I always intend to read, and generally*
> *do read, what I write aloud to some one;*
> *any one almost will do, but he should*
> *not be so clever that I am afraid of him.*
> *I feel weak places at once when I read*
> *aloud where I thought, as long as I read*
> *to myself only, that the passage was all*
> *right.*
>
> SAMUEL BUTLER

Then he takes it to a group of other beginning writers and reads it aloud to them. He listens to what they say. He tries to hold their responses in mind without accepting or rejecting them instantly. At home a day later, he reviews the criticism, follows the suggestions he thinks helpful and ignores those he finds invalid. He writes his fifth draft and submits it for publication or files it with his finished work.

A program for improving writing such as the one presented in this book will not succeed unless the beginning writer becomes experienced through engaging in critical sessions with his peers. The person directing the program needs to encourage the writers to criticize upon their own two feet, and to evolve their own standards; but he also needs to state his own opinions of what is good and bad about writing—both the writing of those who sit with him and that published by established professionals.

He may help beginners become better critics by reading a paper or two before the group, preferably one that has been reproduced for each member, pointing out its strengths, and inviting further comments from the group. Then he can break the group into smaller sections of seven, eight, or nine, and ask them to read aloud their papers to each other for criticism. Nine is an ideal number because it makes a sufficient audience to put pressure on the writer. He hears his words differently when they are read to an audience of that size than he does when he reads to two or three listeners. If most of his nine listeners say his writing is good or bad, he cannot dismiss their opinion lightly. But if he reads to only two or three, he may say, "Well, Jim was just trying to be nice to me" or "Abigail never did like me anyway."

Preferably, small groups should meet in separate rooms, or only two to a room, so that they will not disturb each other; but that is not always possible. When the leader finds time does not permit a reading of all papers in groups as large as nine, he may cut groups to four or five, or even three when the writers have become more trustworthy and honest as critics.

The remarks of critics who take writing seriously are the most valuable response a writer can receive. Marginal comments pointing out slips or mistakes in grammar, spelling, or mechanics are not ordinarily useful to a writer until he is polishing his work in final draft. The experience of thousands of teachers in American high schools and colleges has showed that such reading for correction rather than helpful editing has had little positive effect. Once beginners sense they are improving rapidly and can write papers that move their peers, they take pride and care in their work, which improves every aspect of their writing. A man is not going to learn the fine points of catching a football on the run, over the heads of defenders, or near the sidelines, until he can first hang on to it when it is thrown straight at him softly.

Giving criticism in a small group session asks a great deal of the critic. If he is impressed, he must sense his reaction and make it verbal. Some persons say that criticism must never be vague—"Good," or "I liked that." Those persons were never writers; they don't know what encouragement means. Perhaps they fear such general remarks are mere flattery. If so, the criticism is immoral and damaging. If honest, it is valuable. It will be more valuable if the critic learns to state it specifically: "I liked your descriptions. They were fresh. I wrote down this one: 'The hands looked stiff, as if they had just weeded a garden, and her fingers were yellow and brittle.' "

The wise critic knows that the beginning writer is vulnerable to almost any blow. He has little confidence, is easily knocked out. He feels his writing is all him; he has developed no objectivity. Any criticism of his sentences is an attack upon his self. Therefore the critic who would help a beginning writer, rather than destroy him, starts with positive criticism. He looks for what he can praise. A sentence. A paragraph. An incident. One word. If he can find nothing he can honestly admire, he says nothing but "Keep writing." Everyone has a command of words if he can find the troops that belong to him, and the wise critic finds ways of assuring the beginning writer of this fact.

As the beginner continues writing, he more often speaks with force and tells experiences or ideas that strike with surprise and truth. The critic keeps before the beginner his successes. He tries to move him from success to success.

The critic remembers he is part of a group. He volunteers only two or three criticisms during a half-hour period, knowing that if he talks more than that he will usurp others' time and lessen his chances of being heard with attention and respect. So he takes notes as the writer reads and he selects from all his responses to the writing those he thinks will most aid the writer.

Only when the writer has achieved enough successes to recognize his abilities and potentialities does the intelligent critic engage in thorough and negative criticism. Once the writer senses that a number of honest and keen-minded persons have admired some of his words, he is strong enough to take negative criticism and use it to create a success.

A professional editor demonstrates model behavior. He considers himself not so much a judge as a helper—one who assists the writer in improving a piece of writing that both persons have a stake in. He is not a public critic sounding off to impress others with his wisdom or wisecracks. He is not trying to get one up on the writer he works with.

> He [Ezra Pound] was a marvelous critic
> because he didn't try to turn you into
> an imitation of himself. He tried to see
> what you were trying to do.
>
> T. S. ELIOT

In his manner he must convince the writer he is not out to needle him but to help. Only then will the writer think objectively about what the critic is saying. Striking back at the critic is pointless. At the moment of criticism, no one enjoys being told his writing contains weaknesses. Learning to write communicatively is painful, but if the writer builds confidence slowly and solidly, he will rise to the level where he exclaims in joy with the critic at their mutual discovery of a weakness and how it may be strengthened.

To learn to do something well rather than simply to learn *about* something requires failure. Not final failure, but a number of small failures alternated with successes. The learner who never anticipates failure is doomed to continue without improvement or to collapse into perpetual inactivity. He is fortunate if he has an expert coach who makes sure many of his first small tries are successes.

The wise writer expects his fellows to say they don't like something in his work. He tries to find out what and why. When his writing is praised, he says "Thank you" or nothing. He does not apologize and say, "This is really not very good. I needed to take more time on it," or "You've all probably heard this kind of thing before." If he really possesses such feelings toward his work, he does not bring it to the group for criticism. He presents only what at the moment looks good to him, in the best form he can put it in. He tries to be honest. When he receives criticism he never says, "Well, I wasn't trying very hard when I wrote that." He does not agree with a critic just to be friendly, but he does not engage in long hostile defenses of his work which imply the critic is committing a crime to speak against what he has written.

> *A writer is unfair to himself when he is*
> *unable to be hard on himself.*
>
> MARIANNE MOORE

Disciplining himself in group critique sessions, a writer trains himself to be a better critic of his own work when alone with it. He knows he must stand by his words or change them upon criticism. The critics may praise and censure, rave and rant, but he must make the final decisions. He is ultimately responsible for his sentences.

chapter 10
oppositions

Strong writers bring together oppositions of one kind or another. Kitchen language and elevated language, long and short sentences, fast and slow rhythms. And what they choose to present from life—whether it be object, act, or idea—is frequently the negative and the positive, one thing and its opposite, two ideas that antagonize each other. The result is tension. And the surprise that comes from new combinations. And news.

When you wonder whether you ever think anything worth communicating to others in writing, you need only look at what you have written and ask whether it contains tension and surprise. Put the following short papers to that test:

> This university is the first university I have attended. The university itself is not bad, but the dorms leave something to be desired. I cannot see why the students in the dorms waste so much time fooling around when they can use this time profitably studying.
>
> I'll be here approximately two years. I am going to make those two years the most profitable years of my life and education.
>
> My course of study is that of Food Distribution. I plan and hope to become a supermarket manager for the Brinner Food Company located in Detroit, Michigan.

> I am going to try extremely hard this semester, as a fresh-
> man, to build my grades as high as possible. This is not
> just to show everyone I can do the work, or for personal
> satisfaction, but to build my self-confidence in myself. I
> plan to have both a profitable and enjoyable stay here at
> the university.

About all that can be said of that paper is "Ugh." The incoming
freshman is sure he is going to study hard and be a good boy. No
surprise. Nothing within his paper *speaks to anything else in the
paper*. No tension as there is in this paper:

> During my student teaching in summer school, my critic
> and I would occasionally take the class to the library. The
> first time we went, I was sitting with a confused ninth-
> grade boy trying to explain to him how to do a summary.
> The fat authoritarian librarian stomped over to us and
> whispered at me through clenched teeth, "Either you shut
> your mouth, young lady, or take your books and get out of
> here. You haven't stopped that mouth for ten minutes.
> This is a library, not a place to flirt."

Here the opposition comes up strong because the writer expects the
reader to get the point on his own. (Incidentally, the word *authori-
tarian* above is Explainery and should be removed. The librarian's
ugly language, faithfully presented, does the job, needs no help from
an adjective.)

Most professional writing sets up oppositions that build tension
and pay off in surprises. William Hazlitt, who died in 1830, is still
read today because his sentences are pungent and biting. He called
one of his essays "On the Ignorance of the Learned" (opposition already in the title), and built tension in this way:

> The book-worm wraps himself up in his web of verbal gen-
> eralities, and sees only the glimmering shadows of things re-
> flected from the minds of others. Nature *puts him out*. The
> impressions of real objects, stripped of the disguises of words
> and voluminous roundabout descriptions, are blows that
> stagger him; and he turns from the bustle, the noise, and
> glare, and whirling motion of the world about him (which
> he has not an eye to follow in its fantastic changes, nor an
> understanding to reduce to fixed principles), to the quiet
> monotony of the dead languages, and the less startling and
> more intelligible combinations of the letters of the alphabet.

A beginning writer often says, "But I can't do anything as difficult as that." He can. He already does. In conversation he frequently puts together exciting oppositions—they are what impel him home to his roommate or spouse to tell the news. When writing, a person who has no pertinent news to tell should simply record a fact that interests him. Then he will have something to oppose. A something must be caught by the mind before anything can arise to oppose it. Here's an entry in a college girl's journal.

While I was brushing my teeth this morning, I looked out the rain-splattered window and saw rusty orange leaves falling to the soggy ground. They're like death.

She has put down the something. Nothing surprising—that dead leaves are like death. In fact, that's a stupid thing to say. Better leave it out. But then the writer kept going. She let herself connect those leaves to-someone.

They just fall for seemingly no reason. The men in Viet Nam—do they really know why they are falling?

Now opposition has been brought about. Soldiers are not leaves, but they fall—also without knowing why? (Incidentally, the writer has used an intensifying word that doesn't intensify—the *really* in the phrase *really know*.)

The most available and obvious truths are frequently closed to us because we are not open to possible surprise, to seeing the opposite of the common. One day when Henry Thoreau was describing as precisely as possible how a squirrel runs, he asked himself about the opposite—how the squirrel walks. And as he observed squirrels more and more, he came to the conclusion squirrels never walk. A surprising truth. One day in a Shakespeare class students were trying to decide why they didn't like *Richard II* as much as the other plays they had read. Richard was an effeminate man thrust into kingship who kept turning on and off about whether he wanted to be king. One student said that the play contained almost no humor. A simple observation, but one that told a great deal about this play by a writer who customarily introduced humor into the most pressured tragedies. Richard is a fascinating man, but a man and a play without humor are apt to place second in popularity contests. To see what is there but invisible, to see what is not there but expected, takes a person willing to oppose his habitual opinions and expectations.

> *He who knows only his own side of the*
> *case, knows little of that.*
>
> JOHN STUART MILL

Make it a habit to look for oppositions. You will find suddenly that you are wiser than you thought. Do it automatically. If you find yourself putting down *hot,* consider the possibility of *cold* in the same circumstances; if *simple,* then *complex;* if *loving,* then *hating;* etc. The habit will prevent you from oversimplifying people and processes and ideas. If you're trying to draw a portrait of a person you know and find yourself putting down good traits, ask if he has any bad. Or vice versa. Note how the writer of this journal entry did that.

> I'm not bragging or anything like that, but the fact is I live in a dorm. I also have the weirdest wall-mate. We share the bathroom. Everyone calls him The Farmer. He lives on a farm, no doubt—carries with him the old habits and customs of the ancient farm hand. He's only showered three times since school started back in September. No, I'm not lying, only three times. Now you might be wondering, "How does he know he's only taken three showers?" Well, when most people take a shower it's a commonplace event, but with him I call it a major overhaul. He showers, washes his hair, brushes his teeth, and finally takes off his gold-spotted shirt and puts on his green-spotted one. So whenever he changes shirts, the floor knows he's taken a shower.
>
> It also takes him about an hour in the shower. One day in the Big Three, I was beginning to think he forgot where his body parts were. But the really weird thing is he always talks about crabs. When he comes out of the shower he yells, "Well, those crabs are gone for a while."
>
> Sometimes you forget about his odor and dirt, like when he offers you some of his mother's home-made cookies. They're not so bad if you drink a lot of water. The Farmer usually shares whatever he has, so most of the time we overlook his bad traits.
>
> But when his caustic body aroma strikes you, it's like a spike in your heart; you've got to get rid of it. Right now everyone is on his back to clean up, partly because he stinks, but also because he's really a good guy. Like I always

say, "If you look at a car with a corroded body, it doesn't mean the engine's bad."

In that paper the writer has found oppositions. Now he needs to say more about the good side of The Farmer, let the reader see him in action positively.

When mothers write of their children, they often brag insufferably until the reader doubts all their assertions because the kid simply couldn't be that good. In the following small portrait of a daughter, the writer sees oppositions and thus finds lively truths.

> Karen is twelve, the not-quite, almost, nearly stage. One minute she teases for nylons. "But Mother, all the girls wear them!" The next she insists on a unicycle for Christmas.
>
> She wants a horse for her birthday. Convincing her father wasn't difficult. When she puts her arms around him and tosses that long blonde hair, he'd get her an elephant if she asked.
>
> Her bed is never made before 4 P.M. and her clothes are always in piles around her room. She doesn't throw them there. They seem to come off by some witchcraft. She's always surprised to see them down there on the floor.
>
> It takes her fifteen minutes to clear six cups and saucers from the dining room table and she is the only one I know who sits on the kitchen counter while drying dishes.
>
> When urged to "Please get those dishes done," she replies, "O.K., Mother, dear," in her half-laughing, half-caressing, half-child and half-adult way.

WRITING ELEVEN: Write two 10–15 minute free writings (putting down the words as fast as you can and aiming to fill at least a full page) in which you begin with something and move to an opposition. Keep going, don't stop to reflect long. It makes no difference whether you write more about the first thing or the second, just so they oppose each other. Perhaps they will seem strong oppositions as you begin and almost identical twins when you finish. No matter. Be open for surprises.

You do not need to write about persons. Maybe a place interests you and sets up oppositions for you, or one place opposes another as it did for the girl who wrote this description.

> I often go to the library to the row of study rooms on the second floor. I have no favorite, they all seem identical, although I know they're not. I choose the first empty room.
>
> One wall is completely taken up by a wooden door with a window in it. On an old label on the glass someone has scribbled "Help."

The writer of this paper now continues with more physical details about the room. Probably they will begin to bore you. Remember when you write that description gets boring fast unless shown through some human action or brought alive by oppositions and surprises. The next lines from this paper are enclosed in brackets to suggest they might be left out in a second draft.

> [The wall opposite the door contains a long window looking out onto shelf after shelf of books and other tables where other people are studying. The two remaining walls are unbroken except for a heat register and an electric socket. The floor is paved with black linoleum tiles freckled white, the ceiling with white acoustical tiles dotted black.]
>
> The air vent in the ceiling is surrounded by rings of dirty stains. The yellow walls have been scratched, scuffed, and scribbled on by countless occupants. Some have tried to immortalize themselves: "Steve loves Linda." "Call Betty, 381-8596." "D.W. + J.B." Others are anonymously clever— "G. Houle was here." or philosophical—"Why, why, why?" or sceptic—"Repent sinners." Even the table top is scored with idle carving: "Kiss me," "Mel 1965," "Sigma Phi Epsilon." These writings seem pathetically disembodied, detached from the people who wrote them. Their attempt to make the bare wall and table more personal only advertises impersonality and coldness. The room belongs to no one. Any person can enter, leave his initials, his scuff mark, his cigarette butts, and never return . . .

Now the writer sets up her opposition—the library room against her dorm room:

> Sometimes I stay in my dorm room to study. It seems less severe than library study rooms, but it's not. The smell is of hair spray and unwashed feet. Room 348 is larger than most dorm rooms because four girls live here. But the jumble of furniture and possessions makes it always crowded. Besides the regulation university desks and chairs, we've

added a rocker, a record player, a crowded bookcase, and an orange rug now faded by lint and dust. The window sill looks like a continuation of the desk next to it. Mugs, bottles, pencilholders, pictures, a clock, a Kleenex box, books, papers, and a football pom-pom flow from one onto the other, and the bookshelf at the end of the desk is piled with bright colored volumes. When the brown window curtains are opened, the view is of another red-brick dorm.

The personal touches that a library study room lacks are only temporary here. Nothing will remain of my roommates and me when we leave, except a few more scratches on the desks and tape marks on the walls. But the four of us in 348 don't often think of the depressing impermanence around us, of the unknown girls who have lived here before us, and who will live here after, trying to cover a dormitory room with home. Instead we listen to the music coming faintly down the hall. Sometimes we say a few words to each other about the day's happenings, but my roommates seem as far from me as the people who sit outside the windows of my study room in the library. They walk past my life silently. I see them for one minute or one year, but in time I won't see them at all. And I won't miss them. I like them now, but then I won't care.

The habit of seeing oppositions within one thing or person or between things and persons marks the intelligent man, even the wise or profound man. Shakespeare became famous in large part because he created characters who were round instead of flat. There was room in them for fascinating oppositions. Shylock was a cruel moneylender and a harsh father, but he gave one of the greatest of all speeches against racial or religious discrimination. Today it could have been expressed point by point by any of our leading black militants.

He hath disgraced me, and hindered me half a million; laughed at my losses, mocked at my gains, scorned my nation, thwarted my bargains, cooled my friends, heated mine enemies; and what's his reason? I am a Jew. Hath not a Jew eyes? Hath not a Jew hands, organs, dimensions, senses, affections, passions? fed with the same food, hurt with the same weapons, subject to the same diseases, healed by the same means, warmed and cooled by the same winter and summer, as a Christian is? If you prick us, do we not bleed? if you tickle us, do we not laugh? if you poison us, do we not

die? and if you wrong us, shall we not revenge? if we are
like you in the rest, we will resemble you in that. If a Jew
wrong a Christian, what is his humility? Revenge. If a
Christian wrong a Jew, what should his sufferance be by
Christian example? Why, revenge. The villainy you teach
me, I will execute; and it shall go hard but I will better the
instruction.

Those words from a man who had often appeared unfeeling come as
a surprise to the reader of *The Merchant of Venice*. The whole speech
is based on an opposition—Jew to Christian, says Shylock, supposedly
different, but actually the same in their humanity. Note how easily
Shakespeare sets up opposing words: *warmed—cooled, Christian example*—the reader expects a positive virtue to follow, but he gets—
revenge.

Nothing mysterious about the fundamental of presenting oppositions. Because Shakespeare uses it brilliantly doesn't mean you cannot
use it in your way. If it becomes habitual to you, occasionally you will
slide into statement as strong as Shakespeare's. For example, you may
think of something as ordinary and yet inspired as Shylock's "if you
tickle us, do we not laugh?" which comes on the reader so surprisingly
in the midst of that train of dignified and solemn comparison.

A college freshman once was writing idly in her journal in the
laundry room of a dormitory and put down these words:

I leaned against the washer and as it began its cycle, my
entire body pulsated with it. It was as if I were holding my
heart in my hand, and I was terribly excited. Then suddenly the washer stopped.

She made the jump between the throb of the washing machine and the
throb of her heart. Oppositions frequently gain in power from being
different not only in content or idea but in tone or level as well. We
think of a washing machine as lowly and mechanical and a human
heart, exalted and pulsing.

The passages of student writing printed in this book are almost all
short, of such length that they would not be published in most magazines or anthologies. They are short for two reasons; the first is that
long examples would make the book fat, the second is that beginning
writers usually think they can't sustain powerfully a long piece of writing, and so they seldom try. They can—you can, if you go about the
job the way professional writers do.

They use every possible method. Collect materials and evidence in notebooks. Make tape recordings of what people say. Take pictures to aid their memory. Consult books and magazines. They put to use many of the strategies presented in this book—sometimes four or five in one effort.

Here is a long story about two boys. Right away you may have thought: "Two—probably in opposition." Yes, in both opposition and harmony. It is a big story made up of a lot of little stories. Words and acts speak to each other constantly and remind the writer of others he may have forgotten. It is a story of large opposition and how the writer came to understand its meaning and value.

* * *

NOT ANOTHER WORD

Richard Thurman

Because I was one of the bigger, healthier boys in the class—and also one of the biggest, smoothest liars, and thus apt to set an inspiring example for the others—Miss Devron would often begin the morning's inquisition with me. "Paul Adam," she would say, beaming down upon me, "would you be kind enough to tell us what you had for breakfast this morning?"

Even in the third grade, we were perceptive enough to sense that Miss Devron's inquiries into our daily breakfast menus sprang from something deeper than a mere interest in keeping us healthy. One look at her size and you knew what supreme importance food had in her life, and since we were her children—those she would never have herself, because of age, temperament, and general appearance— she apparently found it necessary to feel her way into our souls by following a glass of fruit juice and an egg and a slice of ham down our throats each morning. It wasn't just her zeal to know us personally through the food we ate that made us guard against her with a series of outrageous lies; she also wanted to know our families—their general way of life, their social and economic status in our small Utah town, and whether or not they lived in accordance with the Mormon doctrines, which were as inseparable from our lives as the mountain

"Not Another Word" by Richard Thurman. Permission the author; © 1957 The New Yorker Magazine, Inc.

air we breathed. And she had a nasty way of pointing out any devia-
tion from her set of standards by interrupting the stream of breakfast
reports. "Hominy grits!" I remember her saying on one of the first
mornings we were in her class. "Did you hear, class? Ronald Adair
had hominy grits for breakfast."

She smiled her closed smile of wisdom and commiseration at
Ronald, and placed the index finger of her left hand like a hot dog
between her second and third chins while waggling her free hand
scoldingly in his direction. "It's a lucky thing for you, young man,
that your parents somehow had the energy to come out West, where
you can get a new start in life," she said. "It's food like hominy grits
that has kept the South backward so long. Out *here* we eat bacon and
ham-and-eggs and hot cereal and fresh fruit juices and good buttered
toast with jam. You're very lucky, young man! My, yes."

With such tactics she soon taught us to lie, and regardless of what
each of us had eaten at home, there in Miss Devron's class we began
to share a breakfast as monotonous as it was sumptuous. It was only
a variation in quantity that crept into our diets from the first student's
report to the last, for if one egg and a modest piece of ham were enough
to start Miss Devron's fingers strolling contentedly over the terraces
of her chins, it took considerably more than this to keep them happy
and moving by the time the class was half through its recital, and by
the time the last student's turn came, Miss Devron's wolfish appetite
responded to nothing less than a gorge. Lila Willig was the last student
on our class list. She looked as if she were made from five laths, and
in the hectic flush of her unhealthiness—perhaps caused by near-
starvation at home—she would sometimes get a little hysterical and
report that she had eaten twenty-five eggs and a whole ham. I'm sure
now that this was not because of any native waggishness in Lila, but
we thought it was then, and we always laughed until Miss Devron had
to pound the desk with her ruler.

"Now, stop that foolishness, Lila," she would say briskly. "Tell the
class right out how many eggs you had for breakfast."

"Five," Lila would say, nervously scratching her frizzled yellow
curls until they stood out like coiled wires. She could have said
nothing else. The boy in front of her had just reported a breakfast
of five eggs; anything less from Lila would have been picked up by
Miss Devron as an example of parental neglect.

"That's better," the teacher would say, her fingers resuming their
stroll. "And as I look over your faces this morning, class, I can already
see the differences that good eating habits can make in one's life.
How much brighter your eyes! How much stronger your backs!"

We simpered back at her, only vaguely and uneasily aware that she was a tyrant who was flattening our individuality with the weight of her righteous self-assurance. In less than a month under her, we were reduced to a spineless group of sycophantic ham, egg, and cereal eaters, with only Lila's occasional lapses to show us what a dull mold we had been crushed into. And then our integrity was rescued in an unexpected way.

The new boy who turned up in our class a month after the opening of school certainly looked like no hero. He was smaller than most of us, and while all of us boys were proudly wearing corduroy knickers, he still wore the short pants we scorned, and in the sharp air of that October morning his thin legs were mottled with a network of blue. We welcomed this pathetic figure with a fine generosity of spirit. "Where you from?" one of us asked him as we walked up to where he was standing, at the edge of the playground.

"New York."

"New York!" we said, and I now had an explanation of why he was such a puny-looking little rat. From the handful of Western movies and cowboy books I had already absorbed, I knew the kind of magic that enters into a man's blood when he is born west of the Mississippi River. His eye is clearer, his nerves are truer, his gait is more tireless, his aim is steadier, and in the very heart of his manliness there is a dimension that effete Easterners know nothing about. All this I knew as I looked down at the new boy's skinny blue legs.

"New York, eh?" I said menacingly, moving up to him until I could have rested my chin on top of his head.

"That's right," he said, lounging against the top rail of the playground fence and casually lifting one foot to rest it on the lower rail. I eyed him with a steely coldness I had learned from a story about a man who had built the Union Pacific Railroad across the plains and who could drive a spike into a tie with two hammer blows. I put my fingers into my belt, just above where my six-shooters should have been. "Who's your old man voting for?" I asked. "Al Smith or Hoover?"

"Al Smith."

"Well, then, I guess I'll have to beat you up."

Perhaps nowadays, what with the broadened horizons brought on by the Second World War, Korea, UNESCO, and the stress on social-adjustment patterns in modern education, a new student from, say, Siam or Afghanistan can take his place unobtrusively in an American schoolroom. I don't know. But I do know that in my part of America in 1928 a new student had to fight his way into school, particularly if

he had come to us from more than five blocks away. It will be understood, then, that I had no unusual political precocity or passion at
the age of eight, and that this difference in our fathers' political
views was only a pretext for me to beat up the new boy, who had
offended every one of us by coming all the way from New York,
with his short pants and blue skin.

We sized each other up for a second. Then he shrugged his thin
shoulders and said "O.K.," and the quickness with which he squared
away for battle gave me a little turn. We circled around each other,
with everyone urging me to get in there and show him what was
what. But just then the bell rang, and I felt a surge of relief that was
just a bit disconcerting to anyone born as far west as I had been.

"I'll finish with you later," I said.

"O.K.," he said, with that same unnerving readiness.

Something more immediate than our father's political inclinations
operated to bring us closer together that morning. Miss Devron put
the new boy in the empty seat just in front of me, and I spent the
first few minutes of class watching his blue neck turn pink in the
warm room, while the pupils drearily went through their recital of
breakfasts eaten that morning.

"And now the new boy, Robert Bloom," said Miss Devron, smiling
down at him. "What did you have this morning?"

He had been listening carefully to what was going on, and once,
when he turned his profile to me, I could see that he was enjoying
himself. The rest of the pupils had answered from their seats, but he
stood up in the aisle. He stood at attention like a soldier.

"I had a cup of coffee and a snail, Ma'am."

There was a stony quiet for a second, and then the dazzling irrev-
erence of what he had said burst through us with shock waves of pure
delight. Miss Devron pounded on the desk with the ruler, and her red
chins trembled in front of her like molten lava. "Class!" she cried.
"Class, we'll have order here! Come to order. Come to order this
instant!"

But she was trying to calm down a madhouse.

"A cup of coffee and a snail, please!" somebody shouted.

"Give me a worm with mine!" somebody yelled back.

And on we went, up that enticing road of suggestibility, until we
were eating snakes on muffins. The special delight, of course, was the
coffee. *There* was the alluring evil and joy of what he had said,
because most of us in that room, including Miss Devron, were Mor-
mons, who felt, in a way beyond reason, that murder was no more
than a high-spirited lark compared to drinking coffee or smoking.

It wasn't until Miss Devron and her ruler and the powers of light finally triumphed over the dark joy in us that we began to realize the outrageousness of what he had said. We slunk back from debauchery to righteousness under Miss Devron's glowering eye, and finally he was left standing there, all alone before the glare of our joint indignation.

"We should never laugh at those who don't know better, class," Miss Devron began, in a carefully controlled voice. "We must share our knowledge with those less fortunate, and help them to know the truth. Robert comes from a part of the country where they don't know about health. Now then, Robert, that can't be all you had for breakfast, can it?" She looked at him with the pity, the heart-spoken prayer, and the tenderness of a missionary meeting with a cannibal for the first time.

"No, Ma'am," he said. "I had two cups of coffee."

The tight breath gathered in our throats again, but Miss Devron was in control now, and aside from a few blown cheeks and red faces there was no sign that we were not with her in spirit.

"Now, class," she continued, "I want to ask Robert's pardon for what I'm about to do, but I think we can all learn a great deal from what he has told us and from what we can see. Very soon now Robert will be as big and strong as any of you, because he will soon be eating the right foods. But look at him now. See how small he is? *This* is what comes from not eating the right foods and from drinking coffee."

We looked him over, almost seeming to pass him from desk to desk, as if he were a mounted disease-carrying bug we were studying. But what a happy, smiling bug! To judge from his face, he considered the attention we gave him an unexpectedly hearty welcome to his new school.

"I don't think it's the coffee, Ma'am," he suddenly added. "My dad says I steal too many of his cigarettes."

During the next couple of minutes, Miss Devron could have fired salvos of cannon shells over our heads without getting our attention. We were like an oppressed people hailing with insane joy the coming of a revolutionary leader. Even the girls in the room were caught up in the exultation of our victory. All the cigars, cigarettes, or drinking straws filled with grains of coffee that any of us had smoked in secret, all our uneasy past abandonments to appetite, curiosity, and lawlessness were suddenly recalled and made more glorious by Robert's cheerful confession. We worshipped him instantly, and at the end of the day a lot of us walked with him, proud to be seen with such a man. We were walking along with him, swearing, talking about smoking,

and making faces at the girls on the other side of the street, when he
stopped and tapped me on the arm.

"How about this place?" he said, pointing to a strip of grass between
two houses.

"What do you mean?" I asked.

"Your old man's voting for Hoover, isn't he?"

"Sure, but . . ."

"Well, let's fight."

I wanted no part of the fight now, but Robert insisted. He proceeded to support his political views with a ferocity I couldn't seem
to match, and it wasn't until he hit me a hard one in the eye that I
brought any personal enthusiasm to the fight. From then on, my size
and strength started getting the better of him, but no one in the
group around us was shouting for me. Those who had been beside
me that morning were now yelling for Robert to kill me, and I must
say that he did his best. But I finally knocked him down and sat on
top of him, and kept his shoulders pinned to the grass until he
admitted that Hoover would win the election. When he was up again,
he expressed some strong reservations about his opinion, but the
election a few days later proved I was right, and, with our political
differences out of the way, we became the best of friends.

For the next two or three weeks, Miss Devron tried her best to
change Robert's breakfast habits, or at least to get him to lie a little
in the interests of classroom harmony. But his incorruptible honesty
soon inspired the rest of us to tell what we had really had for breakfast. Variety returned to the menu, and Miss Devron's discovery that
some of the larger, healthier children, like me, frequently ate what
tasted good for breakfast, instead of simply what was good for them,
seemed to undermine her spirit. She acknowledged defeat one morning when she opened class by reading aloud to us from a book of dog
stories by Albert Payson Terhune. Subsequently, she read to us
whenever there were spare minutes in the day, and the breakfast
lists were forgotten. From that time on, she was one of our favorite
teachers.

My first idea about Robert's father was that he was a sailor in the
United States Navy. Robert showed me pictures of him in a sailor
suit—pictures in which he was leaning against a palm tree; laughing,
with his arm around two girls; pulling a rope; scrubbing the deck of
a ship; or standing on his hands, with a distant and smoking volcano
framed between his spread legs. Then I learned that he was no longer

in the Navy but was selling something—"selling something out on the road," as Robert described it. With only that imagination-tickling description, I developed the permanent expectation of turning a corner in the city someday and seeing Robert's father selling something right in the middle of the road. What he would be selling I couldn't imagine, nor had I a clear idea of how he would be doing it. Salesmen were never allowed in my own neighborhood, and the only prototype of Mr. Bloom I could conjure up was a man I had seen at the circus the year before. He had been standing outside one of the tents—a man with a dark face and a croaking voice, who kept urging us to come in, trying to scoop us up over his shoulder and into the dark tent with a dipping swing of his straw hat. "Selling, selling, selling!" my mother had said to my father. "It's plain disgusting." And so the man with the straw hat became Mr. Bloom, and I always had the feeling that Robert's house, too, was somehow disgusting. But it was also the most exciting house I had ever been in.

The excitement would hit me as soon as I entered the front door—usually in the form of Robert's dog, an overgrown mongrel lummox called Buddy. I think he was mostly a police dog, but any remnants of purebred respectability had worn thin through long association with the underworld of back alleys and garbage cans, and through personal vice, for the dog was a hopeless drunkard. At least once a week, Robert and I would take a bottle of beer from his refrigerator (and how thrilling it was for me to be in a house containing anything so illegal and wicked as a bottle of beer!) and pour some of it out into a saucer for the dog. He would go at it with a ravenous thirst, frothing the beer with slaps from his scooping tongue until the white suds were all over the floor and his muzzle. He looked as if he were mad, and soon he would act mad. He would lurch around the house, bumping into chairs and tables, and endangering ashtrays and bric-a-brac in his weaving course. I would hold him by the collar at one end of the living room while Robert called him from the other end, and negotiating those fifteen feet of open rug held for him all the peril and adventure of a walk on a slippery deck in a typhoon. Once he made it to safety, he would sit down, brace himself against a chair, and look at us triumphantly. We would never get him drunk when Robert's mother was around, of course. That was the one thing I ever saw her really angry about. But she was a person of such unquenchable joy and good cheer that even the sight of Buddy drunk that one time didn't keep her angry for long.

She came home from town unexpectedly that day. Buddy's flank had just crashed into a floor lamp and Robert was juggling it back to equilibrium when his mother walked in the front door.

"Robert, have you got that dog drunk again?" she asked, after one look.

"Yes, Mom."

His truthfulness, both at school and at home, always amazed me. For me the truth was usually a fearful thing; my telling it often seemed to hurt my father or my mother, or someone else. But Robert was dauntless before it.

"I've *told* you not to, Robert," Mrs. Bloom said. "You know I have. Poor Buddy! Just look at him. That's no way to treat a dog."

We all looked at him, and I, at least, was conscience-stricken at what we had done. But none of us could remain remorseful for long. Deep in his cups, Buddy had misgauged the size and slipperiness of the low black leather hassock in front of the rocking chair, and though he managed to plant one haunch on it, it kept sliding off. He would edge it back momentarily, his happy face conveying to all of us his certainty that he was seated there four-square and in perfect dignity. I don't know what there was about him—perhaps a certain slack-jawed serenity—but we all started laughing helplessly at the same time. Robert's mother threw herself onto the couch, and Robert and I rolled on the floor in our laughter, while Buddy watched us out of one open eye.

She recovered enough after a time to continue her scolding, but she couldn't get more than a few words out without looking at Buddy, and then she would laugh again. Finally, she gave us some cookies and milk, and poured out a big saucerful of thick cream for Buddy, which she said would sober him faster than anything else. While Robert was drinking his milk at the kitchen table, she came up behind him and slipped her arms under his and clasped her hands on his chest. She kissed him on his neck and on his cheek and up into his hair, and all this time he went on eating his cookies and drinking his milk. I hardly dared to look at them, but I *had* to see the way she kissed him. She was a young woman, with long, dark hair, and black eyes that opened very suddenly at times, then closed very slowly, the lids seeming to take great pleasure in their long trip back down. The nails of her fingers, clasped on Robert's chest, were buffed to a high polish, and her lips were full and red, and looked wonderfully soft against Robert's cheek. I was the fifth, and youngest, child in my family, and I had only been pecked at gingerly by thin lips pulled tight against clenched teeth, and now I could almost feel that cushioned touch of Robert's mother's kiss on my own cheek. I had no name for the feeling it gave me. I was simply fascinated.

She straightened up, put her hand to the back of her hair, and walked to the refrigerator again. "Boys, boys, boys!" she said, "Little devils, all of you. Little heartless devils, getting dogs drunk, pulling girls' hair, fighting, swearing. You're no good, any of you." As she said it, she dug two big scoops of applesauce out of a bowl and slapped them into two dishes.

"So why do I like you so much?" she said to me as she leaned over the table to put a dish in front of me. She was wearing the kind of low dress she usually wore, but I didn't dare look away from her face. I just looked at her smile, and that was everywhere. Then she leaned over and kissed my forehead.

By the time I left for home, Buddy was on his feet and feeling well enough to walk to the corner with Robert and me.

"I like your mother," I said.

"Ah, she's all right," he said, leveling his toe at a rock and kicking it out into the street.

"You bet she's all right. I'd like to marry her when I grow up."

"She's already married."

"I know she is. My gosh, don't I know that? I just said I'd like to, that's all."

We stood on the corner and kicked a few more rocks into the street. And then we were just standing there. Suddenly there was between us a strip of that infinite desolation that surrounds and crisscrosses life, which children must face without the comfort of philosophy or the retreat of memory.

Robert slapped the dog on the side as hard as he could. "Come on, you," he said to him, and I stood and watched them run down the street. I wondered why he never seemed to like the dog except when we got him drunk. I would have given anything for him, but it had been made clear to me at home long before that our yard was too beautiful to be ruined by a "dirty dog."

Besides Buddy, and Robert's mother, with whom I fell more and more in love as I sampled her cakes, home-canned fruit, dill pickles, candy, sandwiches, and lemonade, there were other charms at Robert's house that made my own seem intolerably dreary. Although it was nearly Christmas and I had known Robert for more than two months, I still hadn't met his father, and yet I had come to feel that I knew him as well as my own, or even better. My father's actual physical arrival at home, after a day spent seeing patients in his office or operating at the hospital or attending a church meeting, was the main thing that impressed his existence upon me. He was so neat, so disciplined in his habits, and so completely without vices, eccentricities, or hobbies that he carried himself completely with him wherever he went. But Robert's father lay scattered about the house in the form of pipes, fishing equipment, shotguns, whiskey bottles locked in a glass-front cabinet, a tennis racket, a set of rusty golf clubs, and a three-foot-long Chinese beheading sword, with a dragon engraved on the length of the blade and a dull, pewtery stain on the bright steel, which Robert said was blood. His father had brought the sword home from China when he was in the Navy, and it hung, with its handle wrapped in cords of scarlet silk, above the bed that he and Robert's mother slept in. I was so taken by the sword at the time that I thought anyone would die of pride to have it hanging above his bed, but I now see what a generous concession to his male taste it was for her to have it there. I remember the room as delicately feminine in decor, but it was his room, too, and he had chosen the exact thing to put his mark on it that I would have chosen if I had been married to Robert's mother.

Mr. Bloom did come home occasionally, but even then I didn't get to see him. He was sleeping, Robert would say, going on to explain how tired a salesman becomes after several weeks on the road. On two or three such afternoons, Robert's mother was also not to be seen, and he told me that she, too, was taking a nap and that we were to tiptoe carefully when we went past the closed door to their bedroom.

Christmas morning came and I was downstairs at 5 A.M., tearing into my carefully wrapped presents with impatient, greedy hands. The unexpected child of my parents' middle age, with all my brothers and sisters grown up and living away from home, I had spent my early hours of the past three Christmases all by myself, and I am certain that the pain of a child getting up on Christmas morning to find nothing under the tree cannot be much worse than the pain of one who finds everything there but has no one to show it to. It was not that my parents were really unfeeling. Indeed, they carefully kept my belief in Santa Claus alive beyond the customary age of disillusionment, perhaps because I *was* the last and

much youngest child—even telling me that all my Christmas presents, except for some clothing from my mother, had come from
Santa Claus. But it never occurred to them to get up early on Christmas
morning in order to share my excitement, and I can still remember
the sick emptiness of the hour and a half between my discovery of
my presents and the first sound of someone else stirring in the house.
That year, as usual, I finally heard the maid come upstairs from
her basement room, and for the next ten minutes I held her captive
while I gloated over each new addition to my wealth.

"Santa was certainly generous to you," she said, and it was so
true that I didn't at all mind her saying it in the middle of a yawn.

"Look what Santa Claus left me!" I was able to say to my
parents at last, when they came down for breakfast. I had been
particularly struck that year by the great number of things he had
given me compared to what my mother had given me, and I
emphasized this difference by putting his gifts to me and hers in
two piles, side by side. But a peck on the cheek and a cursory smile
were all the tribute my parents paid to me, Christmas, and Santa
Claus's generosity before they opened their own small presents
from me, with an air of rather hasty embarrassment, and then
turned to the newspaper and to breakfast.

Still, this year I knew someone who would take a second look at
what I had received. It took some tight crowding, but I managed to
tie all my presents onto my new sled with my new lariat, and I
departed for Robert's house. I wasn't disappointed. Not only did
Robert's eyes pop at some of the individual presents and at the
sheer mass of what I had been given but his mother and, yes, his
father, too, were as excited as Robert himself. Mr. Bloom, who got
down on the floor to play with my new hook-and-ladder fire engine,
turned out to be just the sort of man I had expected. He liked
the fire engine so much that I wanted to give it to him, except
that the idea of giving it up hurt too much. Out of this dilemma
came a sudden inspiration to ask him if he would like to trade
his sword for my fire engine. I was circling carefully about this
idea, trying to approach it in the best way, when something happened to destroy the notion utterly.

It was not surprising that none of us had paid much attention
to Robert's gifts during the first few minutes I was there. All three
of the Blooms were too polite not to have gone all out to admire
a sledful of gifts dumped into the middle of their living room by a
guest as greedy for appreciation as I was. They would have done

this even if my presents had come from the ten-cent store. But my gifts were both costly and impressive, and the Blooms, in their modest circumstances, had no need to be just polite; quite simply, they all gave in to the dream of having enough money to buy what I spread out before them, and wholly enjoyed themselves with my presents. I was too far lost in their appreciation to remember that Robert had also had a Christmas that day. But he soon reminded me of it.

"Look!" he said to me. He held in his cupped hands a bright, gold-colored wheel, suspended on a silver axle within a framework of two intersecting wire circles.

"What the heck *is* it?" I asked.

Robert's mother and father were both down on the floor with us, and while Robert threaded a length of green string through a hole in the axle and then wound it carefully along the axle's length, I could feel their eyes looking from me to the wheel and back, excitedly waiting for my reaction. Then Robert gave the wound-up string a sudden vigorous pull, putting the muscles of his back and arm and the tension of his clenched teeth and closed eyes into it, and brought the top spinning to life. The golden wheel hummed softly within its unmoving world of wire circles. Robert placed the top carefully on the smooth surface of a box lid, and there it rested, poised on its projecting tip like a dancer on one leg.

"Watch," he said, and he picked up the wonderful toy and rested its cupped tip on the point of a pencil his father held up. Once the top was spinning there, Robert pushed it, a fraction of an inch at a time, until it was no longer a continuation of the pencil's length but was hanging horizontally out over space, held from falling only by the quiet humming and the touch of the pencil point on the cup.

"My *gosh!*" I said. "Where'd you get that?"

"Mom gave it to me."

"It's called a gyroscope," she said.

For the next five or ten minutes, we shared the excitement of watching the gyroscope ignore gravity in every position we could devise. I was ready to trade Robert all the solid excitement of my presents for the magic that I could feel spring to life when I pulled the green string. I held the gyroscope in my hand and laughed to feel that quiet, determined will fighting mine as I tipped the wheel away from the path it had chosen in the air. And then, suddenly, the magic would be gone and I would be left holding the toy dead in my hands.

"And what did your father give you?" I asked, staring down at the wheel.

"That Chinese beheading sword."

I gave him back the top, but I couldn't look at him. I could feel the cold, sharp edge of that sword in me.

"Where is it?" I asked at last.

"He hung it over my bed."

"Let's see it."

We stepped around the scattered toys and went into his bedroom. There it was, hanging over his bed, just as I had dreamed it might hang over mine.

"I'm not to touch it until I'm older, but she's all mine," Robert said.

I could easily have cried. My mother had given me ties, socks, gloves, shirts, pants, shoes, underwear—all the things a boy could easily do without. But Robert's mother had given him a gyroscope! And the sword had come from his father, while I didn't even think that my father had given me anything! I seemed to have only one real friend right then.

"What did Santa Claus bring you?" I asked.

"Santa Claus? *Santa Claus?*" he hooted. "There isn't any Santa Claus, you big dummy!"

I had heard there wasn't—but only speculatively, never with this final, crushing authority. I could think of only one way to defend myself against Robert's having everything and my not having even Santa Claus. I hit him twice, once on the chest and once in the face, and then I tied all my presents onto my sled with my lariat and started out of the living room, refusing to answer any of the questions his parents asked me. Robert followed me onto the porch, and when I was half a block away he called out to me, "What did you hit me for?"

"Shut up!" I yelled back, and I went home and put my presents under the tree for my relatives to see when they came around later.

Most of the rifts of childhood are as troubled, as tearing, and as quickly smoothed over as the wake of a small motorboat, and by the time Christmas vacation came to an end I had accepted the death of another illusion and Robert had forgotten my naïveté. We went on as before, with the abrasive honesty of his life wearing away at the hypocrisy of my own until I, too, occasionally knew some emotional truths. With that encouragement of truth which had been given him at home, he was quite free to say, for example,

that he liked or disliked this or that person, this or that book, or a
threatening gray or a clear blue sky. But I knew no such freedom.
Caught within the attitude that this world was God's green acre
and too sacred to be regarded critically by the likes of me, I wasn't
free to decide whether I liked a dog better than a cat, or a mountain
better than a rosebush. Any expression of vital choice on my part
was seen as a blasphemous elevation and denigration of two aspects
of the divine order, and, pressed down by the weight of my blasphemy, I lost the power to make any choice. But Robert restored
this power during the next year of our friendship. He restored it
with a series of shocks that showed me that what he said about something and what I felt about it, way down, were often related. How
exhilarating it was to have him come out with a truth that my
bones knew but my tongue could not say!

"What do you think of Miss Brown?" I might ask him, speaking
about the elementary-school art teacher.

"She's a nice lady," he answered, "but she doesn't know anything
about art."

My heart pounded with the truth of what he had said. I half
knew she didn't know anything about art, but she had been put in
our classroom by authority as an art teacher, so it was certain that
I must be wrong about her. "What do you mean, she doesn't know
anything about art?" I asked—on his side, of course, but still fearful.

"All she draws is mountains," he said disgustedly. "Never people,
or dogs, or flowers, or trees, or boats, or water, or houses, or clouds,
or *anything* but mountains. And it's always the same mountain. You
should have seen the teacher I had in New York. She could draw a
face on the board in two seconds and everyone knew who it was.
Boy, was she an artist!"

If I was impressed at the time by the fearlessness of what Robert
knew and said, it is only now that I can appreciate the full miracle
of his freshness surviving the hothouse atmosphere of souls under
cultivation for adulthood that existed in our third- and fourth-grade
classrooms. Having known Robert, I now seriously believe that the
right sort of parents can emotionally equip a child to survive the
"civilizing" process of education. But my real appreciation of
Robert came mostly in retrospect, and most of whatever I now know
about truth I had to learn the hard way, for in the late winter of
our fourth-grade year—about a year and a half after our friendship
started—I cut myself off from the hope that Robert would go on
indefinitely helping me to find truth.

It was one of those false spring days that sometimes appear toward the end of winter—a sad, nostalgic day, when the air teased our bodies with the promise of games and picnics, and the earth was still locked up and unavailable for our use, beneath two feet of grimy snow. Robert and I were walking home together. "Mom just put up some more dill pickles last night," he said, and suddenly the day came alive.

"First one who gets there gets the biggest," I said, and, with my longer legs, I was on the porch while Robert was still pounding up the sidewalk. We pushed the living-room door open, and when we weren't hit in the chest by a flying, dancing Buddy, we both understood the sign. Whenever Robert's father was out of town, his mother tried to keep Buddy in the house as a watchdog—I suppose on the theory that he might possibly trip up an intruder and break his neck as he frisked about him in indiscriminate welcome. But when Buddy was absent—off on some disreputable scavenging trip, no doubt—it usually meant that Mr. Bloom was home. Robert and I now peered out the back living-room window and saw the car in front of the garage, and he lifted his fingers to his lips. "Come on," he whispered. "Let's go into the kitchen."

We tiptoed past the closed door of his parents' bedroom and past the open door of his own bedroom. As usual, I looked in and saw the sword still hanging over his bed. The sharp pain of Robert's ownership of that sword had been replaced in me by a kind of dull wonder at his exasperating sense of honor. "No, I can't touch it until I'm twelve," he had insisted a dozen or more times that past year—times when nothing in the world but a three-foot-long Chinese beheading sword was appropriate to the game at hand. Now, in the kitchen, Robert whispered, "We better not have any pickles without asking Mom. Boy, was she ever mad the last time we ate them all! How about some apricot jam and bread?"

"Swell," I whispered back.

"Hey, would you rather have apricot or strawberry?" he whispered from the depths of the icebox.

"Let's have both," I said, regaining some of the excitement I had lost in my disappointment over the pickles.

He brought out the two jam jars, spooned large helpings of each kind into a bowl, and began whipping them together with a fork. I stared, hypnotized, at the clean colors as they ran together and faded to a pinkish tan. "Boy, are you ever lucky!" I said. "Eating any old thing you want when you want! Do you think my mother, or that old maid of ours, would let me eat *anything* between meals? No, sir! Our maid says you're spoiled because you're an only child and your mother doesn't know any better."

"Well, maybe," he said, shaking fist-size globs of jam onto the bread. "But Mom told me they're going to try and get me a baby brother or a baby sister pretty soon."

"A baby brother or sister? Which kind would you rather have?"

"Oh, I don't care. They're both O.K., I guess." He returned the jars to the icebox, and came back to the table and picked up his bread and jam. "How about taking these out on the front porch to eat?"

"O.K."

We crept past the closed bedroom door again and went out on the porch, being careful not to let the door slam behind us. When we were comfortably settled on the front steps, with our mouths full of bread and jam, I suddenly decided to ask him a question that had occurred to me many times. "Robert, is there something wrong with your mother and father?"

"What do you mean, 'something wrong'?" he asked.

"Well, you know. The way they're always resting when we come here. Are they sick?"

It seemed to me that they must certainly be sick, or something more than sick. For me, bed was a concept that changed entirely with the time of day. Bed at night was a completely respectable thing, both for myself and for my parents—so respectable, in fact, that I usually put up a spirited fight against going to it. But after the sun rose over the high, gray mountains east of town, bed instantly became something slack and irresponsible, even on weekend mornings, when there was no immediate reason for getting out of it. "What?" my father would say, standing over me at seven o'clock on a rainy Saturday morning. "Not up yet?" He never said it harshly but always with a friendly smile, kept just thin enough to give me the message that bed simply wasn't the place to be at that hour. So grave was this obscure crime that even when I was sick enough to stay in bed all day, I dreaded the long morning and afternoon hours there, and never wholly relaxed until it was 8 P.M. again and really time for bed. If there was one aspect of the irregularity of Robert's house that I did not enjoy, it was this matter of bed in the afternoon. There *was* something sick about it.

"Heck, no, they're not sick," Robert said. "Dad gets tired out on the road. I *told* you that. And Mom likes to be with him.

They're just taking a nap. Or maybe they're trying to find me that baby brother."

I stopped in the middle of a bite and stared at him. If he had spoken the last words in Latin he could not have lost me more completely.

"They're trying to find a baby? In *there?*"

"Well, of course," he said, stuffing the last of his bread and jam into his mouth. And then the full extent of my darkness must have shown on my face. He swallowed with a little choking cough. "Oh, my gosh!" he said. "You don't know about *that,* either, do you?"

"Of course, I know about it," I said angrily. "I just didn't know what you meant."

But I couldn't cover up my ignorance or my need to know the truth, for he proceeded to tell me all about it. He told me in adequate detail and finished by saying that all babies were "found" in just this way.

"*All* babies?"

"Yep—me, you, everybody. That's the way everybody's parents get their children."

I jumped up, and, seeing the expression on my face, Robert stood up, too, and then I hit him twice—once on the chest to knock him down and once on the nose as he was falling. In its most impersonal sense, the idea he had given me was just barely tolerable, but in relation to my parents it was an unthinkable blasphemy. After all they had done for me, hitting him seemed the very least I could do. I stood over him, breathing hard and with my fists clenched. He looked up at me from the top step, where he had fallen, and slowly rubbed his nose.

"You big damn dumb!" he said at last. "I'll never tell you another thing as long as I live!"

"You just better not," I said. "You just better never say another word to me if you know what's good for you!"

And he never did. From that day forward, I was on my own.

WRITING TWELVE: Try to pull together, dredge up, or get flowing enough memories of someone to write a long story about him consisting of many little stories, like "Not Another Word." Take several weeks to work on this writing. You might write one or two of the little stories every day and then piece them together, throwing away those that don't fit. You may find yourself dealing with two persons who oppose each other in some way, as did the boys in Richard Thurman's story. Or you may find yourself dealing principally with one person. Whatever, be sure you are hooked into an opposition that keeps you discovering incidents that reveal the person or persons you're writing about. If you don't find such an opposition, you probably cannot write a long story without padding it.

Persons are easier to write about than places, but if a place calls you, answer that call.

> *It is much easier to sit at a desk and read plans for a billion gallons of water a day, and look at maps and photographs; but you will write a better article if you heave yourself out of a comfortable chair and go down in tunnel 3 and get soaked.*
>
> STUART CHASE

There was a Boy...
                    many a time
At evening, when the earliest stars began
To move along the edges of the hills,
Rising or setting, would he stand alone
Beneath the trees or by the glimmering
    lake,
And there with fingers interwoven, both
    hands
Pressed closely palm to palm, and to his
    mouth
Uplifted, he, as through an instrument,
Blew mimic hootings to the silent
    owls...

                    WILLIAM WORDSWORTH

chapter 11
through facts to large meanings

DISTANCE AND MEANING

REMEMBERING CHILDHOOD is not childish, but wise and sweet and necessary. We go back because we loved those years of play. We go back because remembering moves us closer to the children around us today. We go back because in writing through these years we gain a second life.

The best writers take this journey. Mark Twain wrote *Huckleberry Finn*, a novel about a boy with a gifted tongue, who once said:

The widow she cried over me, and called me a poor lost lamb, and she called me a lot of other names, too, but she never meant no harm by it. She put me in them new clothes again, and I couldn't do nothing but sweat and sweat, and feel all cramped up. Well, then, the old thing commenced again. The widow rung a bell for supper, and you had to come to time. When you got to the table you couldn't go right to eating, but you had to wait for the widow to tuck down her head and grumble a little over the victuals, though there warn't really anything the matter with them. That is, nothing only everything was cooked by itself. In a barrel of odds and ends it is different; things get mixed up, and the juice kind of swaps around, and the things go better.

After supper she got out her book and learned me about Moses and the Bulrushers; and I was in a sweat to find out all about him; but by-and-by she let it out that Moses had been dead a considerable long time; so then I didn't care no more about him; because I don't take no stock in dead people.

Pretty soon I wanted to smoke, and asked the widow to let me. But she wouldn't. She said it was a mean practice and wasn't clean, and I must try to not do it any more. That is just the way with some people. They get down on a thing when they don't know nothing about it. Here she was a bothering about Moses, which was no kin to her, and no use to anybody, being gone, you see, yet finding a power of fault with me for doing a thing that had some good in it. And she took snuff too; of course that was all right, because she done it herself.

J. D. Salinger wrote about another boy with gifted tongue, who cherished his little sister Phoebe:

She was laying there asleep, with her face sort of on the side of the pillow. She had her mouth way open. It's funny. You take adults, they look lousy when they're asleep and they have their mouths way open, but kids don't. Kids look all right. They can even have spit all over the pillow and they still look all right.

These men wrote of childhood at the height of their mature powers. If you are under twenty, you need even more than they to write of childhood. A writer requires some distance between him and the events he recalls—not always, but usually. Then he is unfamiliar enough with them to feel the need to relate them fully for his readers and for himself. If he writes of yesterday's or last year's events, he usually remembers them so well he leaves them shrouded in his near-by intimate memory, which the reader does not share.

> *But don't expect to write well about the love affair that you are in the midst of, or have just mailed a letter to break off. One principal figure in that situation you can't see. At least one. Probably two. You are "involved." You don't surround it. You suffer or you triumph; you do not comprehend.*
>
> *Later, all those feelings will become your knowledge. They will be of your knowledge and your wisdom when they no longer possess you. Your subject must be something you possess and can move all the way around. The former feelings that come together in your subject may include the most glorious or devastating that you ever had. And you will re-experience them. But you must emotionally enclose and dominate them.*
>
> SIDNEY COX

In most truthful accounts of childhood by adults, a tension builds between the childlike way of doing and perceiving and the writer's present ways. Like most tension in communication, it often breaks open new insights for the writer and reader. The child can never know the adult completely or vice versa, but in the act of writing the adult momentarily constructs a bridge. There is danger for you as a writer walking there. But also the chance you may get over to the other side where you have never been before.

In a small way the following story about childhood play brings to life the difference between a child's perception of the world as a play place and the adult's perception of it as a threatening and hence socially bound place.

BLINDED

It was getting dark as I finished putting away the last of the dinner dishes. There in the kitchen drawer lay three

flashlights, complete with batteries. I yelled for Jan and
Judy. We slipped from the house, flashlights in hand. After
chasing each other around a while, we ran toward the
Memorial Park on the corner. There is a sprawling bush
right near where two streets cross, a perfect place to hide
for shining flashlights into car windows.

We looked all around to make sure no one saw us, then
headed for the bush and jumped in. A pair of headlights
shone in the distance. The three of us shifted into position
while the car approached the stop sign. He stopped, then
came toward us. The car was almost in front of the bush.
Out into the dusk shone our three lights. We were tense,
afraid someone would find us, or stop and yell at us. But
because we knew it was wrong, we kept waiting for the
next car to come. Two of them this time. Our lights were
all but lost in the oncoming glare of headlights, but the
tension mounted. My legs were beginning to get cramped
so I shifted to an ever denser part of the bush.

Straight ahead, yet still a way off, the lights beamed.
They stopped; we tensely waited. Now they were coming
straight for us. Flash! Our lights beamed back. The car
slowed and pulled over. A guy got out and came running.
Jan crouched behind a branch while I scooted under some
thin, well-covered branches and lay flat on my back. Judy
took the hint and crawled under a branch next to me. The
man found Jan right away and yelled at her. Didn't she
know better than to shine lights in peoples' eye while they
were driving, and didn't she realize that it could blind the
driver, and he could run off the road?

Then he turned around and started through the bush
after Judy and me. He was right next to me when he
spotted Judy. Stepping on the branch I was under, he
grabbed her arm and yanked her up. I was just dying.
I knew he would see me or hear my heart throbbing. I
didn't even move to breathe. Judy was looking right down
at me while he gave her the same lecture. I was sure he
would see me then. Thank God she was too scared to
talk, otherwise she would have told on me for sure. He
turned, stepped down from my stomach and left, telling us
to stop and never do it again.

I waited until the car sounded far away, then dragged
myself out from under the branches. Whew, that was close!

We all sat down behind a branch and began to breathe
once more. Some lights were coming. Still shaking we
looked at each other.
Flash! Out shone our lights.

JOY PEPPER

The secret of once is operating in that story—*one* night's escapade
comes alive; the writer does not generalize about many nights.

To tell large truths about childhood and how it differs from adulthood may seem an impossible task. But when you put down a telling
fact that draws others to it, you may be able to go through them to a
significant finding about childhood. If you don't come up with such a
larger truth, a significance, you may still have an account that takes
your reader back into your childhood and brings it alive so much that
he finds himself also moving back into his. Here is another childhood
memory.

CATCH THE BALL

It was warm, the sun flashed through the branches of the
tall trees looking like flash bulbs going off in the sky. I
didn't know where I was, but I was with my parents, so
it didn't matter.
Dad had parked the car out on the street, and we had
walked up a long driveway edged with greens and flowers.
Past the big red brick house of English Tudor was a high
wooden fence. My parents had opened the gate of the fence
and there I stood, looking into the sky, counting the suns
that sprinkled through the branches of the huge trees. The
landscaped yard of flowerbeds and lawn chairs formed a
circle around an old dirty cement bird-bath. It was full of
blackish water left from the spring rain, and offered
neither refuge nor pleasure to the small summer birds.
"Jack, Donna." I saw strange people coming toward my
parents; they seemed to be smiling at me for no apparent
reason.
"This must be little Bobby," said a tall ugly woman in a
white dress that held a sap stain just below her knee.
Mother started introducing me to the smiles. "Bobby, this
is Mrs. Morrison, Mrs. Agrestrom, and Mr. Agrestrom . . ."
I watched my dad take a bottle of beer from a cooler of
melted ice. I was ushered to a lawn chair through little
clumps of people all talking at the same time.

Someone gave me a bottle of Coca-Cola. It was wet and dripped on my pants. There were no other children in the whole yard. I looked for my father and saw him walking towards me with a big baldheaded man. The man wore yellow bermuda shorts and shower thongs; the sun reflected off his bald head, making it look wet and shiny. They motioned me into the middle of the yard where they stood by the useless bird-bath that distracted from the smell of grass and flowers.

"You remember Uncle Otis, don't you Bobby?"

I said yes even though I'd never seen him before.

We started tossing a red ball around. Dad kept telling me how good I was every time I managed to catch the ball. Uncle Otis said the cubs needed me, whatever that meant. The ball was tossed at me and it skidded along the ground and jumped through my legs. It came to rest next to the bird-bath. I ran after it. I heard Otis yell that he was going to get me. As I bent down to pick up the ball, I felt Uncle Otis's hands grab me around my waist. He picked me up and lifted me over his head.

I looked around from within the grasp of his strong hands, the people were laughing, even my father. Otis moved a hand down to my ankle, grabbed it, and held me upside down.

The branches of the big trees were on the bottom of the yard. If Otis dropped me, I would fall into the top of the trees, through the branches and out into the sky.

He lowered my head into the bird-bath. As I felt the water on my head, I heard the people laughing around me. I still stared into the inverted sky.

"Now you'll be bald like me," said Otis, laughing, as he put me down next to the bird-bath. I was dizzy. I looked into the bird-bath and saw the black waves Otis made with my head splash over the sides.

The laughter died. I looked at my father. He wasn't smiling any more. I ran. Out the gate and into the driveway. I felt the water drip from the top of my head down my neck and face. I thought the dirty water the birds wouldn't use would make me bald. As I ran into the street and towards the car, the water made my shirt wet and the back of my neck cold, and it ran down my cheeks with my tears.

Once again the child and the adult are perceiving an experience differently. For Uncle Otis, the incident was carefree play; for the little boy, terror.

Here is a childhood story by a college freshman who in her class papers customarily recorded facts with brutal force even when she was speaking love and tenderness.

WE WERE GETTING ALONG

I was to stay with my Aunt Bertha, where good schooling and manners would be taught. What Mom needed was understanding and someone to talk to, since her brother recently died in an auto accident. She was always alone, with nothing to do while we kids were in school.

If only I had kept my whale of a mouth shut, she would never have had to leave Jim, Joey—my brothers—and me. Mom and Dad were divorced at the time. Since Dad was living away, I slept with Mom whenever I could because her bed was much bigger than mine. Sometimes she would say, "Go to your room!" but if I nagged at her enough, she would give in and let me sleep in her big bed.

Earlier that night, Jim and Joey got into a spat over what show we were to watch. Mom never said a word. We stayed up that night till the 11 o'clock news came on and we even made our own supper—peanut butter and banana sandwiches with Kool-Aid. "All you can eat. Mom's sleeping," Jim said, peeking into her room, then closing the door quietly. I washed the dishes, Jim dried, while Joey, the youngest, cleared the table, only breaking one dish— that was good for him.

Dad called to see how we were getting along, because he knew Mom wasn't feeling her old self. "We're fine, but Mom's still sleeping," I said. She slept about sixteen hours a day before we started complaining. We thought she had tired, iron-poor blood and needed Geritol, because on the Amateur Hour, they would come out with, "Are you tired? Rundown? Get enough sleep? Try Geritol!" The next day we went to school, pooled our money ($2.97), and Jim went to the store and bought a bottle. Mom was sure surprised when we tromped into her bedroom. I handed her a spoon. "Here, Mom, I don't like it when you're not yelling at Jim and Joey for picking on me."

Joey said, "You always ask for it!"

Mom was so thrilled about receiving the Geritol she started to cry and told us she would use it later. That was the night before I told Dad on the phone that she was still sleeping, but she wanted us to wake her in half an hour.

"Well," Dad said, "OK, if you get frightened, just call 381-2001."

"Sure, Dad. Bye," I replied as if he were kidding. Me get frightened? After all, I was nine years old.

That night it started to rain. I crept into her room, knocked the book from the bedstand onto the floor. Mom didn't move, just made a groaning noise. I climbed into the huge bed, snuggled next to her, back to back, and covered my head with the sheet, which made me feel better.

It seemed four hours later (really, it was about twenty minutes) when a tree limb cracked down onto the roof of the house. Lady, our collie, started barking and ran around the house. It was droopy, black, and noisy from above the sheets. Then Mom started to groan as if she was in pain, someone pulling her hair out, strand at a time. All I could think about was Dad telling me to call if I got frightened. Me scared of a little old storm? Huh! After another hair, I asked Mom if anything was wrong.

"They're coming to get me! Run, get in the house! The plane will hit me!"

"Are you all right, Mom?"

She went on and on. I didn't want to frighten Mom, so I called 381-2001. Dad answered and I told him what had happened.

"Uncle Milt will talk to you till I get home. Call him. You hear me?"

I called Uncle Milt, told him what had happened. After Dad arrived, then he came over to help.

Mom never got up during the night. Just lay in her big bed. I felt like a fool calling everyone at 2:00 A.M. and getting them out of bed.

"Your mother's just having a bad dream," my Aunt Bertha said when she arrived. She was Mom's sister, the old hag. Always wanted you to do something for her. "Make the beds! Clean the floors! Kids were made to be seen and not heard." Jim and I knew Mom wasn't just having a bad dream. Joey, being only seven, slept through the whole affair.

About 7:00 A.M., Pastor Jones came to pray with Mom and talk to the elders. He patted me on top of the head. I got mad, walked away, and tried to talk to Mom, but everyone kept me away as if she were poison.

A while later, an ambulance came. Two men got out, and started walking toward the house. Lady bit one man on the back of the leg. There was a "Beware of Dog" sign on our front tree, so the man just bitched. I was glad Lady bit him.

The two men walked into the house as if they owned our place and grabbed Mom. She made a fuss. Then they slowly walked her through the living room and away. Everyone was staring at her as if she were some kind of animal. I knew she was still my mother.

GRACE WENDELL

Such a piece of writing tells so much truth that it may hurt the persons mentioned in it, although what it says is worthy of the attention of many readers. (The names in this story, including the author's—as in many other stories in this book—are changed to protect persons.)

BEGINNINGS AND ENDINGS

Most good published pieces of writings have been created in several drafts—each version tighter and sharper than the last. What you see in print is almost never the first effort. No professional writer expects to dash off a piece of writing that is beyond improvement. Each version he thinks of as preliminary to another better version until finally he has had enough of drafting and says, "Done."

About eighty percent of the time, professional writers and editors find that the beginning of their first draft is no beginning at all. It is a mess, a series of false beginnings in which the starter's pistol goes off once, then twice, and the runners burst from their blocks only to stop and come back again. A writer must expect these bad starts because when he first meets his reader he has been thinking through *all* that he wants to tell him, not just the beginning of it. So he tells him too much—what concerns the end of the story or the chain of ideas, as well as the beginning—or too little, on the false assumption that the reader has just gone with him on this journey of reflection. In fact it cannot for the reader be a journey of memory. It must be a trip into an unknown woods in the partial dark where the stumps and branches leap at his feet and the hanging spider webs clutch his face.

Look at the first draft of your story. Is there some place on the first page where the reader could begin satisfactorily? Look for a spot where the story itself starts up, not simply where you began to write.

> *I write my first version in longhand (pencil). Then I do a complete revision, also in longhand . . . Then I type a third draft on yellow paper, a very special certain kind of yellow paper. No, I don't get out of bed to do this. I balance the machine on my knees. Sure, it works fine; I can manage a hundred words a minute. Well, when the yellow draft is finished, I put the manuscript away for a while, a week, a month, sometimes longer. When I take it out again, I read it as coldly as possible, then read it aloud to a friend or two, and decide what changes I want to make and whether or not I want to publish it. I've thrown away rather a few short stories, an entire novel, and half of another. But if all goes well, I type the final version on white paper and that's that.*
>
> TRUMAN CAPOTE

Here is the opening of the first draft of a childhood story that took too long to get going.

I had gotten Alice for a present on my fourth birthday. We had finished my cake and Mommy told me to go into the living room. I had just settled down in the big chair when Daddy came out with a box. I opened it and threw away the tissue paper and there she was—all dressed up in a pretty pink chiffon bonnet and pinafore. She had booties and real socks, too. Mommy gave me a nightie and a blanket she had made for her. That was in the box, too.

That's not a bad opening, but nothing in it surprises, and nothing hints at the tough attitude the narrator is going to take later; so a reader might quit reading after that first paragraph, thinking he was going to read a gooey little girl's story. The story ends with such strength that such a beginning as this doesn't fit. It is commonplace. When a child gets a doll, she takes it out of its box.

In the final draft of the story, which follows, the reader is quickly taken on a walk with a baby carriage and soon finds the little girl treating her doll as if it is her baby—which is the central attitude exploited in the story. Upon the advice of an editor, the author dropped the original paragraph given above and started at a later point, in this way:

ALICE DEAR

She was the prettiest doll I had ever seen so I gave her the prettiest name I knew then, which was Alice. But *Alice* wasn't enough, so later I attached the last name, *Dear*.

One day Mommy took baby sister out for a walk in the carriage and I asked if I could take Alice Dear along. Mommy showed me how to wrap her up like baby sister and how to carry her so she would be comfortable, and we went for a walk. Whenever someone looked at baby sister, they had to peek under Alice Dear's covers, too. Everyone thought she was the prettiest doll they had ever seen, just like they thought baby sister was the cutest baby.

I had three dolls—Alice Dear, Patty, and Judy. Alice Dear was the oldest and my favorite. Patty was a nice doll, but she was big as a real baby—much too hard for me to handle. She had a hard plaster head, rubber arms and legs and a cloth body. You couldn't spank Patty very hard, because every time you did, she'd always cry at you—WAH WAH! I couldn't bear to hear any child of mine cry like that. Judy was a more grown-up doll. She would walk, but her body was hard and you always had to treat her nice because Mommy said she cost a lot of money. Alice Dear was more timid than Patty or Judy. They could take care of themselves pretty well, but Alice Dear needed me. She could be any age you wanted her to be, but Patty was always a baby and Judy was always seven years old.

Alice had an all-rubber body and I could give her a bath, which I did every day. She had rooted hair and I could comb it and set it. When I spanked her, she always knew it was for her own good and that it hurt me more than it hurt her. She could take it like a lady. She didn't cry back at me like that ole sissy Patty did.

Alice Dear was cuddly. She was just right in my arms. I could take her to bed with me, and if she landed on the floor at night, she didn't mind because she knew I loved her. Patty would get mad at me, I know, because Mommy told me once that if she ever landed on the floor, her head would break. I couldn't even consider taking Judy to bed with me. Her hard body always poked me and sometimes she'd get stubborn and stick up her leg.

The years soon took their toll on Alice Dear. She began to wear out from all the baths and her rubber skin got all black. Though Alice never grew up like normal children, she got bald from all the times I washed and set her hair.

One hot July day of my ninth year, Alice Dear got a spanking for being naughty. Her soft body couldn't take it any more, and she split right up the back. All her foam rubber stuffing fell out.

I looked at her in surprise. Alice Dear didn't cry, she just gave up. All those shots in her behind from the times we played hospital together, she the patient, I the nurse, stood out like bruises. Suddenly I cried for all the times Alice never did.

I ran in the house and told my mother what happened and she comforted me. Then she took a paper bag and a broom and cleaned up Alice from the garage floor. She saved Alice's head. Alice Dear had a pretty face—rosy cheeks and blue eyes and a dimple that was nice to kiss. I set her head on the window sill in my bedroom for a couple of weeks and then asked Mother about doll factories that take parts from broken dolls and make them into new dolls. The next day, Daddy took Alice's head away.

It was right around that time that I lost interest in dolls.

JULIE TEITELBAUM

Consider the openings to all the papers you have written. They should open the story—swing open, and let the reader in. In the story "Catch the Ball," printed earlier in this chapter, the writer spends several lines setting the scene, but he does so with originality that prevents boredom. Instead of writing the tired phrase, "It was a warm, bright day," he says:

> It was warm, the sun flashed through the branches of the tall trees looking like flash bulbs going off in the sky.

The metaphor probably earns the respect of the reader. It suggests that this writer can produce a telling fact even in an opening description, so chances are good the story will develop some hard and valuable truths.

In the first two sentences of the story "We Were Getting Along," the writer sets up a contrast between "good schooling and manners" and "understanding" and forecasts the probing she will do into the acceptance of the mother by the daughter and the relatively cold concern of relatives and institutional officials.

In writing an opening beware of the windy generalization:

> Everybody likes hot rods and I am no exception.

Not true. Many persons detest hot rods and consider them the most likely transportation to Hell. Don't turn off the reader by pretentious or coy behavior. In the beginning you establish your voice. If you begin squeaking like a monkey or thundering like an elephant, you have ruined your chances with the reader, who will be astounded later to find you writing in natural human voice. Beware of phony introductions, voice changes, and unnecessary apologies.

An opening often gains by being new, surprising; but if your writing is crammed with surprises all the way through, you may do well to begin quietly and conventionally. You do not have to amaze or stun or mystify your reader at the beginning. But you have to avoid alienating him with emptiness, phoniness, or unsuccessful attempts at humor. You may simply begin factually:

> East High School is located two miles from the center
> of the business district in Clarksville.

but don't use that fact unless it makes a point relevant to your story. Later in this story, the distance from the school to the business district should come up.

Think hard how your reader will take your first words. Consider this opening:

> **What's going on? This question might have gone through
> the minds of the grocery store owners when the students of
> Mr. McMahon's psychology class went to the different stores
> for an assignment that was done over vacation.**

"What's going on?" is a question that might be asked by anyone in any situation. Here the reader is required to wait too long before the question gains any significance.

Revision: "What's going on?" said the grocery store owner when he saw twenty-five students from Mr. McMahon's psychology class walking up and down the aisles writing in their notebooks. They were carrying out an assignment during Thanksgiving vacation.

When you have found or created a good beginning to your story, consider its ending. At both ends of a piece of writing, a writer is driven to explaining, almost as if he wanted to give advice to the reader on how to read what he has written, and nothing is worse than advice. If the Explainery comes at the beginning, it is lost on the reader who does not know the story yet. If it comes at the end, it tastes like soggy bread. The reader has read the story and is insulted by being told what he has read.

The first draft of "Alice Dear" ended like this:

> It was right around that time that I lost interest in dolls, so I put Patty and Judy away to rest. They're still very stiff and unfriendly, but maybe my daughters will like them more than I did, so I save them and take very good care of them. They still look like new after all these years.

This last paragraph took up points unrelated to the preceding sentence, which was "The next day, Daddy took Alice's head away." That sentence by itself might make a pretty good ending, for it jolts the reader and continues the humor established earlier. But as an ending it may leave the reader wondering whether the narrator ever saw Alice again. The whole paragraph suffers because it takes up Patty and Judy again, when by now the story is all Alice's. When an editor saw this paragraph, he suggested that the writer had already written a good ending with the sentence "It was right around that time that I lost interest in dolls" but hadn't had the courage to stop when she had scored.

It's pleasing to create a smashing ending to a piece of writing, but ridiculous to try for one and miss. As you will see when you read on in this book, one of the fundamentals of good writing is alternation— of kitchen and elevated style, of fast and slow action, of idea and example. The practiced writer who senses that his writing must have early hit the reader hard often plays down the ending, understates it, so that it really is an ending, not just a stopping of something that has remained at one level all the while. The author of "We Were Getting Along" did this in her next-to-last sentence.

> Everyone was staring at her as- if she were some kind of animal. I knew she was still my mother.

This ending carries a great deal more feeling in its simple expression than would supercharged sentences like these:

> My God! Didn't they have any sensitivity? Their behavior was absolutely cruel and vicious and they didn't realize the horror of it.

After you have let your first draft of a childhood story cool a while, look it over for a spot near the end that is exciting or surprising. Consider stopping a little before you believe your reader will expect you to. If possible, find a good detail near the end or one of the main feelings or ideas in your story; chop everything else off that follows it, or move the good passage to the end position.

Don't drool an ending. Wipe your mouth, say the last word, leave your reader.

WRITING THIRTEEN: Choose an incident or several incidents in your childhood and reconstruct them with telling facts. If possible, go through those facts to some larger meaning, a view of childhood or the relationship between children and adults, which goes beyond your experience to speak to your readers' experience.

Think about the voice in which you write. Are your purposely mixing the manner of adult and child as Richard Thurman did in "Not Another Word"? Or are you trying pretty much to capture the sound of a child talking? Does your ear allow you to include as part of the story the dialogue of children who appear there?

Repeat: *to double, re-double, renew,
parallel, echo, match, mirror, reproduce,
regenerate, reincarnate, multiply, revive,
reaffirm, reassert, accentuate, emphasize,
build, hammer, slap, thump, beat, bang,
punch, jab, convince, charm, lull, caress.*

chapter 12
repeating

WEAK AND
STRONG REPETITION

IF SOMEONE you love keeps saying he loves you, the repetition is beautiful. But if someone you dislike keeps saying he loves you, the repetition is unbearable. And there are places and moments where you don't want to be told you are loved. Even the heartbeat, with its repetitious but slightly irregular liveliness, can become monotonous—for example, if recorded day after day in a laboratory.

Repetition can comfort or bore, clarify or confuse, astound or outrage. Consider these repetitions:

> **I think Ethel was rebelling when she refused to follow my
> suggestion. She was rebelling against her ability to recover,
> her ability to heal, her ability to retain her youth. She had
> lost her youth, yet she was still fighting. Fighting for a lost
> cause.**

They clog the passage rather than emphasize what needs to be emphasized.

The professional writer reads his work aloud to himself and to others. He hears repetitions his eyes did not see. The beginner and the professional need to find ways of getting inside their writing and hearing it objectively. One way is to listen for repetitions, which are easily detected. Those that the writer is surprised to find are usually weak: he didn't intend them. They may become valuable to him as flags indicating other failures or surrenders. If he didn't notice

them before, he probably missed other weaknesses. Read the following passage aloud and you will find weak repetition. It will help you
spot other weaknesses.

> One of the specific aspects of the speech was the question
> and answer period. I feel that the panel during the ques-
> tion and answering period was very biased in their questions
> to Governor Barnett of the state of Mississippi. In so much
> as the questions directed toward Governor Barnett were
> mostly concerned with segregation in general.

The passage needs massive cutting. Here is a possible revision:

> In the question and answer period, the panel was biased
> toward Governor Barnett of Mississippi. Most of the
> questions concerned segregation.

In another part of his column, this writer ran into a snag with the
word *fact*.

> Governor Barnett has said that the North is just as segre-
> gated as the South. This is of course an overstatement of
> fact, but it still does contain a certain amount of fact.
> There are no signs forbidding Negroes from using a drink-
> ing fountain or from buying a bottle of Coke from a vend-
> ing machine, but I have experienced prejudice in the North
> and even helped the cause of segregation in Lansing, Michi-
> gan.

The second sentence might be revised in this way:

> This is an overstatement but still contains a certain amount
> of fact.

Note that in both excerpts from this column, the writer employed
weak repetition when he was generalizing, not when he was giving
particular evidence. His last sentence in the second excerpt ("There
are no signs . . .") is well written. In it he has found his voice and
speaks with his natural powers.

Often weak repetition blooms when a writer tries to impress his
reader, as in this passage:

> When one sits before an open hearth and can see the
> flames shooting from the burning wood, hear the crackling
> of the fire as it engulfs its source of fuel, and feel the

> warmth given off, one enters another "world," a "world"
> which is quiet and peaceful . . . You may ask why we
> spend so much time by the fire, and that should be a diffi-
> cult question to answer. But I believe it is the "mystery" of
> the fire that intrigues us. This "mystery" of the fire has a
> way of captivating your thoughts and putting you in a
> trance-like atmosphere.

Here again words appear close to each other in ineffectual repetition.
To show how unprofessional he is, the writer also puts quotation
marks around *world* and *mystery*—which he uses in the commonest
way—and insults his reader. Instead of saying the crackling fire
"engulfs its *wood*," he says "engulfs its *source of fuel*." He so feared
repetition that he went to ridiculous lengths to find a synonym. Wood
is fuel, but here the general subject of fuel is not being discussed.
If the writer cannot stand to hear the word *wood* repeated, he should
remove its first use, not its second. Then the passage would read:

> When one sits before an open hearth and watches the
> shooting flames, hears the crackling as the fire engulfs the
> wood, and feels the warmth given off . . .

Avoidance of repetition sometimes leads writers to silly substitutions
for a key word in a passage. If the principal subject of your writing
is *cats,* use the word *cats* frequently. Don't say *cats,* then *felines,
furry friends,* and *four-legged bundles of fur.* Sports writers often sin
with this "elegant variation." For example, a good sportswriter in a
student newspaper began his article with *The Rich track team.* Then
he calls them by their name *The Olympians.* Next he says, "Then
the squad began to show." Up to that point his variation in naming
is inoffensive, but next he says:

> Still improving, the Central cindermen then overran T. F.
> South and Lockport West, finishing the season in grand
> style. The Olympians captured nine firsts . . .

By that point the paper's regular readers are probably fatigued by
the writer's attempt to avoid repetition, and an outsider is probably
lost, wondering whether *the Central cindermen* still refers to *the Rich
track team* or to one of their opponents.

The writer who has found a voice that belongs to him repeats
words with power, not with weakness. If he wants to hit a word
hard, he repeats it. Dr. Seuss does:

Then Horton the elephant smiled. "Now that's that . . ."
   And he sat
      and he sat
         and he sat
           and he sat . . .
And he sat all that day
And he kept the egg warm . . .
And he sat all that night
Through a *terrible* storm.

Thomas Paine, the pamphleteer who helped persuade colonists to join George Washington's army, wrote:

> I call not upon a few, but upon all: not on this state or that state, but on every state: up and help us; lay your shoulders to the wheel; better have too much force than too little when so great an object is at stake.

These repetitions helped create the United States.

In Shakespeare's *Macbeth,* Macduff speaks to Malcolm, reminding him of the sad state to which Scotland has fallen under the rule of the murdering King Macbeth:

>   Each new morn
> New widows howl, new orphans cry, new sorrows
> Strike heaven on the face, that it resounds
> As if it felt with Scotland and yelled out
> Like syllable of dolor.

Here the word *new* murders husbands, fathers, happiness, and creates widows, orphans, sorrows. It is not at all like the *new* which appears on so many packages of detergent, toothpaste, and shampoo in the supermarket. The manufacturer thinks the word will sell his product and he changes the product ever so slightly once a year, or changes it not at all, and stamps *new* on the package. Too many *new's* on packages have killed the force of them all.

Professional writers usually avoid starting a sentence with the same word that ends the preceding sentence:

> I found out his name was John. John was an engineer.
> The last topic on the program was rehabilitation. Rehabilitation is an urgent matter in Michigan because prisons are overcrowded.

In his second or third draft, the professional writer looks for repetitions of this sort—he knows they will be there—and expunges them. But frequently he achieves his best repetition unconsciously. An idea, or a fact, often epitomized in a key word, dominates his mind. He repeats it when he writes.

A good way to utilize repetition without being dull is to shift the form of the repeated word, or play with it in some way. Here a writer makes the word *uncivilized* speak to the word *civilized*:

> **I don't like picnics. That's against the great American tradition, I guess. I don't like to combine the civilized way of eating with uncivilized surroundings.**

When you write out a first draft hurriedly, you may find one key word appearing again and again. Before you eliminate the repetitions of it, think twice. Some of the repetitions may give strength to your writing and let the reader know what objects or ideas dominate your thought. Here is a memory of childhood that needs cutting. It contains too much good writing to be allowed to remain in this state marred by weak repetitions. But some of its repetitions are essential; for example, of the word *outside,* which is central to the writer's point. (Some of the major repetitions are indicated here in italics.)

> **Summer seems more fun during childhood. I remember those *screen-door days*. The back *door* to my house was covered with two sections of *screen* that bulged from being pushed by an endless chain of small hands. I doubt that the *door* was ever shut without a *bang*; in fact it seemed to be there for the sole purpose of shutting with a *bang*. To butt out that *door* without hearing the familiar b-r-r-zing *BANG*! would have been as unnatural to me as giving my sister some of my candy—well almost. I was always in a great hurry to get *outside*. Summer is an *outside* time. I had an outside mind. I could only think in *outside*. Sometimes in my haste to join my mind *outside*, I would fly at the *door* only to discover, too late, that a security-conscious grandmother or some such menace of childhood had locked it. I would come to a tire-tearing halt, like a cartoon car stopping on a dime. I had to peel my face off the *screen* like a waffle, and looking very much like one only with much smaller squares. I would *cuss* at whoever locked the *door*. If I did not know who the culprit was I would *cuss* at**

everyone just to be on the safe side. However my anger was silent, or mutterings at best. My mother's children left much to be desired where brains are concerned, but she did not rear any of us to be *stupid*, at least not so *stupid* as to be caught *swearing*. My father was a great strong *swearer*. He could invoke deities and conjure up demons that made my bottom sore before the *belt* was even off his waist. I was always puzzled by the fact that I could say "*god-darn*" this and "*god-darn*" that depending on whatever I wanted *God* to mend, and yet "*goddamn*" always removed the belt from my father's waist. The sin was in the "damn" not in the "God." I always wondered what God thought about it and how big a belt he had.

MICHAEL MANUEL

In this reflection on childhood, the notion of *outside* is crucial to the story because it is the urge to get outside quickly that led the boy to swear and to confront his father and think upon the effects and causes of profanity. But too much emphasis on *outside* and the screen door makes the ending discussion of profanity seem like an afterthought rather than the major subject the writing builds toward.

Here is a revision of the story with a number of the repetitions cut out:

> The back *door* to my house was covered with two sections of *screen* that bulged from being pushed by an endless chain of small hands. That *door* seemed to be there for the sole purpose of being slammed. To butt out it without hearing the familiar b-r-r-zing BANG! would have been as unnatural to me as giving my sister some of my candy.
>
> I could only think in *outside*. Sometimes in my haste to join my mind *outside*, I would fly at the *door* only to discover too late that a security-conscious grandmother had locked it. I would come to a halt like a cartoon car stopping on a dime and would peel my face off the *screen* like a waffle. Then I would cuss—at everyone, just to be on the safe side—but silently, mutteringly. Mother did not rear us to be so stupid as to be caught *swearing*.
>
> Father was a great strong *swearer*. He could invoke deities and conjure up demons that made my bottom sore before the *belt* was off his waist. I was always puzzled because I could say "*god-darn*" this and "*god-darn*" that,

> depending on whatever I wanted *God* to mend, and yet
> *"god-damn"* always removed the belt from Father's waist.
> The sin was in the *"damn"* not in the *"God."* I always
> wondered what *God* thought about it and how big a *belt*
> he wore.

Repetitions remain but they are necessary, therefore not tedious
but powerful. To gain their full effect, some words should not be
repeated at all. The writer should save them strategically for one
best moment. In the above story if the word *bang* is to sound loud,
it should be heard only once.

Rhyme is a form of repetition, of sound, not word. It can be
used in prose if the writer remembers that its effect there is customarily humorous. Lilian Moore wrote a book she called *A Pickle
for a Nickel* in which she had Mr. Bumble say truly, "Boys like noise."

REVISING FIVE: Examine your story about childhood. Omit the
weak repetitions and consider adding strong repetitions. Use penciled
brackets so that you may restore words or phrases should you later
change your mind.

WRITING FOURTEEN: Dash off two 10- to 15-minute free writings
in which you play frequently with repetition. Repeat words in as many
different patterns as you can. Repeat a word three times in a row,
then repeat it as the key word in three phrases: "He was a bumbling
carpenter, a bumbling father, a bumbling fisherman." Then separate
the repeated words even more from each other. Try repeating all kinds
of words—verbs, adverbs, prepositions, adjectives, nouns, etc. Use a
word once with one meaning and then with another meaning. If you
feel stalled, study advertisements in magazines and commercials on
television to find still other ways to repeat. Study poems; almost all
good ones repeat words skillfully. In all your practice in repeating,
do not make up nonsense phrases or sentences that are lists of words
unrepresentative of thoughts or feelings in you. Try always to say
something you mean but play while you do that. Play around—seriously.

PARALLEL CONSTRUCTION

One of the fundamental beats in all good writing is parallel construction, which is based on repetition. No competent writer's ear is
deaf to it. Take this statement:

> **George liked Jean and often walked beside her on the way
> to school. Jean was also sometimes accompanied to school by**

Ronald, who also liked her, but who often could be seen walking behind her.

Here is a shorter version:

George liked Jean and often walked beside her on the way to school. Jean was also accompanied by Ronald, who walked behind her.

But it is still awkward. Seeing that the sentences compare George's and Ronald's walking with Jean, the professional writer would cast each part of the comparison in parallel form:

George liked Jean and walked beside her to school. Ronald liked Jean and walked behind her to school.

Tightened and paralleled in this fashion, the sentences now emphasize that Ronald was bashful. They could be paralleled in another way:

The boys liked Jean. George walked beside her to school and Ronald behind her.

At the same time that most parallel patterning throws into simple and dramatic comparison two or more ideas or persons or things, it shortens a statement so severely that it requires work from the reader. This is an ideal combination of qualities: challenge and delight.

The writer who wonders how his words will strike his reader need only ask how they strike him as he patterns them. If he finds himself unchallenged or bored, he should know he is not writing well. His words should speak to him as well as to his audience—and to each other. Parallel patterning helps give them voice. Here is a beginning writer making words speak to each other:

I like to bounce when I get into bed, and pick up my pillow and throw it down, then pick up my head and drop it into the pillow, like someone picking up a little kitten and dropping it in some out of the way place so that it won't get *under* foot. Good thing I've got the upper bunk . . . I couldn't be any more *out* from *under* foot.

Train your ear so you hear a word when you write it, and then ask whether it needs an answer from another word soon. Here is a beginning writer who was listening as he wrote:

Why not be natural, free, untimed, unlimited?

Here is a professional advertising writer listening as he wrote:

> You ought to watch Longchamps meat experts buying
> beef for your dinner. They stride through the refrigerators,
> sniffing and poking each rib on the rack. They know what's
> what. So butchers give them their best. Well marbled steaks,
> tender as butter. Naturally aged meat, with a rich, beefy
> taste. Longchamps experts are tough. That's why Long-
> champs steaks are tender . . .

All writers who want to hammer an idea employ repetition and
parallel construction. A high school girl gets out her hammer in the
following article from the Lakeview High School *Crystal* of Battle
Creek, Michigan (May 6, 1966):

NASTY NAZI SYMBOL OR HARMLESS FAD?

> **Most teenage fads are inoffensive and short-lived. A current
> fad in Battle Creek is far from inoffensive and should be
> stopped at once.**
>
> **Teenagers are adorning themselves with symbols of Ger-
> man militarism such as German army helmets. Some are
> wearing an Iron Cross on a chain around their neck. Else-
> where, the Nazi swastika is in style.**
>
> **These symbols recall the death of 291,000 Americans and
> the slaughter of six million Jews.**
>
> **They recall an upheaval during and after the war, started
> by a man who used the swastika as the symbol of an evil
> philosophy.**
>
> **Human memories are short, but not so short that they
> blot out this devastating period of history.**
>
> **These military symbols are probably just an expression
> of rebellion. Some kinds of rebellion are healthy. This kind
> is sick.**
>
> JANICE NEMRAVA

IMITATING ONE: Practice parallel patterning so you can see how
easy and hard it is. Read the following examples and imitate their
structure while you are writing thoughts of your own:

1. Every day, the sun; and, after sunset, Night and her stars.
   Ever the winds blow; ever the grass grows. Every day, men and
   women, conversing—beholding and beholden.

   RALPH WALDO EMERSON

2. We have rates by the hour, day, week, month, or by the job.

DICK'S KALAMAZOO JANITOR SERVICE,
YELLOW-PAGES ADVERTISEMENT.

3. Other people cannot see what I see whenever I look into your father's face, for behind your father's face as it is today are all those other faces which were his. Let him laugh and I see a cellar your father does not remember and a house he does not remember and I hear in his present laughter his laughter as a child.

JAMES BALDWIN

4. Cut flowers at proper stage of development. Dahlias when fully open; gladioli when first floret is open; peonies when petals are unfolding; roses before buds open. In general, cut while in bud.

The Pocket Household Encyclopedia

5. Remember that young uncooked spinach makes a good salad; that cooked buttered spinach and grapefruit salad are an ideal reducer's luncheon; and that cooked spinach greens are superb with Hollandaise Sauce . . .

IRMA S. ROMBAUER AND MARION ROMBAUER BECKER

Pursue, keep up with, circle round and round your life, as a dog does his master's chaise. Do what you love. Know your own bone; gnaw at it, bury it, unearth it, and gnaw it still.

HENRY THOREAU

chapter 13 keeping a journal

"WHAT a square idea," you may have said to yourself when you read the title of this chapter. A journal! You kept a diary in high school and took it out the other day and looked away in embarrassment—

> This was the greatest day of my life. I met Tim. He was standing outside the dime store, this tall, handsome boy—a dream that's what he was—and I thought—"He ought to be on TV—and then Jeannie introduced me and I thought I'd die. I couldn't believe it. Before I knew what was happening I found myself being walked home by him. He's just absolutely—I can't say what he means to me already.

Or if you're a man, your diary went for two days and stopped. The entries looked like this:

> Played ball this morning. Had lunch at 12:30. Didn't do much the rest of the day.

The writer of journals like that can't say or won't say. The reader gets no telling facts and so can't go through them to essentials or significance. No oppositions, no tension, nothing to grab or be grabbed by. A few years later even the writers of these diaries will be unable to get any valuable meaning from them.

In contrast, here's an entry from a journal kept by a person who constantly tried to put down truths.

I have drained six cartons of lemonade and twelve glasses of tap water since this afternoon, and two quarts of milk. I have a fever but am on my feet, slushing off to class—reading, writing, and I get paid today.

Like the entry about Tim, this one is intensely personal, but it records telling facts which take the reader through the door into some essences. Reading this entry twenty years later, the writer might sense the tremendous swallowing vigor of his youth. There is a tension between his fever and his elation. Not a developed or highly significant piece of writing, but it scores, it characterizes.

All good journals observe one fundamental: they do not speak privately. They can be read with profit by other persons than the writer. They may be personal and even intimate, but if the writer wants an entry to be seen by others, it will be such that they can understand, enjoy, be moved by. The trap has sprung on the writers of the first two entries quoted in this chapter. They heard of secret diaries and thought they should write secretly in their books. So they went Engfishing, writing in a pseudodramatic manner but supplying the reader none of the oppositions that create drama.

Society presses on the writer to say nothing in his journal. A weird country we live in, where, as George Riemer points out in *How They Murdered the Second R* (1969), over six billion greeting cards were sold in one year to people who couldn't bring themselves to write anything of their own to friends and relatives. The Engfish teachers have done their job. But you know how to tell truths that count for you, and to make one truth breed another.

The man who dreams of becoming a writer spends his time dreaming of becoming a writer. The man who intends to become a writer keeps a journal and works the mine. You may say you don't intend any such thing, but you are one already if you have taken yourself through the program thus far in this book. That is, you write a lot, and some of what you write moves other persons. If you keep a journal, you can make your letters and school writing better, for it not only provides practice ground, but also gives you entries you can combine into longer work. Henry Thoreau did that and called the book *Walden*. Samuel Butler did that and called the book *The Way of All Flesh*.

Asked to write a full portrait of someone, a class of writing students found they couldn't open up to tell enough. Most of the papers disappointed the students and the professor. One young married man read the class this entry from his journal:

1

My wife's Aunt Sadie died yesterday, and the wheels of grieving were set in motion. Six months ago she wasn't even sick (we didn't know it, anyway). She and K.C. (her husband, whom we call Case) lived in Sellers, which is a little dot on a township map. When Sadie complained of being tired, her doctor (small town and country variety) told her to take iron pills to fortify her blood because she was at about that age for her change in life. So she took iron till she rusted when it rained and then went to another doctor after a year or so. He found out she had a form of leukemia.

Mary's ma and Sadie were sisters and super close. They were both cut out of the same hunk of gold. Whenever I saw Sadie and Case, Sadie would hug me with one arm and start shoveling food at me with the other, and Case would open me up a beer and start getting out a new (or an old) gun to show me. Real folks. Sadie always talked loud and real fast so I couldn't keep up or disagree, just like Mary's ma . . . and Mary. But I never wanted to shut Sadie up. She was always where it was at. Before I could agree with her, she'd hand me a bowl to lick or the last slice of ham, or Case would slip me another beer. I remember holding bowls of food in my lap all the way back to Kalamazoo when we'd come from Sellers.

Now I have to go to her funeral. I don't like funerals because of the people that lots of times go to them. That's why if I want to pay respects to someone, I go to the home and sit by them when I'm alone. Some people actually rejoice at the sight of a person crying at the death of another. They think the greater the display of emotion, the higher the reading on the love meter. The reaction of one person to the death of another is a personal thing. Some people cry for the dead person's suffering. Some cry for their own guilt feelings about their treatment of the deceased. Some cry selfishly at their personal loss and future inconvenience. And maybe some people just cry.

There is so much energy wasted at crying. Sadie at least fed people, and she couldn't have always felt as good as she acted. Probably the worse she felt, the better she cooked. But her worst probably doubled most people's best.

Isn't it barbaric to put dead people on display? Tomorrow we are going down there a full twenty-four hours before the funeral so that Mary's two youngest sisters can get used to things—what they mean is get used to seeing a corpse. I say a person should be allowed to remember another person in the way they want to. About all I can remember about my grandmother is how she looked in her casket and how her hand felt so cold and wax-like when I kissed "Nonnie" good-bye. The corpse shouldn't even have to be present for a funeral gathering. Having a group of people standing around watching a person being buried is like having friends in to witness a birth. There should be glad things doing at a funeral gathering. Sadie couldn't have stood to see all those people without feeding them. They should all talk about her and sing and toast to her good things.

And now I don't think my favorite dessert that Sadie used to fix me will taste good any more because everyone's going to spoil it and I hope she understands that I'm just a minority of one, but I loved her quite a bit for an aunt that's just adopted.

DAVE CONNOR

The students liked that writing. One said, "Write more. I want to know still more about Aunt Sadie." The writer promised, but did not force himself to continue the story right away. When more strong feelings hit him the next day, he wrote another entry.

2

I'm in Sellers. Everyone has seen Sadie at the funeral home. I wonder why they call it a home. I stayed there for about an hour and every time a new bunch of relatives would get there, the crying and sobbing would start again. The parlor has overflowed into two extra rooms with flowers. This evening, Mary said that people just kept coming in and there have been several hundred through there since yesterday. Tonight Mary said that there was little sadness displayed and that all of Sadie's friends were talking and visiting and I think sharing some of the love that all these people had for Sadie. She was such a worker. She

helped everyone and never sat still long enough for anyone to do anything for her. I think she wanted them to do
something for somebody else and start a chain letter of
doing good things. And it is sad now that she can't do things
any more. When Becky, my fifth-grade aged sister-in-law,
was crying so hard this afternoon, I talked to her because
she's never been in a funeral situation before—all of her
grandparents are still living. I asked her if she ever saw
Sadie cry, and she kind of whispered "No," and I said,
"Sadie didn't let people stay sad when she was around, did
she?" And I got another "No." "I think it might make Sadie
sad if she saw that she was making you so unhappy," I
got a soft head on my shoulder and a hug from one skinny
arm half-way around the middle. I told her that Sadie had
been in a lot of pain when she was sick and felt very badly
even after the doctors had done everything they could,
and shouldn't we be thankful that she wasn't feeling badly?
"Now she can rest and be peaceful and we should be happy
for her."

Maybe I sounded like a preacher and maybe it wasn't me
talking, but she needed someone to hang onto who wasn't
already tear-soaked. Mine were the only dry eyes in the
house at the time. My wife is one of five girls and my sister-
in-law's husband and I are big brothers quite a lot. I'm a
big brother anyway, except I only have one sister, and she's
the youngest in my family, so I don't know much about
little girls.

Sadie would be happy if she could see the kitchen at her
daughter's house. It's piled full of food that people have
been bringing over all day long. There's like ten pies, six
cakes, five potato salads, four beans, eight Jello things,
and about three dozen home-baked dinner rolls. Small
town folks help so much. They come into Nancy's house
after each group leaves and wash up all the dishes and
clean up the house. Nancy's got her dad to tend to now
and so many things to do. She's a pretty strong person. It's
hard for an only child to shoulder the bulk of a load like
she's got now because Sadie took care of Case and the
bookwork for his garage and she did all of Grandpa and
Grandma Lewis's cleaning and washing and then some.
But I think Nancy inherited her mother's will to do good
things, come hell, high water, or locusts.

I don't think tomorrow's going to be as sad as I thought at first.

Waiting a few more days, the writer felt moved to complete the record of his changing feelings about funerals. He wrote this entry:

3

We buried her today. Lots more family came and I saw the rural roots of their upbringings emerge in their sincerity, frankness, and strength. Few of the people were verbal wizards or well-versed, and few were under forty. They were tanned from years of exposure or from their retirement quarters in Florida. As I shook hands with them during the day, I could sense their feelings. The men were big and grasped my hand firmly, and extended their friendliness and welcome in their simple and straightforward greetings. My hand felt small in the grasp of these working hands that were still calloused and showed the marks of their toil. Streaks of gray were common in even the sons of the older men, but the gray was apparent only on the outside. The men were dressed neatly and each man filled his jacket through the shoulders so that you didn't notice the missing button-down collars and herringbone suits.

The women were stout and unpretentious. Their hands too had steered many a tractor and pitched more than a few bales of hay. Their dresses were fitting to the occasion and to the women wearing them—not a lot of style, but a lot of class.

After the funeral and the graveside service there was a gathering at the American Legion Hall, where we ate some more and where I watched people a lot. The atmosphere was pleasant and I think it helped people to relax from the tension and emotional strain and start getting back to the matter of picking up from where they were so sadly interrupted.

The minister who gave the service was a carpenter and a minister—a becoming combination. He spoke to a full house about the privilege that it was for all of us to help—each in his own way—to share the burden that had come to the family. We can all be strengthened by the love that Sadie had spread to so many in her life and that abounds

even at her death. He talked a lot about walking the path
of life and how great it was for all of us to take a step
together in that atmosphere so filled with love.

The sun was bright and you could tell that winter was
just about over and something was getting ready to happen to all the farmland we passed on the way to the ceme-
tery. The line of cars stretched a long ways down that tarvy
road, and parked cars were wound all through the grounds
while the minister read the last simple words.

During the service there were a lot of private tears running down already red and swollen cheeks. Mine had remained dry until almost the end of the service when I put
my arm around skinny little Becky, who sat next to me.
This time when her head pressed on my shoulder, it was
me who was trying not to cry. I felt the grief of the family
then and didn't care much about why I was upset. Lots of
people had wept openly in the past two days when I had
not.

I love a lot of those people like I was a blood relation,
and feel only now I was really part of them. During the
service I had flashed ahead to my aunt's funeral, or my
folks' deaths, and I began to understand a little better and
to feel the feelings that everyone had. I cried too because
I'm not an omniscient narrator . . . . I'm just a little slow
to feel.

When the writer and his professor looked at the three entries together,
they saw they made a record of a whole journey from the writer's scorn
for funeral rituals to his acceptance of them, and how and why he
moved from that place to this place.

> *Look sharply after your thoughts. They
> come unlooked for, like a new bird seen
> on your trees, and, if you turn to your
> usual task, disappear; and you shall
> never find that perception again; never,
> I say—but perhaps years, ages, and I
> know not what events and worlds may
> lie between you and its return!*
>
> RALPH WALDO EMERSON

Students in school seldom have the opportunity to consider an experience or idea over a period of time and from different and developing viewpoints. That's one of the reasons they seldom write moving, deep stories or discussions. Keeping a journal forces a writer to put something in the sock every day or so. Often when he reviews what is there, he sees materials that fit together and build. He can work with them.

All sorts of odds and evens and ends can go into the journal sock. Here are some lines from Henry Thoreau's journals, which ran to fourteen volumes when printed.

1

April 22, 1851. Had mouse-ear in blossom for a week. Observed the crowfoot on the Cliffs in abundance, and the saxifrage. The wind last Wednesday, April 16th, blew down a hundred pines on Fair Haven Hill.

Having treated my friend ill, I wished to apologize; but, not meeting him, I made an apology to myself.

It is not the invitation which I hear, but which I feel, that I obey.

You may say those lines don't amount to much. The hundred pines down on Fair Haven Hill make a fact, but what does it tell? The last two sentences are generalizations and do not bring a person or act alive. True, when the mouse-ear came into bloom may not be significant, but then again for Thoreau it may some day bloom again in conjunction with another thought of his. Think of your journal as a place where you may write anything, even a fact that doesn't tell. It's a chance book, where every phrase put down might later speak to you or to another phrase recorded days or months later.

The last two sentences in Thoreau's entry #1 are generalizations, and therefore run the risk of being empty or boring. They do not reveal the persons they must have been based on. Yet they contain oppositions, so they are more than half-hearted remarks. In your journal, record simple facts, opinions, preferences—anything that counts for you at the moment. Here are entries from college students' journals:

A

Lines I liked: When Queen Mab drums in the soldier's ear and he, awakening suddenly, "swears a prayer or two and then sleeps again." (63:87) Seems to me probably just what a soldier does.

I also like Benvolio's line on 47: 131, "Being one too
many by my weary self." Sometimes I feel the same way.
I don't even like my own company.

B

My son turned over today and I never imagined the happiness that an apparently trivial move like this could bring.
I guess I'm growing up faster than he is.

Here's Thoreau characterizing one of his neighbors in his journal.

2

October 4, 1851 . . . I was admiring his corn-stalks disposed about the barn to dry, over or astride the braces and
the timbers, of such a fresh, clean, and handsome green, retaining their strength and nutritive properties so, unlike the
gross and careless husbandry of speculating, money-making
farmers, who suffer their stalks to remain out till they are
dry and dingy and black as chips.

Minott is, perhaps, the most poetical farmer—who most
realizes to me the poetry of the farmer's life—that I know.
He does nothing with haste and drudgery, but as if he loved
it. He makes the most of his labor, and takes infinite satisfaction in every part of it. He is not looking forward to the sale
of his crops or any pecuniary profit, but he is paid by the
constant satisfaction which his labor yields him. He has not
too much land to trouble him,—too much work to do,—no
hired man nor boy,—but simply to amuse himself and live. He
cares not so much to raise a large crop as to do his work well.
He knows every pin and nail in his barn. If another linter is
to be floored, he lets no hired man rob him of that amusement, but he goes slowly to the woods and, at his leisure,
selects a pitch pine tree, cuts it, and hauls it or gets it hauled
to the mill; and so he knows the history of his barn floor.

Farming is an amusement which has lasted him longer
than gunning or fishing. He is never in a hurry to get his
garden planted and yet [it] is always planted soon enough,
and none in the town is kept so beautifully clean.

He always prophesies a failure of the crops, and yet is
satisfied with what he gets. His barn floor is fastened down
with oak pins, and he prefers them to iron spikes, which he
says will rust and give way. He handles and amuses himself
with every ear of his corn crop as much as a child with its

playthings, and so his small crop goes a great way. He might well cry if it were carried to market. The seed of weeds is no longer in his soil.

He loves to walk in a swamp in windy weather and hear the wind groan through the pines. He keeps a cat in his barn to catch the mice. He indulges in no luxury of food or dress or furniture, yet he is not penurious but merely simple. If his sister dies before him, he may have to go to the almshouse in his old age; yet he is not poor, for he does not want riches. He gets out of each manipulation in the farmers' operations a fund of entertainment which the speculating drudge hardly knows. With never-failing rheumatism and trembling hands, he seems yet to enjoy perennial health.

Thoreau found telling facts and significant oppositions between the way Minott and other men lived. He brings the reader up sharp with the last sentence, saying that a man with rheumatism and trembling hands enjoys perennial health. After the whole account of Minott's solid way of life, the pressure on the last two words is so strong that they speak of more than simply physical well being.

You may never match the depth and vigor of Thoreau's journals. You don't have to. No one is requiring a *Walden* from you. But you will write a valuable journal if you practice the fundamentals presented in this book. Note how these entries from beginning writers' journals come alive:

C

I worked again and about seven Ed came into the store. Until three months ago, he was drinking four to six quarts of beer every night. Then one night he choked on his phlegm (he has bronchial asthma), fell over backward into the bathtub, breaking his pelvis, and almost choking to death—when he got to the hospital, the doctors diagnosed also a weak heart, bad liver, and almost shot kidneys. His doctors warned him to stay away from alcohol or die in five years. He bought only Coke for about a week after he got out of the hospital.

Then one night that I happened to be working, he walked in—twenty pounds thinner and looking like death warmed over, and ordered one bottle of Pabst. I involuntarily hesitated but I'm not there to be a moral judge, so I sold it to him. He bought four last night, and I figure that gives him about four years and nine months.

A constant charge made by professors is that students do not relate what they read in class to their own lives. True of Engfishers, but not of students who have found their own voices and are willing to put down their truths. A line sticks in their minds and helps them see better at a later time, in another place. Here are two journal entries in which that happens.

D

In class once we talked about how much we forget of each day and it's still true. A few days ago I was walking through Bronson Park and noticed a cigarette butt squashed into the pavement still wet and soggy from the melting snow. The brown paper that covered its filter was faded. I thought how many other times I'd seen ugly cigarette butts smeared on sidewalks and forgotten them, but this one I remembered. Oh joy! Then I reached the street and gazed at the brown parking meter that clashed with the green lamp post and the purple car. Usually I would ignore such a color combination and walk on oblivious, not to be avoiding seeing it, but forgetting it as fast as it was seen. Kierkegaard said in one section of *Either/Or* that there is an art to forgetting just as there is to remembering. And I wondered how much of one day's comprehensions do we train ourselves to forget.

E

"Every man is the builder of a temple, called his body, to the god he worships, after a style purely his own, nor can he get off by hammering marble instead. We are all sculptors and painters, and our material is our own flesh and blood and bones."

While sitting in church three weeks ago I saw an example of what Thoreau is telling us in the above statement.

Mrs. Churchpillar came into our church and sat down beside me. I was *indeed* privileged, for everyone praised Mrs. Churchpillar as a large contributor to the new church. We happened, *in fact,* to be sitting in one of the *very* pews donated by the Churchpillars. But, *somehow* I found it difficult to praise Mrs. Churchpillar because of the sight of her own temple, the one Thoreau talks about. *Her own temple was a mess!*

The artificial paint on her face was so thick that if I were to chip it with hammer and wedge I could not reach flesh.

> Her dress was so tight that if she had left it on for any
> length of time her circulation would have been paralyzed
> from diamond choker to spike-heeled alligator shoes. Her
> breath was still clouded, and her head, too, from the
> whiskey-sours of Saturday night. But, *such as it is,* her
> body is her own temple to God.

Like most first versions of writing, this entry could be cut to its advantage. The words italicized above might go. "Her own temple was a mess!" is a giveaway line that prevents the subsequent description from surprising the reader.

WRITING FIFTEEN: Keep a journal for at least two weeks.

REVISING SIX: Revise and sharpen two or five entries you think carry truths and oppositions and present them for criticism.

Do not feel that everything in your journal should be excellent, or that right now you should be able to tell what is good and bad. A journal is a place for confusion and certainty, for the half-formed and the completed. Thoreau said:

> Of all strange and unaccountable things this journalizing is
> the strangest. It will allow nothing to be predicated of it; its
> good is not good, nor its bad bad. If I make a huge effort
> to expose my innermost and richest wares to light, my
> counter seems cluttered with the meanest homemade stuffs;
> but after months or years I may discover the wealth of India,
> and whatever rarity is brought overland from Cathy, in that
> confused heap, and what perhaps seemed a festoon of dried
> apple or pumpkin will prove a string of Brazilian diamonds,
> or pearls from Coromandel. [January 29, 1841]

You too.

chapter 14

sound
and
voice

ALL PERSONS employ sound skillfully without being taught. In a speech given to American teachers in 1966, Edmond Wright, a British schoolteacher, pointed out that under extreme emotional stress all persons speak in strong rhythm and often with alliteration.

David! You're a *dirty*, low-*down dog!*

He told students to write down what persons at home said under stress: they found considerable alliteration. One student complained that he didn't hear any, so Mr. Wright suggested he go home and pour a glass of milk over his brother's head and then listen to his father. He did. He heard considerable alliteration.

Knocking around in every person's head are the sounds of his native language: spoken or muted echoes of what he has read, the lullabies his mother sang him, the rich cursing of men hunting or playing games, the formal rhythms of a trained voice reading in church or synagogue, the skip rope song, the hurried swallowed phrases of other children singing the "Star Spangled Banner" or chanting the "Gettysburg Address," the taunts they sang in the street:

Simpy Sam is a stupid old man!

Without trying, most persons can write rapidly such sound effects as these by a high school girl:

134

> I like to go fishing. But I don't like to touch worms or slippery, slimy fish. They wiggle. I went with Anne three years ago. That was fun until she broke her promise and made me take the fish off. Then it swallowed the hook. It was terrible. It wriggled and writhed in the bottom of the boat. Then it just lay there. Dead.

This is not an exceptional piece of writing. The seventh sentence suffers from It-ache. In the sixth, *it* refers to the fish; then suddenly *it* refers to the whole struggle of the fish with the hook. But in sound, the passage is strong. *Slippery* and *slimy* and *wriggled* and *writhed* alliterate with force and their sounds echo the sense of what they say. The last two sentences allow the record to run down appropriately, and *Dead* stands by itself, final—in its position, its shortness, and its two hard *d's*.

In the phrase "bottom of the boat," the writer has repeated the *b* sound skillfully. You may say that she did not mean to hit that sound hard and that it adds nothing to the passage because the *b* sound does not suggest *boat* or *bottom* as the *sl* sound in *slippery* and *slimy* suggests the squirming fish. True, but one of the marks of a strong writer is that through his sentences appears from time to time an occasional repetition of sound that gives his words a strength like the "bone" in spaghetti cooked not too soft by an expert Italian cook. Note this pattern of sound repetition in these next passages. The authors were probably not trying for any effects, but they achieved them nevertheless.

> Men are *h*orri*b*ly *t*edious *wh*en *th*ey are good *h*us*b*ands and a*b*omina*b*ly concei*t*ed *wh*en *th*ey are no*t*.
>
> OSCAR WILDE

> It's like *wh*en you break up *w*ith a girl and you've explained all your reasons to her *wh*y. And *sh*e *s*ays, "I *s*till don't *s*ee *wh*y it *w*on't *w*ork." And you've *s*een *it* ou*t* and you've hi*t th*e *b*lan*k* har*d* col*d w*all of *s*olid no*th*ing.
>
> HIGH SCHOOL STUDENT WRITING FREELY

Another way to create faithful and exciting sound in your writing is to try to put down what you hear. The sound of a bullfrog? In *Walden,* Thoreau calls it a *trump* and put it down *tr-r-r-oonk*! In his *Journals* he describes the pigeon woodpecker's "whimsical ah-week ah-week." In *The Field Book of Ponds and Streams,* Anne Haven Morgan writes the American toad's call as "wheep."

When she heard the sound of traffic on a nearby street, a mother
working in a beginning writers' course remembered her children's
youth through sound:

HOME

> At noon, traffic on Stadium transmits an even, steady
> sound, the passing of many cars blending together in a
> deep, harmonious hum. At two o'clock in the morning, a
> single car creates a gradual crescendo as it approaches, a
> diminuendo as it moves into the distance.
>
> One car at night carries a lonesome, nostalgic sound. I
> am reminded of times I've lain awake waiting for teen-
> agers to return. In the deep quiet of the country night I
> can hear the first faint sound of a car coming down the
> highway a quarter of a mile away, slowing down to turn
> the corner onto the gravel of our country road, the gradual
> increasing of sound as the car approaches; then a momen-
> tary lowering as it slows for the bump of the little bridge;
> an increasing again for the rise of the little hill where our
> house stood. I can remember lying tense and breathing
> lightly, waiting for the moment when the noise of the car
> would continue on past the house into the distance. Or—
> it would pause, diminishing abruptly as the driver pressed
> the brake and the car coasted with its own momentum into
> our driveway. I heard the final beat of the motor, the quick
> staccato of young feet, first on the porch steps, then on
> the stairs. Soon the hall light, always left on for the last
> one in, was snapped off.
>
> My child was back under my roof again.

GERTRUDE ANDRESEN

Here the writer not only remembers sounds but evokes some of them
by her choice of words and building of sentence rhythms. The statement

> then a momentary lowering of sound as it slows for the
> bump of the little bridge

employs the word *bump* perfectly—a short word with a little burst
and closure in it, coming in the middle of the statement so that
it sounds exactly like what the writer is describing. Maybe *bump* was
the only word that came to the writer's mind, luckily right in sound

for her purposes. Maybe she also thought of saying *slight rise in the road, ripple,* or *protuberance,* and discarded them because they did not contribute anything in sound. Often a writer doesn't know how he achieved his good sound effects. Sometimes he doesn't hear them until a reader points them out. Yet they are there and he has a right to take credit for them.

You may train your ear by reading aloud good writing. Then when you read aloud your own writing you are more likely to hear skillful sounds. In reading a second or third draft you can change a word here or there.

To write fully, you must use all your senses. Remember how places and objects smell, the taste of the back of your hand, the touch of concrete, the sound of a laugh—an American's laugh, a Southerner's laugh, a Northerner's. Such variety.

The representation of sounds in words can become conventional and even trite—"bang!" "screech," "eek!" Here is a beginning writer recording sounds in fresh words:

> I like the quiet crackling of root beer foam; the swish, then flap of the net as the basketball passes through . . . squeaky popcorn; slept-on mattress . . . moccasins treading soft sand, crisp as toasted linen; steel door weightlessly slammed shut; secret roar of sea shell; whirr of a movie reel; the ps-s-s-t of freshly opened coffee . . . whirr and buzz of the WALK signal; a Band-Aid coming off . . . creaky wicker chairs . . .
>
> SISTER MARY LOIS GLONEK

IMITATING TWO: Put down in words a page of sounds you like and dislike. Study the passage above by Sister Mary Lois. Note her accuracy and restraint. She avoided the obvious and conventional representations of loud sounds. You may follow her direction or others. Like all symbolizing of experience through words, the representation of sounds is complex and subtle. Sometimes it is almost a precise rendering of actual sound; sometimes a satirical conventionalization, as in the *Batman* series—"Zowie! Blat! Pow! Bam!"

The most significant sound in life is that of other voices. The best writers seem born with an ear's memory for the way a person speaks, and if they write down the conversations of a dozen persons in one story, all speak recognizably differently. Maybe this is a natural gift, not to be learned. But you may try, at least, to see whether you have it.

The following two statements by William Carlos Williams differ completely from each other in sound. They move differently—that is one of the effects a writer can achieve by controlling sound.

THE DANCE

In Breughel's great picture, The Kermess,
the dancers go round, they go round and
around, the squeal and the blare and the
tweedle of bagpipes, a bugle and fiddles
tipping their bellies (round as the thick-
sided glasses whose wash they impound)
their hips and their bellies off balance
to turn them. Kicking and rolling about
the Fair Grounds, swinging their butts, those
shanks must be sound to bear up under such
rollicking measures, prance as they dance
in Breughel's great picture, The Kermess.

POEM

As the cat
climbed over
the top of

the jamcloset
first the right
forefoot

carefully
then the hind
stepped down

into the pit of
the empty
flowerpot

Dr. Williams' mastery of sound should come as no surprise to readers who know he was a poet. A practicing M.D., he wrote poems in his office in between seeing patients or on the way to visit them in their homes.

In "The Dance," Dr. Williams writes only two sentences, listing again and again a few nouns joined by prepositions, or a verb form ending in *-ing*. Once he says they go round and round, his parts of sentences repeat and repeat and thus go round and round themselves:

the squeal and the blare and the tweedle
a bugle and fiddles
their hips and their bellies

One way he gets the parts of sentences to swing is to join them with *and,* a word he uses six times.

Read aloud, the poem almost flies off the page, because Dr. Williams has employed so many sound effects—alliteration and assonance, the repetition of *ound* in *round, around, impound, Grounds, sound.*

Dr. Williams' second sentence is not actually a sentence but a jamming together of the parts of several sentences which do not keep straight their subjects and verbs. For example, the shanks are not "swinging their butts"; the dancers are. Dr. Williams knows what a sentence is, but here he deliberately violates grammar in order to increase the feeling that the speaker is himself breathlessly swinging around and around rather than reciting a carefully composed statement at a speaker's podium.

In the second poem about the cat, Dr. Williams has arranged his words to slow down the reader as he speaks the lines. Instead of the constant repetition of words ending in *-ing,* he uses many words ending in sounds that stop rather than prolong sound: the word *top* not a word like *new,* the word *jamcloset* not a word like *see.* Also many of his words begin with hard sounds: *cat climbed, flowerpot.* In "The Dance," he wanted beer-drinking peasants to swing in circles; in "Poem" he wanted a cat to step precisely and carefully. The sound of words is the poet's business. He must be able to control it as a pitcher controls a curve.

You may hate poetry or fear it because you have been tossed too many knuckleballs, those slow and slower mushy pitches that take forever to reach home plate. Because of that possibility this textbook has not asked you to write poetry, although to learn to write some poetry is to learn to master language, and thus to write any sort of statement, whether a business letter or a novel, with power. If you have urges to write poetry, give in to them.

But know what contemporary poetry is before you try it. Not a bunch of vague private thoughts about reforming the world or feeling sorry for yourself because you're lonely. Like all good writing, good poetry puts you somewhere in reality—perhaps in the mind of a real person. It's alive. You can see what William Carlos Williams wrote about, a Flemish painting he liked and an American cat. Lois Berg wrote about learning to ride a bicycle.

Write about your experience. You don't have to try poetry; but if you do, remember it is first of all concentrated form of expression. Pack the word. Pack the meaning. Play with words. Make one phrase say three thoughts or feelings. Remember, sound should speak the feeling you wish to communicate. Use rhyme if you wish, but keep it alive, fresh, surprising. If it comes out blue, true; moon, June, swoon —give up. Poetry must have guts and bone, whether it is delicate or slambang. It must have all the attributes of good writing discussed in this book, only brought to their ultimate concentrated power. That way, underneath, it carries truth.

> *Poetry is a response to the daily neces-*
> *sity of getting the world right.*
>
> WALLACE STEVENS

VOICE

In free writing a person frequently finds that his pen or typewriter seems to have taken over the job of writing and he is sitting there watching the words go down on paper. A writer should do whatever he can to help bring about this state. In his book *Making It,* writer and editor Norman Podhoretz says:

> The poem, the story, the essay, and even something so ap-parently inconsequential as a book review (I mean one which is approached with seriousness), is already *there,* much in the way that Socrates said mathematical knowledge was already there, before a word is ever put to paper; and the act of writing is the act of finding the magical key that will unlock the floodgates and let the flow begin.
>
> .   .   .
>
> . . . The key, I believe is literally a key in that it is musical . . . it is the tone of voice, the only tone of voice, in which this particular piece of writing will permit itself to be writ-ten.

Mr. Podhoretz goes on to describe a writer who has found a voice right for what he wants to say.

> In this beatific condition, he will sit with a pen or at a type-writer and watch, in delight and amazement, sentences mysteriously shaping themselves into rhythms he *knows* to be right . . . He will find that he has not only been permitted to uncover things he did not know he knew, but that he has also been allowed for the first time to say many things he knew he knew and had never been able to get onto a page because they had never *fitted* anywhere and only what fits is allowed.

There is nothing so good as *feeling* to control actions. Lots of talk flying around these days about developing intellectual control, but to learn to tap feelings so they control actions and words is far more useful. If you can find the feeling that belongs to a piece of writing you want to create—your feeling toward the subject and the persons you are writing to—then the composing may be accomplished almost without your help, and it will be true in tone, and compelling. Note how feeling holds together the following passage.

> A sun-bleached beach in Monterey, California, that's where he wrote the letter. He said the moon was full, and beautiful, and it hit the ocean just right, that he was glad it was a weekend and he didn't have detail, that he was wearing the sweater I got him for Christmas and was drenched in Pub, which I also bought him, that he thinks he's landed the radio job, that he wishes he could be home in Michigan and be going to college again.
>
> He asked me if I liked the valentine he sent and the flowers and do I miss him and think of him and how did I do on my chemistry exam?
>
> He said it was getting too cold to write outside by the ocean, so he better leave. He was going to San Francisco for the weekend and would I stay home over the weekend because he was going to call Saturday night? I did. He didn't.

Finding the right voice will help you write better than you ever thought yourself capable of writing. The author of the following passage wanted to defend a basketball player for losing his cool during a game. Once he put down the words "you are high on the tempo of the game," he slid into a rhythm that perfectly reproduces a basketball game—the players submerged in a sea of crisscrossing waves and currents.

> Spencer Haywood, the Olympic basketball star who now plays for the University of Detroit, got suspended for a week. That cat's got himself in a little jam, but people are coming through for him. It is an unbendable fact, however, that attacks on officials cannot be condoned. I know what he felt at the time, however, and it is a very difficult thing to cope with, you are high on the tempo of the game and your total absorption and involvement in it. Then that whistle blows and that blankfaced impersonal black and white striped jerk starts bellowing his judgments that are

not personal in creation but are so in effect. And you can do nothing about it once he says it. When it leaves his mouth, it is law, it is absolute, it is irreversible. You go from high back to earth and inside yourself and outside the situation and inside the ref and over to the coach and into your teammates' eyes and under their sweaty skins and sometimes you come up with no sense of judgment or what to do and you strike out at something or someone and it will always hurt you in that situation. Spencer is hurt but he is being dealt with by human beings who have displayed their qualities of humanness in their judgment.

DAVID SIMPSON

The rhythms in this comment about a basketball player are not fancy stylistic tricks but the very pulse of what the writer has to say. Yet in his sympathy with one player the writer has not forgotten the game. He still sees the need of a referee with absolute authority.

Before you write your next paper, sit still a moment and listen to yourself speaking inside. If you hear a voice that takes on a clear tone— happy, calm, humble, arrogant, loving, irritated, enraged, soothing, or ironic, listen as you write and get it on paper.

> *I've never liked the conventional con-*
> *ception of "style." What's confusing is*
> *that style usually means some form of*
> *fancy writing—when people say, oh yes,*
> *so and so's such a "wonderful stylist."*
> *But if one means by style the voice, the*
> *irreducible and always recognizable and*
> *alive thing, then of course style is really*
> *everything.*
>
> MARY MCCARTHY

Finding a true voice gives a piece of writing unity. Everything seems to belong together and the whole speaks in one rhythm that cannot easily be denied or forgotten. And it keeps the sentences pouring out and thus gets by the danger of stopping somewhere along the line wordless, and then stopping again, and perhaps becoming absolutely stopped, so the writing can never be finished. In the following letter by a mother, there is no doubt that the writer is going to finish her statement.

Dear Mrs. Grint:

My son Robert is in your music class. As you know, he left his music book on the school bus last Friday. Robert has

searched the bus, asked the drivers, the principal, the janitor, his teacher, even the school cook—without success.

You told him you could not understand how a nine-year-
old boy could be so careless, irresponsible, and ungrateful
and strongly suggested that he lacked proper home training.

Robert is careless and irresponsible, and most of the time
I wouldn't change him if I knew how. He's careless and irresponsible, Mrs. Grint, about your values and mine, not his.
Robert's world consists of baseball, frogs, snakes, bubble
gum, and more baseball. He takes his mitt to school every
day and doesn't lose it. He spends hours down at the pond
collecting frogs and snakes.

Ungrateful! Why should he be grateful to you for driving
out every natural musical desire he has ever had? Sending
that damn book home to be covered is a case in point.
You've made it a sin for a child to have an uncovered book
in your class. You shout at your students, humiliate them
before their friends if they sing a wrong note, or sing too
loud or not loud enough. If their attention wanders, you
assign them an extra report on Bach or Mozart.

It is true, as the school administration points out, that
your students learn music—music theory, music history, and
music antagonism. I'm sorry for your students, Mrs. Grint.
They've been cheated. They've had to pay too high a price
for learning to sing on pitch. I'm sorry for you too. You've
paid too much for the covers on those music books.

A writer's tone should be natural to him in the circumstances, and
above all it should be justified. Nothing is more ridiculous than a
person who takes on the wrong tone—unless he is doing it as a joke.
The prissy schoolmarm who pretends to be offended by a bit of gossip
that you can see her licking her lips over becomes a buffoon. When
the author of this textbook was in the army, he knew a corporal who
was always affecting a pompous delivery and then misusing big words.
Once he shouted at several soldiers talking noisily outside the captain's
office, "All right now, cut out the levitivity!" Another time, explaining
the rules of the Geneva Convention for behavior of war prisoners, he
said, "Give the enemy officer only your name, rank, and serial number;
and then step forward one pace and lay your prudentials on the
ground."

In the following letter, taken from a campus newspaper, the writer
tries to speak in a condescending voice to persons he thinks his intel-

lectual inferiors, yet he does not command his own elevated language firmly enough to deserve the superior position he has given himself. He berates a columnist for not getting down to criticism, but he himself does not make a clear statement of what was bad about the columnist's writing. He is showing off his vocabulary rather than using it powerfully, so the tone is arrogant, but ill-founded.

> To the Editor:
> I do not imagine that it is the usual thing for graduate students to seek to disturb the lethargy which has obviously enveloped the undergraduate staff of The Daily Orange, but having in mind the high cost of newsprint, I feel obliged to speak out against its unforgiveable waste as noticeable in some sections of your paper.
> I speak here directly of one column, authorized by a chap named "Bernie," and which purports to be a critical review of television offerings. More specifically, I am concerned with the column as it appeared on Tuesday, Dec. 11.
> Such writing as appeared in this item is, I fear, only too typical of collegiate journalism on the whole, and of the undergraduate "critical" mind in particular.
> The subject of these review columns is not criticized, but, rather, serves as a springboard for the author's inane solecisms, painfully born in a vacuum, and nurtured by insipidity.
> The use of Irish orphans as the basis for a crude observation on the televised appearance of Elvis Presley is only a gross example of stupidity compounded with poor taste.
> The criticism directed at Kate Smith made claim to intelligence only in that it was written in fairly correct grammar, (though it should be said that the hyphen is still considered a part of English grammar).

In that last sentence the letter writer makes fun of a columnist for not being perfect in grammar and himself errs in punctuation by putting a comma before a beginning parentheses mark. The intelligent critic allows other human beings a few slips in form, lest he leave no place for himself to stand. To continue the letter to the editor:

> In pertinence to material, descriptiveness of such relevance, and the other accepted canons of artistic criticisms the column was woefully lacking and the author, apparently, equally ignorant of the existence of such.

But the world has had its great writers and, I suppose, we must have our Bernies. However, as the editor of a college newspaper, you, sir, should feel exceedingly culpable for allowing such execrable prose to reach your pages.

It degrades not only your capabilities and those of the rest of the staff, but also offends the intelligence of all connected with a university that sponsors writing of this calibre.

There is enough wrong with the "Ed Sullivan Show" that it provides ample material for stimulating criticism. Resorting to pseudo-witticisms for a few strained laughs is a luxury which no publication can, economically as well as aesthetically, afford.

Whew! A graduate student Engfisher. He really had nothing to say except that he was superior to this stupid "chap" Bernie. When that is the message, the tone cannot be anything but affected or arrogant. When you have something to say you know will be of value to others, then you will respect words and choose them honestly. And they may take on a tone you want them to have.

Here's an essay that won a hundred dollars in a contest sponsored by a national sorority for women educators. It's all marble or plastic, like most of the winners of contests asking for statements on "Why I Am Proud to Be an American" or "Why I Believe in the United States." The writers presume the judges want Engfish and give it to them. Then the judges are left with the job of deciding which is the best paper among several hundred or dozen hopeless, dull statements.

WHY I WANT TO BE A TEACHER

I want to be a teacher because, by teaching one can help students toward the world of tomorrow—of the 100-year life, of supersonic speeds, of visits to the moon, and yet maintain and enrichen the American Teaching traditions.

"Help!" you may be saying. "Already I can't stand it." But it gets worse:

A teacher can help to guide the future businessman, the scientists and the leaders of our country toward the future

Where else would they be guided to? Perhaps the businessmen to jail for violating antitrust laws or the scientists to Hell for inventing diabolic engines of death?

in an era when education has become a vital part of the American life . . .

Was there some era in which education was a deadly rather than vital part of American life? If it taught this girl how to write, perhaps that era is the present one. The essay goes on in that platitudinous way and becomes more fatuous in the later paragraphs.

> I want to teach because I like people and I like to work with people. One learns by teaching; each day holds a new experience, problem or personality. One meets people of different backgrounds and with new ideas.

Where does a person meet only people of the same background and with old ideas?

> Through her years of teaching, each teacher experiences many different personalities. She has the opportunity to help develop these personalities and become more enriched from the experience. With the guidance of a good teacher, students learn more than math, history, or whatever the subject, They can learn a lesson in living.
>
> Getting students to think original thoughts, feel honest emotions, listen, respond and arrive at their own conclusions is a rewarding experience in itself . . .

Trouble is, this girl hasn't the first notion of what it is to think original thoughts or feel honest emotions when she is writing. Her voice is borrowed, and badly. She's an All-American Engfisher.

As a writer at times you may not feel close to your subject: it does not produce love or hate in you. You may not feel close to your audience; you are not entirely sure who makes it up. The subject or the occasion may seem so mechanical or formal that any appropriate voice you choose does not belong to you. At these times you need more than ever to search hard for a voice. Remember the directions written by the teacher taking trippers to Chicago in Chapter 3. She found a light voice in which to speak ordinarily heavy instructions. Here is a part of a pamphlet titled "How to Take Care of Cats," published by the American Humane Association. How would you describe the writer's voice?

> There are few greater compliments than the friendship of a cat. You can't *buy* friendship from a cat. You can't *force* friendship. You get affection and respect from a cat only when you earn it—and a cat's standards for human conduct are high.

The cardinal need, in making a friend of a cat, is to understand cats.

For example, you should understand that punishment has almost no effect upon a cat—except that the cat may get indignant and leave home. A folded newspaper, banged loudly on a table *before* a cat jumps on the table, may make the cat decided not to jump. But a smack on the tail, *after* the jump, will merely convince the cat that *you* are an objectionable person. The cat won't connect the blow with the fact that it is on a table.

Don't expect to get "obedience" from a cat. Cats simply don't recognize authority. The word "obedience" isn't in their vocabulary. If you ask a cat to do something that it wishes to do, it will consent very graciously—and that is the best that can be had.

If this characteristic irritates you, try a tankful of fish instead of a cat.

So many of the strong voices in this chapter speak in anger that you may think a person writing with dignity and control cannot sustain a voice that will give unity to his words. Here is part of a speech delivered by one of the most eloquent men of the nineteenth century, Frederick Douglass. A slave until the age of twenty-one, he was largely self taught and therefore did not always use Engfish as did some of his better educated contemporaries. He is here dedicating the Freedmen's monument in memory of Lincoln in Washington, D.C., April 14, 1876.

We fully comprehend the relation of Abraham Lincoln both to ourselves and to the white people of the United States. Truth is proper and beautiful at all times and in all places and it is never in any case more proper and beautiful than when one is speaking of a great public man whose example is likely to be commended for honor and imitation long after his departure to the solemn shades, the silent continents of eternity. It must be admitted—truth compels me to admit—even here in the presence of the monument we have erected to his memory, that Abraham Lincoln was not, in the fullest sense of the word, either our man or our model. In his interests, in his associations, in his habits of thought and in his prejudices, he was a white man.

He was preeminently the white man's President, entirely devoted to the welfare of white men. He was ready and willing at any time during the first years of his administration to deny, postpone, and sacrifice the rights of humanity in the colored people in order to promote the welfare of the white people of this country. In all his education and feeling he was an American of the Americans. He came into the Presidential chair upon one principle alone, namely, opposition to the extension of slavery. His arguments in furtherance of this policy had their motive and mainspring in his patriotic devotion to the interests of his own race. To protect, defend, and perpetuate slavery in the states where it existed Abraham Lincoln was not less ready than any other President to draw the sword of the nation. He was ready to execute all the supposed constitutional guarantees of the United States Constitution in favor of the slave system anywhere inside the slave states. He was willing to pursue, recapture, and send back the fugitive slave to his master, and to suppress a slave rising for liberty, though the guilty master were already in arms against the Government. The race to which we belong were not the special objects of his consideration. Knowing this, I concede to you, my white fellow citizens, a preeminence in this worship at once full and supreme. First, midst, and last, you and yours were the objects of his deepest affection and his most earnest solicitude. You are the children of Abraham Lincoln. We are at best only his step-children, children by adoption, children by force of circumstances and necessity. To you it especially belongs to sound his praises . . . But while in the abundance of your wealth, and in the fullness of your just and patriotic devotion, you do all this, we entreat you to despise not the humble offering we this day unveil to view, for while Abraham Lincoln saved for you a country, he delivered us from a bondage, one hour of which, according to Jefferson, was worse than ages of the oppression your fathers rose in rebellion to oppose.

The voice in which Douglass speaks (he wrote his speeches for delivery) is dignified. Many sentences are of about equal length and start in much the same way. The language and the effect are elevated, befitting words spoken at a highly formal occasion. But Frederick Douglass was not showing off his vocabulary as was the graduate student writing about Bernie. Douglass never for a moment forgot his truth. He spoke hard words about Lincoln, and many whites have

been shocked by them. His statements gain in surprise because they
are delivered in grand tones. Like everyone else who has ever spoken
a word, Frederick Douglass and you have at your command a number
of different voices. Use them.

> *Concentration upon honesty is the only*
> *way to exclude the sounds of the bad*
> *style that assault us all.*
>
> DONALD HALL

WRITING SIXTEEN: Do two 15- to 20-minute free writings on any
subjects that strike you at the moment. Whether large or small matters, you must know them and care about them if you are to find a
voice that speaks rightly your feelings. If this task intimidates you,
look back over the chapter and see how different subjects brought
on different, but real, voices for writers like you. Don't expect too
much. If you write one paper of the two in an authentic voice, you
have done well.

chapter 15
writing
critically

THE BEST CRITICS help their readers see better and entertain them in the process. They provide oppositions, tension, surprise, news, as any other good writer does. Of Shakespeare, William Hazlitt wrote,

> His plays alone are properly expressions of the passions, not descriptions of them. His characters are real beings of flesh and blood; they speak like men, not like authors. One might suppose that he had stood by at the time, and overheard what passed. As in our dreams we hold conversations with ourselves, make remarks, or communicate intelligence, and have no idea of the answer which we shall receive, and which we ourselves make, till we hear it, so the dialogues in Shakespeare are carried on without any consciousness of what is to follow, without any appearance of preparation or premeditation. The gusts of passion come and go like sound of music borne on the wind.

What Hazlitt says Shakespeare does, and what Hazlitt himself does here, is what more critics ought to try to do. But most college students have no notion of any such thing, they write Engfish, sometimes so agonizingly pretentious—like the paper quoted below—that at the outset the reader doubts whether they are ever going to get down to saying anything about their subject.

A critic is a person who differentiates between the good and bad qualities of some piece of work through his reasoned

opinions. He can be in total agreement or disagreement in regards to merit or fault. In short, he is either for you or against you. It has been said that every story has two sides of which a critic could be a mediator or arbitrator to this point of view.

A leading film critic from the city of Chicago, Illinois, is Roger Ebert. He expresses his reviews for the *Chicago Sun-Times* newspaper every week in his movie column. The articles he writes are very outspoken and articulate in their composition. He is considered to be one of the foremost critics in the film industry today of which his work shows to prove. This paper is dedicated to a review written by Mr. Ebert for the Showcase and Travel Section of his newspaper. It is a very interesting literary work that he portrays in this particular article. I will give a general description of what he has written in his column and then give my own personal commentary as to how I think he expressed his analysis . . .

Abominable writing. Pure blab. All those words and the writer hasn't gotten down to saying what Mr. Ebert said about any films. How could anyone waste his readers' time by telling them that a critic might be totally for or against something? Or that Chicago is a city and the *Sun-Times* is a newspaper?

The only answer is that the writer must be scared. He doesn't know enough about what the critic is judging to judge the critic. He shouldn't have written about him, or he should have gone out and seen what the critic is talking about so he can judge what he says. This paper shows how a writer's language becomes unnatural when he doesn't know what he is talking about. The sentences read like a foreigner's attempt at English, or a bad translation from Latin; but the writer was a hundred percent American college student, frightened out of his language. Here's more:

Mr. Ebert's article is entitled "New York Film Festival Begins by Digging Up Old Paydirt." He begins his composition by stating that movies are constantly rediscovering themselves and are beginning to break up some of the old ground of the early film industry. By this, I believe, he means that the films of today are trying to achieve the greatness and superbness of the art qualities that the yesterday movies possessed. As works of art, films are trying to portray the exquisite characteristics of their tradition that

have given them an overwhelming acceptance as a bene-
ficial means of personal entertainment and enjoyment.
They are classics of our time . . .

No more. You will be spared the rest of the paper, which went on
for three pages in a special brand of Engfish that might be called
Pseudo-Objective. Apparently the writer borrowed some of Mr. Ebert's
words, but they didn't fit into his sentences.

> *Objectivity does not mean detachment,*
> *it means respect; that is, the ability not*
> *to distort and to falsify things, persons,*
> *and oneself.*
>
> ERICH FROMM

Good critical writing is not that hard to produce. If truth is your
concern, both in what you say and how you say it, you will find a
voice and begin writing like this college student did in a Shakespeare
class:

> Being Jewish myself, how objectively can I view Shylock? I
> can't honestly deny that when people refer to some as
> "Jewish" when they mean cheap, stingy, etc., I can't help
> take offense—even though I know the remark is not
> directed to me. I'm the first Jew some have known, or
> known well. They may say, "He really acted Jewish—" then
> catch themselves and apologize to me. They mean no harm,
> but it hurts for the moment, just the same. Yes, I identify
> with Shylock for many reasons. It's hard to be objective
> when you are part of a similar setting, although I'm sure
> the little anti-Semitism I've encountered is nothing com-
> pared to what Shylock must have had to bear with a
> patient shrug.
>   Shylock is definitely a Jew first. I know the type well.
> Jessica running away and marrying a *shikzo* (Yiddish for
> non-Jew, not meant to be too complimentary) really hurt
> Shylock. I've known people to literally go into mourning in
> similar situations. Better their son (daughter) should die
> in an automobile accident than marry that *shikzo*.
>   I cannot agree at all with that attitude. I have been
> having a running argument for probably at least six or
> seven years with the parents of one of my friends on the
> subject of intermarriage.

> But I feel I can empathize well with Shylock. This act,
> his daughter marrying Lorenzo, could easily have caused
> him to try to take his pound of flesh . . .

In that critical passage, a beginning writer uses a voice that belongs
to him. An editor might suggest cutting a few wasted words, but he
would value the passage because it helps a reader understand Shylock.

One fundamental of writing criticism is to consider how much the
reader needs to know of the thing being critized. Here's a critical
comment about a boy's response to a movie scene. It's one of those
passages in which the writer puts down two telling facts and lets the
reader infer what they are saying. The fundamental observed by the
writer is that he has presented the first fact—the sequence of shots in
the film—fully enough so the reader can figure out what the boy's
response signifies.

> There was Frank Sinatra kissing this frigid Creative Writ-
> ing teacher who really liked him but was too serious about
> being a writer to live. It was afternoon and they were in a
> summerhouse. The lights dimmed. He plucked one hairpin
> from her hair and tossed it away.
> All at the same time—
> Her hair dropped around her shoulders,
> her eyes had twice as much mascara,
> and the hairpin clattered to the studio floor.
> I laughed and said, "What a move!"
> The fifteen-year-old boy across the room didn't hear my
> laugh, but answered, "Yeah, he's really got it!"
> I looked at him—searching for his sarcasm.
> He wasn't looking at me. He hadn't moved his eyes from
> the TV.

The same fundamental applies to a criticism that comments on another critic's remarks. Both the writer's remarks and the work they
are based on must be given in enough detail to allow the reader to
judge the judgment of them he is being given. Note how the writer
of the following critical paper quoted the critic he was disagreeing
with.

> On the contents page of *Newsweek*, October 28, 1968,
> listed under the movie section, appeared the line: *"The
> Boston Strangler: a sickening joke."*

Paul D. Zimmerman begins his criticism assuring the reader "No one need be surprised at the emphasis on slaughter and sadism in *The Boston Strangler*." The fact that no one was surprised was because the emphasis was not on sex and violence. If the critic thinks that this movie was simply presented to show slaughter and sadism, he must have seen a movie like *Psycho* by Alfred Hitchcock, or any other that dwelt on blood and horror dripping from a butcher knife gash, draining and spotting on white porcelain. *The Strangler* didn't show any detailed death; it showed a woman beaten but not killed, and a woman viewed up to the moment of death, and nothing more. The sickening, perverted sex was not shown, but only hinted at—the viewer saw glimpses of what followed, but never saw a perverted sex act or a person dying. If the critic was correct, why wasn't a *Bonnie and Clyde* type murder shown? The critic states that the producer spares the viewer "eleven of these [thirteen killings] by shutting off the camera at the last minute." If this was a movie based on "slaughter and sadism" why didn't the producer take advantage of eleven more incidents of death? Obviously this wasn't his purpose.

The critic then states that "most of the film is one great laff-fest at the expense of the mentally deranged."

True, the audience laughed at the peeping Toms and the obscene phone call—they laughed until the last sick pervert was presented. This poor man made love to women's handbags and then washed his hands in a toilet bowl. Nobody laughed at this. The man cried when he saw that the police were only interested in arresting him and not sincerely helping him. Sure we laughed at the previous perverts, because the movie wanted to show that we laugh at them instead of help them. Then, at the last, it brought us face to face with our stupidity. The critic ends this section by saying, "What time isn't devoted to the freak parade is snatched up by phony television bulletins." Evidently the freaks made him laugh, including the tears of someone who wanted to be helped. If he laughed, as he believed the audience did, the freak parade was simply humor to him. He revealed what the movie wanted people to reveal —their fine sense of humor.

The critic then states that the main actor, Tony Curtis, does "an admirable job in the title role, his face clearly charting the inner battle" and showing "the sick self that wants out." The sick man is shown—the critic admits this. What more is expected of a movie? If the audience can see this and understand, the movie has achieved a great purpose. Maybe now people can see why a "nut" like DeSalvo isn't getting what he supposedly deserves—death. Do we kill the sick or help them? The movie says we shouldn't kill.

The critic says the technical points made by the psychiatrists are "voodoo, all to legitimize the film as something more than a thrill." Tony Curtis's acting legitimizes the film (the critic even says it is "admirable"). How can he compliment fine action that reveals a sickness that deserves attention and still say technical terms are needed to legitimize the film? The movie at the end even states its purpose, which the critic said is achieved by fine acting. The critic is saying that minor details overshadow major details. The movie is saying that minor insight allows major insight to be neglected.

The director employs "multiple-screen technique that allows us to see seven women lock their doors at once. But all this just dresses up what remains essentially a long sick joke, or, better, a sickening one." The critic fails to see that a multiple technique may provide the viewer with a multiple insight. For the critic this is just a part of a "sickening" joke. The critic sees slaughter and sadism where it is not, he sees humor in a common pitiful disease, he sees deep technique as being shallow, and he sees fine acting as fine, but not a major purpose. Does he want a dry documentary presentation? I doubt if this would even penetrate his shallow perception.

There's no doubt about opposition arising here—it's the opposition of the writer to the critic he differs with. And no doubt about the voice with which the writer speaks. He lets his words speak to each other: "The movie is saying that minor insight allows major insight to be neglected." And at .times he makes the critic's own words speak back. "The critic fails to see that a multiple technique may provide the viewer with a multiple insight."

The liveliness of this critical paper comes not from some unusual ability of the writer. Frequently his style does not sound professional, as when he refers to "the critic" instead of employing the critic's name. But he was angry at Mr. Zimmerman for what he considered an unperceptive response to a good film, and so he talked back honestly and passionately, and he made things in the professional critic's review and the film talk to each other.

Another fundamental of critical writing is to refrain from presenting the whole work being criticized, to refuse to write one of those outrageous exercises called *book reports* that put the reader off from rather than on to the work under review. Remember your seven-year-old sister answering your question, "How did you like the movie?"

> Well, you know, this man had a little boy who owned a rabbit and this rabbit was in a cage in the back yard and one day the postman came and opened the cage and forgot to close it and the bunny ran out. The next-door neighbor saw the bunny run away. The neighbor's name was Jones, and he had a little boy, too only this boy had freckles, and when the bunny got to the woods . . .

And you couldn't get your sister stopped and she got mad at you for interrupting and trying to find out why she thought it was a good movie. And she answered,

> Well, I don't know, it was though, and when the bunny got to the woods—

From that experience you can probably appreciate that critical writing can perform a service. You wanted to know what had proved exciting or memorable for your sister. You didn't want to know everything, or just anything. Valuable critical writing doesn't try to cover; it focuses.

The fundamental involved here is to keep before the reader your feelings and the facts of the work that gave rise to them. If the work did not stir you, you should not write of it. That is, not unless you expected it to and its failure to stir you was news to you and might be news to your reader. But if that is true, then you were stirred, and you did have feelings about the work.

> *What I wish to do is to plead for passionate criticism for the sake of the passionate itself. Just as passion reveals the*

artist, so does it reveal the critic . . . To
write passionately, the critic must invent,
or, to use a more accurate word, he must
create his criticism so that it reveals a
work of art, through the critic's feelings.

BARNETT NEWMAN, PAINTER

Here is a student in a Shakespeare class respecting her feelings and using them to deepen her understanding of a play. Do not presume she has forgotten the first fundamental of critical writing because she does not tell fully enough the parts of the plays crucial to her argument. She was writing for students who had already read and discussed the plays several times. But for your benefit, Richard II inherited a crown he was not fitted for, and in the play he shifted back and forth between wanting the power and glory and not wanting their responsibilities. In *Hamlet* the scene at issue is that in which the young prince tells off his mother in her bedchamber for marrying the man Hamlet knows killed his father. Here's the paper. Actually it was written as two entries in a journal, but they speak to each other.

1

Speaking of indecisive people brings to mind a conversation that roared between my mother and me the last time I was home. Because I was defending the Blacks, my mother questioned whether or not I would marry a Black.

Mary: Yes, if I loved him.

Mother: Do you mean to tell me that you would go against all that I've done for you and marry a nigger?

Mary: Yes.

Mother: After all I've done, moved to a *better* neighborhood, sent you to *good* schools, and you tell me this. What are they teaching you in that school? Don't you want to be with your own people?

Mary: Who are my own people? Dad's Polish. You're part French, Indian, and German. What does that make me—who are my people?

Mother (glaring): The WHITES!

Mary: Come on, Mom, what whites? Caucasoid, Mongoloid—are you including Orientals, or are they different? As far as I can see it, I have no people. How can you say you have people? You're not a pure anything.

Mother: And you're in college.

Mary: Yeah, trying to get educated. What about you?

Mother: What about the kids? They'll be outcasts. You're just being selfish, you're not thinking, you don't know what you're talking about, you haven't lived! I worked with niggers when I was young and I don't want to marry one.

Mary: Look, I haven't worked with Blacks, but I go to school with them. What's your beef, only their color?

Mother (hautily): Yes, their black color!

Mary: You can't stand them only because of their color. Well, I can't see the difference in color. I choose my friends from our similarities—black or white. Mother, they can't change their color! And if you think you can skirt the issue by moving to a different neighborhood and then sending me to a multi-racial school, you're only fooling yourself.

Mother: If that's the way you think I'll pull you out of that school!

Mary: Go ahead.

The conversation continued for quite a while and I couldn't get past my mother's color ban. Later my boy friend and I were discussing the above conversation and he told me I was a pansy.

. . .

Henry: Why didn't you either keep your big mouth shut or tell it to her straight?

Mary: What do you mean?

Henry: Why didn't you ask her, "What the hell makes you think you're so much better than anyone else?"

Mary: I don't know, maybe because I love her.

I felt like King Richard in this situation. He was a king, but stripped of his power to rule; I am a student, but stifled from becoming educated. I backed down; I did it to keep peace in the family. Did Richard back out of his power to keep peace in his kingdom?

2

Why was Queen Gertrude passive and indecisive? She saw her fault; she begged Hamlet to speak no more, "Thou turn'st mine eyes into my very soul, and there I see such black and grained spots as will not leave their tinct." She did nothing to amend the situation. Why? Possibly Gertrude had had an affair with Claudius [Hamlet's uncle, her brother-in-law], perhaps she didn't love her first husband as Hamlet thought she should. She didn't relieve Hamlet of his anxieties; she only thought of him as insane. Here I am like both Hamlet and Gertrude. I couldn't push my mother as far as Hamlet did, yet my mother thought of me as insane or brainwashed by the university. I tried to unveil her inmost part, but I failed, because she, like Gertrude, did nothing. Yet I can see why Gertrude keeps still.

I love my mother, as Gertrude does her son; but I also love my life away from her, as possibly Gertrude enjoyed her new married life. But why else? I felt I was fighting a losing battle, like Richard. I continued hitting my head against the wall. Gertrude was in a situation where she might lose any way she turned, her son if she upheld Claudius' scheme, her husband if she followed Hamlet's advice. I would lose too if I turned completely from my mother. I'd lose some of her love, her financial support, her domestic comforts. If I turn from my friends and passively follow my mother's bigoted ideas, I would forego my intellectual beliefs and my social friends. Both Gertrude and I love, but my love may mean an intellectual, rather than a physical death.

That paper helped everyone in a Shakespeare class including the professor to understand the indecisiveness of King Richard and the inability of Queen Gertrude to take action on the side of her new husband or on the side of her son once she knew this husband had killed her former husband. For centuries professional critics have been arguing these points in the two plays. This student shed light on them by examining her own feelings in circumstances as frustrating as those experienced in the play.

Another fundamental in criticism: You may bring in your own experience which you think parallels or contrasts with that in the work you are criticizing, but you are bound to the truth of both experiences. You cannot distort your experience to make it seem exactly like that in the work. And you cannot distort the work to make it seem like your experience. Making distinctions of this kind is difficult, but such difficulties are the kind worth taking on.

Now for some working techniques of writing critical papers. Remember term papers in high school? You went to the library over

Christmas vacation and stuffed long quotations into your paper like
bread into a turkey until you had reached the specified fifteen or
twenty pages. When quoting other writers, the professional critic uses
the smallest number of words necessary to make his point. Sometimes
just a phrase or a word he lifts out and puts in quotation marks. This
is not a difficult technique to master. Note how this student restrains
herself in quoting.

> I believe that Jessica's primary function in the play is to
> add to the evidence which Shakespeare presents to con-
> vince his reader of Shylock's almost completely malignant
> character. He creates the "sweet, gentle" daughter who says
> she is of "his blood" but not "his manners" (69:18). She
> can be pardoned for what she does because she cannot
> condone his vile actions—she must escape. But what about
> the robbery? Without it, Shylock would lose much of his
> diabolism, for when he screams "I would my daughter
> were dead at my foot and the jewels in her ear!" (88:83),
> the Jew can sink no lower.

How did this girl know which phrases and sentences to choose from
the play? No mystery. She chose to write about Jessica and her father
because the relationship interested her. Because she was caught up in
it, she wanted to read and reread all the lines that presented or touched
upon that relationship. When she sat down to write, she knew what
she was talking about, and her strong attitudes became the selectors
of the words and phrases she quoted from the play.

Another technique of the professional reviewer is to take notes and
to gather any kind of material that will help him reconstruct what he
is reviewing when later he sits alone writing. Here are two excerpts
from the work of a professional critic:

1

> But around me the audience laughed at the expected and
> unexpected right places. They laughed with McQueen and
> at him, richly appreciative of his panting, unheroic climb of
> the stairs to Miss Wood's apartment, small bouquet in hand,
> his pause before the door with finger extended to ring the
> bell, slow body movement forward, and missing the bell by
> four inches, partly from clumsiness and partly from lack of
> courage.

2

Pennsylvania Station sits heavily on its haunches along Seventh Avenue in Manhattan's West Thirties; the thirty Doric columns on the facade are dead weight. In the crowded circle of airline terminals at Idlewild, the Trans World Airlines Terminal crouches like a bird alighting. The one is huge and massive, the other small and light; both are superb buildings. They do more than house passengers; they know their place in the world and they speak it.

The writer of the first passage saw the film twice and took notes; to write the second passage he stood on the other side of Seventh Avenue and counted the columns across the street.

WRITING SEVENTEEN: Choose something you've read or seen that hit you so hard you wanted to talk to someone else about it— and write a critical paper about it.

One of the simplest ways of providing opposition in a piece of critical writing is to record your responses as a journey. You saw this thing or read this book. How did it hit you at first? Same reaction as it went along? At the end did you see something you missed earlier? Change your feelings? Give your reader a record of your emotional and intellectual journey. You may have been surprised there were no surprises for you. Report the news. Here is a criticism written in a student's journal, and it's a journey.

> Today in class we read and discussed a paper which said: "Lady Macbeth is both a natural and an unnatural being, and I cannot accept her as real." My immediate reaction to this statement was opposition. "How ridiculous! Everybody has two sides to their personality. Villains are not consistently evil; neither are heroes always good." The instantaneousness of my reaction is surprising considering a journal entry I had made while reading *Macbeth*.
>
> My reaction at that time was, "This play is a little bit unbelievable. More precisely, the characters are hard to accept as being real because of the drastic personality changes. In the opening scenes of the play, Macbeth is seemingly a good friend of Banquo's. He is a rather mild man, and honest. What a change to see him later become heartless, even to the extent of killing Banquo, his friend."

I saw in Lady Macbeth an equally drastic personality change, but this time from the opposite direction. "She first appears heartless, cold, and completely self-seeking. ('Make thick my blood,/ Stop up the access and passage to remorse . . .' (51: 44–45). But later she is full of that remorse she so disdained. Such a sudden reformation is hard to swallow."

In short, today I found myself strongly opposed to the very same ideas I held three weeks ago. How can this be? Is it due to a "drastic personality change" within me. I doubt it. To what then?

In thinking about this contradiction, I keep returning to one explanation. Real flesh and blood people have conflicting characteristics, true. But they *vacillate* between these. They are constantly moving from one mood or conscience to another and back again, just as the sun cavorts behind the clouds.

However, Macbeth and his Lady undergo a *terminal* overhaul. They change once and that is the end of it. So I return to my first reaction: Macbeth and Lady Macbeth do not seem completely real. Their characters are too fixed to allow me to see them as flesh and blood.

CONNIE BAILEY

> *Writing must be as immediate as life, or there are no juices, no chance to involve yourself or others in your vitality.*
>
> RAY BRADBURY

The journey form of writing worked for that writer. Try it if it seems to fit your thoughts and feelings about something you've seen or read. If not, go at writing critically in some other way. When a person writes critically out of interest and knowledge, the task does not place impossible requirements upon him. Once he has a clearly realized point to make, he can click it into position as he would turn to a television channel, remembering what evidence led him to the point, and then he can use the fine tuning controls to bring up clarity, definition, and degree of brightness of details.

chapter 16

creating
form

PATTERNS

A RECENT TEXTBOOK on writing says:

> Since learning to outline is one of the most important
> steps—perhaps the most important—in writing well, we
> want you to make at least four outlines.

The man who wrote that must never have talked to a real writer.
Eight out of ten writers say they never use outlines and the other two
say they use them only in late stages of writing, in the second or
third draft when they have all the materials captured and need only
to rearrange them strategically.

In the first place, outlines freeze most writers. Professionals are
looking for ways of breaking up the ice and poking around in new
waters. They want writing and ideas to flow.

> *I have often at the beginning of a book
> found myself very uncertain what I
> would do, and appalled at the difficulty
> of knowing what to put where, and how
> to develop my incidents. I never have
> that feeling now because I have always
> found that there is some one point or
> other in which I can see my way. I im-
> mediately set to work at that point and*

> *before I have done and settled it, I in-*
> *variably find that there is another point*
> *which I can also see and settle, etc.,*
> *etc. . . .*
>
> SAMUEL BUTLER

In the second place—Wait a minute. The second place. By their form, outlines always imply there will be a second place. Maybe there won't be. Or shouldn't be. I.a., I.b., II.a., II.b. "Express all your points in the outline in the same style, all complete sentences or all phrases." The Outliners are full of stuff like that. They get a writer so interested in the form of the outline that he quits thinking of the writing he is outlining.

Yet a reader needs some form or he becomes confused, gets lost, gives up. Making anything—a table, a fishing fly, a piece of writing—involves a struggle between form and content. Only the dull assembly-line maker can avoid that struggle by drawing up a perfect plan, or outline, before he begins creating. Punched out, every one the same, no surprises anywhere. A good planner allows for departures from plan, sidetrips down alleys full of discovery. The best trip you ever took in your life—could you have written an outline for it beforehand?

Yet the reader and writer need form, some direction, some over-riding mood, or they will sense only chaos. When the folks at home send George on a trip, they expect more than a bagful of chaos spilled on the kitchen table when he returns.

Many professionals say that the more experienced they become, the more certain they are of where they're going before they start. But they still keep their eyes and ears open as they go, hoping for fortunate accidents.

Beginning, you may find a direction, even a conclusion, flowering in your mind. Then all you do is find experiences to embody it and bring it alive. But if there is not an example or experience clinging to the idea or direction when you first get it, the chances are you will never bring it alive. Better start with something already alive and kicking. A butterfly caught and squirming in the net, wings flapping wildly. Not a lot of preserved specimens lined up in the glass case neatly and systematically labeled.

But the glass case is good. Something to enclose the things flapping around in your mind and experience. Place something else with the butterfly. Does it go with him? Or does it contrast in some significant way? Is it a leaf in shape—half of the butterfly? And then a bird. Look at him. How do his wings differ from the butterfly's and the leaf's? Let these pieces of experience knock around against each other in the case and in your mind.

> *It doesn't matter which leg of your table*
> *you make first, so long as the table has*
> *four legs and will stand up solidly when*
> *you have finished it.*
>
> EZRA POUND

If what you are thinking about doesn't fit into a case, you may simply jot down the elements in a list, informal, like the one you take to the supermarket.

Any piece of writing needs a point. What that means is hard to say but easier to sense. Everyone knows the meaning of the word when he listens to a person talk on endlessly through boredom into sleep, and someone says, "He talked on and on but to no point." What *point* is and why it is needed can be seen by reading most term papers written in high school and freshman college classes. They have subjects but no points. For example, Harry Smithers writes "about Switzerland." His paper is dead already. The facts he has read about Switzerland or the things he has seen in Switzerland do not make a paper simply because they concern one country. What about Switzerland? Do any of the facts he has collected do anything to each other? Contradict? Surprise Harry in some way when compared with facts he knows about other countries? If he thinks he will write about Switzerland because the library has a number of books on it, or because no one else has written about it recently in school, or because he once heard that watches are made in Switzerland, his paper is doomed. When he starts in on a good piece of writing he will have an itch or he will never scratch hard, with purpose and enjoyment.

Switzerland might be Harry's subject, but never his point. To cover Switzerland would be to write an endless number of volumes, describing its government, postal system, watchmaking industry, role in European and world wars, people's dress, food, social customs—all with that dreadful emptiness of a travel brochure or a bad children's encyclopedia. Take this statement by a writer in a political magazine:

> The Swiss make watches, speak many languages, act as
> peace arbitrators, never commit themselves to the cause
> of right in any war, and act as holding companies for all
> sorts of high-level financial wheeling and dealing, aiding

persons all over the world in avoiding taxes and financial responsibility.

Maybe this statement is not true. But it is full of assertions, of points that could be pursued with genuine curiosity. It was not made by the Chamber of Commerce trying to attract tourists, but by a man puzzled and inquiring who said what he truly believed. If you came upon this statement as the opening paragraph of an article, you would probably suspect that the writer was going to take you on a journey.

An editor of a university press once said that most Master's and Doctor's theses submitted to him for possible publication were unpublishable. No one would want to read them, he said. Some contained ideas and material that could be brought together with point if the author could bring himself to see why anyone might want to know what he had found in his research. When he came upon such a thesis, the editor said he returned it to the writer with the query: "So what?" If the writer could rewrite his thesis so that it answered that question, he had made what could be justly called a book.

To construct a good piece of writing you need to go somewhere in it. If you haven't taken a journey, no amount of outlining or structuring can make the writing live. Whatever the type of writing—article, essay, story, case-history, poem—it must contain surprises and questions. Else it will remain dead for you and the reader. They must be genuine surprises and questions. Many beginning writers are affected by the worst, most gimmicky writing. They spin a long description of a man they have known, disguising who he is and where they have known him, and then in the last sentence they say: "There he was, smoking his pipe in the big rocking chair in the living room—my father." Surprise is valuable, but it must make a point or give truth to experience. This trick ending about Father does neither. If the writer told of a man exhibiting behavior shockingly unlike his father's, then as indication of the shock the writer himself felt, he might properly hold back the identity of his father until the end. The first-rate writer produces surprise after surprise for his reader, in his expression, in the events he records, in the thoughts he comes to through comparisons. But he does not play practical jokes on his readers.

What shape will you give a piece of writing? Or better yet, what movement? It needs a pattern. Formlessness is too hard on human perception. You will lose your reader if he has no hint of what journey you are taking him on. He needs surprise and wondering,

but he cannot stand one question after another with no intimation
of answer or direction. As a writer you need form, a limit which will
force you to invention. Henry Ford did not say one day, "I think
I will invent something great" and then build one of the first American motor cars. He was thinking about a form—a wheeled, self-pro-
pelled vehicle; and a purpose—faster travel on roads than was provided
by horse-drawn carriages.

What is the right form of your piece of writing? There is no
manual in which you may look up the answer. Like all good questions, this one cannot be answered simply. If you remember that a
good piece of writing is composed partly through plan and partly
through accident which the writer keeps himself ever ready to exploit,
you may guess that a good form involves both discipline and freedom
for the writer and the reader. It gives the reader a feeling that he can
see the path at times, at other times that he has to work hard to
open it up. Occasionally it will lead him astray on exciting side trips.
Give the reader a small sense of direction for the journey, but don't
keep nudging him in the elbow—This way! No! Over there! Now back
again!

Professional writers are often mystified by the way they put together
writing. They know it has a form but they seldom know its origin.
They are afraid of outlining because they want things to happen
to them as they write. Nevertheless their final draft usually possesses
sure form, a movement that gives power to the events they have
written about. Some emphasize freedom to discover. Some emphasize
the need for plan. James Thurber said of Elliott Nugent, with whom
he wrote the play *The Male Animal*:

> He could plot the thing from back to front—what was going
> to happen here, what sort of situation would end the first-
> act curtain, and so forth. I can't work that way. Nugent
> would say, "Well, Thurber, we've got our problem, we've
> got all these people in the living room. Now what are we
> going to do with them?" I'd say that I didn't know and
> couldn't tell him until I'd sat down at the typewriter and
> found out. I don't believe the writer should know too much
> where he's going. If he does, he runs into old man blueprint
> —old man propaganda.

Because Thurber wrote this passage doesn't mean that he never paid
attention to the shape of his writing. He rewrote his stories dozens
of times until he got them moving right.

Probably the reason professionals are so unsure in discussing form is that good form always comes out of the materials of a particular piece of writing. As he gains experience, the writer comes unconsciously to a sense of form for his materials. Always he holds in mind a few simple, fundamental forms that will limit him wisely and give his reader a sense of certainty among all the surprises he encounters.

> *A plot is a thousand times more unsettling than an argument, which may be answered. It is not a pattern imposed; it is inward emotion acted out. It is arbitrary, indeed, but not artificial. It is possibly so odd that it might be called a vision, but it is organic to its material: it is a working vision, then.*
>
> EUDORA WELTY

Here are a few such fundamental forms or patterns of movement. They may be useful if you do not let them bind you. Allow one to dominate your complete piece of writing and at the same time introduce several of the others to shape small pieces of the same work if you wish.

(a) *Simple Comparison.* X is different from B. You may show how X's arms differ from B's, then the legs of both, the shoes, etc. Or you may describe X completely and then B completely. As you make your observations and as you write, keep thinking: So what?

(b) *Before and After.* It was *this* way once. Now it is *that* way. You may emphasize the difference. You may ask why the difference. You may tell how the difference came about.

(c) *The Journey.* I (he, or it) started here and went through this experience or that country and came out there. Chronologically. First this happened, then that.

You may present the whole matter as story, or occasionally interrupt to explain significance. Show. Give the story. Tell. Explain why or discuss the significance of an act. But don't interrupt a story to tell or comment unless you do so frequently and regularly.

The Journey pattern is useful in writing about ideas (as well as events) which are apt to become confusing to the reader unless controlled. If it is your idea, you may show where it came from, how you took it on, and what you did with it over the years or days. If it means a good deal to you, the tale of your journey with it should be exciting, for the truth is that the journey was full of surprises—traps, bogs, a mountain with a view.

(d) *David and Goliath.* David has only a slingshot and courage against a gigantic warrior armed with spear and shield and wearing a coat weighing as five thousand shekels of brass. Any little or deprived or disadvantaged person against great forces. Who will win?

(e) *Will It Work?* An idea, a plan, an invention new and untried, or old but now standing against the established order—a variation of the David and Goliath story. The odds are against it because it is not now the accepted thing. Will it win through?

In deciding upon a form, a writer constantly juggles

1. the needs of his materials (they may cry out for a certain treatment),
2. the weight of his purpose,
3. the limitations and potentialities of his medium (is it a letter, an article in a picture magazine, a paper to be read aloud or silently in class?),
4. the knowledge and needs of his audience.

The professional knows he is writing to other human beings, who can be bored, who are often insulted by gimmicks, who have normal human needs for rising excitement, for hoping that every trip they take will pay off.

THE HOOK

A good device to remember is the fishhook. It rises slowly and then hooks back, so it will dig in and stick. It is barbed. Its curve points back to its beginning, to remind itself and the reader where it came from.

Many professionals employ the Hook in their writing: They begin with a word, action, or symbol and at the end of their article or story come back to it. All that has intervened between the first and second mention makes its second appearance more exciting or significant than its first. For example, in Chapter 6, on Fabulous Realities, the student who writes about meeting Fred again after three years' separation speaks of being *twenty-one* in his second sentence. Then at the end of his recollection, he comes back again to that word after he has shown how things have changed in his relationship with Fred.

It was good to be outside again, walking in a different direction from my friend, being *twenty-one*.

The writer of the next paper in that chapter also employs the Hook. She begins by saying, *"Privacy* up here means taking a shower . . . ." and ends with the words *"by myself."*

In the chapter following that, the writer of the case-history "Through the Gates" hooks his story by beginning with the narrator speaking of walking past the experienced workers to his first day on the job ("everybody was watching") and feeling uncomfortable because no one smiled. At the end of the story the narrator walks out past the newly arriving morning workers, and he doesn't smile at them. All the events between those two moments explain the lack of smiles at the beginning and ending.

The Hook is a natural way of forcing the reader's attention on what you want to emphasize. The repetition of a word or act at the end of a developed piece of writing will probably please rather than bore your reader; for what you say is yours in some way and must be unfamiliar to him. The hook allows him to experience something that is familiar now to him.

The Hook is only one of the strategies available to you as a writer. Often you will use it without planning to. Sometimes you can improve a paper by consciously introducing the Hook into your second or third draft to drive your major point home. But it is only a possible strategy, not an inflexible rule. It can become a cheap trick that does not arise out of the materials or needs of the writing. At times a story or article must provide a setting or present a preliminary action before it gets into the major act or idea. Then a Hook would snag the lines of development, and should not be used.

So there are no sure-fire formulas for shaping a piece of writing. But the strong writer keeps the pressure of form upon himself. He keeps asking:

Where is this going?

Does it arrive somewhere?

Does it add up?

Is something happening between things here?

Have I made clear, directly or indirectly, why I wanted to write this?

What did I want to say? Did I get it said?

WRITING EIGHTEEN: Choose one of your free writings you like and shape it more powerfully. You may have to expand or contract it radically. Does it already follow one of the patterns discussed in this chapter? Can you improve it with a Hook?

THE ALTERNATING CURRENT

Bad preachers do not use the Alternating Current. They drone on in an unrelieved elevated vocabulary. Bad editorial writers do the same. They have no sense of the lightness that can be achieved in writing that discusses a solemn subject in sober setting.

We hold these truths to be self-evident . . .

This statement from the Declaration of Independence would be spoken by few persons in their kitchens, but

all men are created equal

might well be there. Speaking of King George III, the writers of the Declaration said:

He has plundered our seas, ravaged our coasts

in language again not of the kitchen, but the rest of the sentence might have been said there:

burnt our towns, and destroyed the lives of our people.

Note the alternation of language in Robert Lipsyte's baseball article:

METS BEAT GIANTS 8-6, ON SWOBODA'S HOMER IN 9TH

Ron Swoboda, who won it in the ninth inning with a three-run pinch-hit home run, said: "It was a story-book game. Holy Cow!" And it was just that.

Most of the crowd of 41,038 at Shea Stadium sat stunned yesterday long after the Mets had beaten the Giants, 8-6. Swoboda's drive cleared the leftfield fence and the 22-year-old outfielder jogged around the bases in a mood he later described as "elation . . . the epitome . . . my greatest thrill!"

More than 24,000 in the crowd had bought their tickets just before gametime because the great Juan Marichal was starting for the Giants. For almost six innings they got what they paid for—perfection from Marichal and something less than perfection from the Mets.

The 27-year-old Dominican righthander, out of action recently because of a sore finger, had registered his 17th victory Tuesday night, by the official scorer's decision, after retiring the last four Mets. Yesterday, kicking high on a dusty mound, he retired the first 17 Mets.

3 OUTS ON 6 PITCHES

In the second inning, with six pitches, he put out the side so quickly that he had to wave his sleepy outfielders back to the dugout. In the third, facing Dennis Ribant, the busy little Met starter, he was worked for his first full count before Ribant lined out to Willie Mays, a well-hit ball that Mays had to hustle to catch and gave a few plaintive voices reason to holler, "Let's go Mets."

In the sixth, Ribant bounced one over Marichal's head for a single, and the crowd prepared to console itself with a brilliant one-hitter instead of a perfect game.

The Giants, meanwhile, were doing what was expected of a team that started the sunny afternoon game leading the National League and fresh from having beaten the Mets three times in a row. They scored a run in the fourth on Willie McCovey's 21st homer of the year, a run in the fifth on Marichal's double and Jim Davenport's single and a run in the sixth on Jim Hart's 24th homer.

GIANTS GAIN 5-0 LEAD

In the seventh, San Francisco made the score 5-0. Tito Fuentes drove one of Ribant's pitches into the leftfield corner. Larry Elliot dropped it in foul territory and examined it, apparently thinking the ball was foul, while Fuentes went to third, credited with a double. Ossie Virgil, who had replaced Davenport at third base, then singled and McCovey walked.

With the bases loaded, Darrell Sutherland replaced Ribant, and Mays singled home two runs.

In the last of the seventh, the Mets began to move at last. They needed three singles and a throwing error by Marichal to get one run. The people who had come to see at least a shutout went home.

Tom Haller hit a homer for the Giants in the eighth, making the score 6-1, but it was a wasted gesture. In the bottom of the eighth, the Mets charged.

Jerry Grote reached second on a two-base throwing error by Virgil, and John Stephenson, a 25-year-old catcher pinch-hitting for Dallas Green, the third Met pitcher, blasted his first homer of the season. Singles by Chuck Hiller, Al Luplow and Larry Elliot made the score 6-4.

In disbelief, the crowd froze.

HAMILTON IS VICTOR

Jack Hamilton, the winning pitcher, put out the Giants in the ninth. Then Marichal strolled back to the mound. He demanded that it be dampened because he was kicking dust into his own face. A little man with a green sprinkling can scurried out and dampened the mound.

Satisfied, baseball's best righthander pitched two balls and a strike to Ken Boyer. Boyer hit the fourth pitch over the fence for his 11th homer of the season, and Marichal was pulled out for some showering of his own.

"Let's go Mets." There was no plaintiveness now, no whine. There was hope.

Ed Bressoud, who had been playing an erratic shortstop for the injured Roy McMillan, singled to left. Ron Hunt, pinchhitting for Grote, bunted, forcing Bressoud at second. Stephenson, hero of the eighth inning, hit a wrong-field single to right. There was one out, two men on base, and the score was 6-5.

The roar was swelling now as Bill Henry, a left-hander, replaced Lindy McDaniel, a right-hander. The next scheduled batter, Chuck Hiller, was called back for a right-handed hitting replacement and Manager Wes Westrum said to Swoboda, "Get a bat."

Swoboda later admitted he was excited because "that's it, when everybody's relying on you." He kept telling himself to "stay loose" and he forgot that the last time Marichal had started against the Mets, on May 20, Swoboda had won the game with a tenth-inning homer against the same Bill Henry.

The first pitch was high; it would have been a ball if Swoboda, overanxious, hadn't swung and missed. The second was a ball, low and inside. The third, waist-high and fast, was thrown with the stuff that dreams are made on.

Kitchen	*Elevated*
they got what they paid for	perfection from Marichal
hustle to catch	plaintive voices
The people who had come to see at least a shutout went home	a wasted gesture
Marichal was pulled out	In disbelief
he was kicking dust into his own face	an erratic shortstop
There was one out, two men on base and the score was 6–5	The roar was swelling now

Elevated language is usually more precise than kitchen language and comes to us trailing associations different from those carried by kitchen language. In many ways it is superior as a vehicle of expression, but no one wants to hear it steadily throughout a lecture or a column. The ordinary speech of the common man is our anchor, and no good writer forgets it.

The Alternating Current is not difficult to turn on in your writing. The secret lies in the genuineness of its juice, the speech you already have in your unconscious memory. If you remember your native dialect—the language you learned at Mother's knee—and alternate that with the language of writing you have picked up through reading and listening to teachers in classrooms, you will find the current naturally coursing through your prose. Finding it is again a matter of honesty. What is your voice? Do you hear how you speak when you are not thinking of your language? Listen to the country, the Kitchen, the ball game, the streetcorner talk in your life. Introduce it sparingly into your writing. At the same time you will find yourself varying the length of your sentences, and that is another form of Alternating. You often talk in shorter sentences than those written in books.

The Alternating Current flows in this quick piece of writing: rich, full descriptions and then short iron, mannish sentences.

> **I used to hunt with Gramp. He didn't hunt like my father. We would walk along the cramped, hollowed-out cowpath. The bushes and weeds would push out at us from both sides. I always walked behind. It led along the murk-filled brown-greenness of the channel that connects his two lakes. I would wait for something to break. He taught me never to kill anything unless I was going to eat it. He helped my brother shoot a pigeon once. He would have eaten it if it had not smelled so much.**

When the hunting was poor, we would go down by the lake and shoot beer bottles that some ass had left behind. There were always some there. Gramp would sit on a rotten stump and remember. He used to shoot pickerel as they pulled their heavy egg-filled bodies up the narrow channel. He said that they would spawn near the roots of the silver-gray pussy-willow trees. They're gone now; so are the pickerel. He would sit and laugh. And tell how the warden had chased him for two miles up to his slate-gray house. He had hid in the barn until he had left and then fried the warm fresh pickerel on the old black stove that was the heart of the house on a cold misty morning. We all learned something from him although he never taught us anything. I never knew it until he left. Tomorrow is never the same.

TOM CRONK

This is the way writers keep their writing alive. Tom Cronk may not have known that he was following an age-old tradition, but he was. Preachers use this method, poets, men who tell stories around pot-bellied stoves.

Whenever you write, consider using the juice provided by the Alternating Current. In the next chapter in what is called an Idea Paper, it is often needed to provide small shocks.

The things, in fact, which a boy is set to learn at school, and on which his success depends, are things which do not require the exercise either of the highest or the most useful facilities of the mind.

WILLIAM HAZLITT

chapter 17
out
of your
mind

AMERICAN CHILDREN take part in the great, long, dishonorable tradition of writing Engfish themes. It is part of the system, and the teacher is as much a victim of it as the student. He went to school once himself. There he was taught to write Engfish. When he became a teacher, his job was obviously to make the students do what he had done. He upheld the tradition.

No one enjoys Engfish papers. No one learns from them. And only teachers read them. This is an empty, mind-rotting tradition to follow. But it is followed.

Outside class, the student often writes in another tradition, which is not empty. He speaks his mind in the letters-to-the-editor column of the school or university newspaper. There he frequently appears at his best—humorous and persuasive, employing evidence that gets to his readers because it is detailed and local. The best of these letters know their audience. The worst don't. They are dull and pointless or narrow and blind.

It is in the best tradition of letters to the editor that the student should write when he is dealing with ideas in the classroom. He should write out of his mind, not out of other persons' minds he has encountered in books or lectures.

Often in the classroom a student is asked to make a case for something. The evidence cannot always come from his own experience. Some must be taken from books or lectures by other persons. But what the student does with those ideas—how he agrees or disagrees with them or shows they agree or disagree with each other—usually should represent *his* informed opinions, based on the best evidence available to him, much as it does when he writes a letter to the editor.

One of the principal reasons beginning writers can quickly shake off Engfish and write lively and telling free writings is that to do so they slip into the tradition of relating a story, which is the basic form of communicating for all human beings: They tell little stories to each other, in the kitchen, on the street, in the dormitory.

That is the structure of most good writing of ideas. The writer tells a little story and then states a point. He maintains his pattern—little story, point, little story, point . . . Beginning writers can do this. Here is a college girl writing ideas.

As I write . . . I am fighting the urge to either jump from my third story window, light a match to this place, or strangle one of my fellow coeds. All are normal responses, I believe, to the frustrations of having been kept awake— despite a need to study early tomorrow morning—for the past hour by the screams, slamming doors, uproarious laughter, and "running down to the bathroom" parties of those girls with whom I am forced to live in close contact.

Considering the circumstances, of course, I feel that these girls are rude, inconsiderate, bitchy bores, but as the saying goes, I'll defend to the death their right to be rude, etc. Despite my resentment I don't believe that legally my right to sleep or study should carry more weight than their right to scream at 1 A.M. Therefore, I would be the last to propose that more rigid rules concerning dorm conduct be instigated.

What I do propose however is that immediate attention be given to changing the rules so that one may choose his own living conditions. Thus, if one enjoys the "beautiful comaraderie" of dorm life he may choose it, and if one feels the need for more privacy he may live in a cave if he so desires.

By the same token, if one has not acquired the habit of eating breakfast, or if one doesn't have the appetite for well-done pork chops on a particular Tuesday from 5–6:30

P.M., there is no sufficient reason he should have to remold
his personality. For although no one will force him to eat,
there is the implanted knowledge that the $20 per week
has already been paid and he had learned from Mom and
Dad that one doesn't order a big meal at a restaurant and
not eat at all. So, a decision—eat at the Union and feel
guilt, or ignore the pork chops and fill up on mashed
potatoes.

The university marches on—seemingly more concerned
with subverting individual freedom of choice in both
flagrant and subtle ways, than with fulfilling their only
legitimate function—that of supplying an education. It is
my hope that more students will wake up and reject their
involuntary second class status, for therein lies the means
to democratically restructuring the most elite university
system.

Those lines made up a letter to the editor written by a university
student. She had no difficulty writing ideas wtih a light touch. She held
onto her natural ability to make words speak to words ("my right to
sleep . . . their right to scream") and to play with clichés ("I'll defend
to the death their right to be rude . . ."). The letter is full of oppositions that produce surprises. How could she write so brightly when she
was dealing with ideas—those paralyzers of so many beginners'
sentences? She was able to find a voice of her own because she felt
right. She was writing within a student tradition of lively letters to the
editor. Anyone who has spent a few months on a college campus knows
the letters-to-the-editor column in the student newspaper carries the
most laughs and the most pointed writing.

Note the pattern of this girl's letter. *Little story*: She suffers an
hour of screams and laughter that kept her awake. *Point*: I don't want
more rigid dorm rules, but freedom to live where I desire. *Example*:
One eats what he doesn't feel like eating because it has been paid for,
or he buys a meal out and feels guilty. *Point*: The university's function
should be to supply an education, not rule a student's private life.

You may think the letter needs to go on to say how the university
might be restructured to do this. That would help, but perhaps the
writer didn't have the space. It is not a perfect letter, but it connects
ideas to experience. It keeps the reader awake. It is not written in
Engfish.

Here is a column from a student newspaper. Note how its ideas are
presented through three little stories—an account of what a novelist

and poet said and did on a campus visit and of a bus trip the columnist once took. Points, or ideas, are interspersed along the way.

REVIEWPOINT

Reynolds Price was on campus two weeks ago giving a reading from his work, discussing *Calliope* [the student literary magazine], and talking with faculty and students. He came from North Carolina by airplane, probably a jet; he wore a well-fitting dark suit and a respectable snappy tie. He read with a steady, drawling voice, talked smoothly, with wit, and criticized curtly, professionally, without compromise.

Back in mid-February poet Robert Sward came to Western to record and read his poems in 2303 Sangren Hall. He went on stage in wrinkled khakis; his long beard looked like he had slept on it. In fact, he had just then wakened from a nap which he needed because he had driven his Volkswagen all night to get here. He shouted his poetry with springs in his knees, trying to catch his breath, gulping water, and gasping air.

Sward read his poetry like he was spitting hot coals. We took it that way, our hearts heating, ready to explode. We walked out of Sward's performance with new ambitions to make poems about pillars on Sangren Hall, the WALK/DON'T WALK lights, pencils, cars, and classroom doors. In the glow of our enthusiasm the world looked like it had been waiting for our own powerful sensitivities to interpret it. We saw a man who had made it, who was good enough to be in the Big Leagues with the likes of Ginsberg; we saw he wasn't so different from us and we knew we might be able to stretch ourselves up to reach that.

Price got to us in a very different way. We went out of the *Calliope* discussion with arrows sticking in our sides. He really let us know where the writing was weak. We knew we'd have to search and sweat to get good. Price said when he was in college he could never judge his writing from his friends' and professors' comments; it took Eudora Welty, a visiting author, to make him sure he was any good. He told us he thought his function here was to be a disinterested outsider bringing that hard, impartial light on student writing.

Sward showed us that we, everydamnbody, have powerful feelings.

Price showed us that to reach professional caliber we must get out of our skins, clarify, rework, step back.

I was riding the Bronco Transit last week, leaning forward in my seat because I was late, when suddenly the driver pulled in at the Roost for a hot dog. Christ, were we mad. We all muttered and swore, resolving to do something about it. When the busdriver got back on he apologized and explained he'd been driving for five hours straight and hadn't had any supper. We got out of our skins when we saw Bronco Transit drivers were people.

A good case of stepping back was Kathy Connellan's chairmanship of the Student Association Housing Committee last year. She came to that job full of a thousand ideas and a million springs of energy, but she says it wasn't until the faculty advisor put her in harness and guided her to work through the proper channels that she was able to get much done.

Robert Koehler's essay "Look Your Best—We're Coed" in the last *Review* was powerful because Koehler was angry and it was smooth because he cut and tightened and rewrote.

It looks like outsiders don't tell us anything we don't already know. We just don't know it well enough.

                                                                B.G.

The ideas for that column came up to the surface after swimming through a lot of experience. Students in school often write badly of ideas because they have just met the ideas in a book and haven't got to know them. Spend a few hours with them, come back to see them next Saturday, before you write.

> *. . . I always try to write on the principle of the iceberg. There is seven-eighths of it underwater for every part that shows. Anything you know, you can eliminate and it only strengthens your iceberg. It is the part that doesn't show. If a writer omits something because he does not know it then there is a hole in the story.*
>
> ERNEST HEMINGWAY

The girl who wrote the prize-winning Engfish essay quoted in Chapter 14 on why she wanted to be a teacher may have spoken the truth, but it was truth not new. The reader expected her to say she wanted to teach because she likes to work with kids and thought she could help them. No news there. If she had nothing surprising or valuable to say, then she was under obligation to save it by fresh and exciting expression. But she clumped along: "I want to teach because I like people, and I like to work with people." Prove you like people, the reader is apt to say. Prove you can help young people help themselves. Sounds as if you never knew a kid well. If you had, you probably would have shown how one or two of them got to you in some special way, or showed they could help themselves.

That essay writer chose the topic because it was required by the contest. She had no sense of herself and her audience as she wrote. Probably was thinking of the judges of the contest all the time. Probably won the prize because of all the papers submitted hers was the least awful.

A writer of ideas who wants to convince others habitually tries to *anticipate the objections of an opponent.* He recognizes this fundamental as an obligation to inspect even his most casual or minor assertion. Some teachers have not learned by teaching, yet the prize-winning essayist wrote: "One learns by teaching . . ." The thoughtful person looks for oppositions constantly. Suppose he picks up the campus newspaper and reads comments by two members of the Students for a Democratic Society. One says that

. . . because the average American only reads about one book
a year and because the news media are managed, people are
unable to acquire intelligent information about the system.

and the other urges people to read the current issue of *Look* magazine "if they wish to understand the SDS and the current student movements," then something is wrong somewhere. One SDS member is saying the mass media are "managed," implying they do not print truths he believes in, and the other is recommending a mass medium as a truthful source of information about SDS.

The idea paper presented below originally appeared as a column in the campus newspaper at Western Michigan University. It was written by Tom Randolph, an All-American in track. In it he moves from idea to example and back. He anticipates the objections of a possible opponent. Unlike the essay on wanting to become a teacher, his provides some of the experience that establishes his right to make his assertions. He has a sense of his audience. He is a young black man addressing white readers. No doubt of that. He takes the reader slowly and simply on a black journey and does not deliver the hard blow to the reader until the end of the column when he has prepared him to accept it.

NATURAL ATHLETES, NATURAL RHYTHM

Many people believe that black people are born with some sort of "natural" rhythm which automatically makes them good dancers and superb athletes. The evidence, they argue is everywhere. Aren't most black people able to dance with those tricky, provocative movements which are so difficult to imitate? Don't most black athletes possess unusually fine coordination which allows them to excel at sports? The answer to both questions is yes . . . and no.

The stereotype of "natural" rhythm is a widespread one. But it is simply not true. There is no such thing as an in-born trait possessed by black people which allows them to become better dancers or better athletes than anyone else. It is probably true that on the average, black people dance better than whites. The reason, however, is entirely environmental. From early age, music and dance play an important role in the life of black people. Black churches place a strong emphasis on music and singing. It is not too unusual to find black children not yet old enough to enter grade school, but able to dance all the latest dance steps.

Black teenagers in America are the pacesetters for the new dances which evolve among the young people of this country. By the time white teenagers pick up the current dance, it changes quickly to something new. Just when white folks had the Twist mastered, black folks dropped it and went on to the Mashed Potatoes. After that came, in order: Hully-Gully, Boogaloo, Slop, Monkey, Jerk, Horse, Dog, Funky Broadway, Four Corners, and the Popcorn.

There are hundreds of examples of the supposed supremacy of black athletes. The finger is pointed at Jesse Owens, Willie Mays, Joe Louis, Jim Brown, and Wilt Chamberlain as some of these. Figures are quoted which show that black athletes are overly represented in college and professional sports. These figures are true. For example, Western has only one black student for each 33 white students. Yet Western's basketball, football, and track teams have a much higher percentage of black athletes than these numbers would indicate. The reason for this is the same as for the dancing. To the extent that black people excel in sports it is due to environmental influences.

The environmental effect on black athletes is clearly shown when one looks at the small number of black athletes that are proficient at golf, tennis, bowling, swimming, and archery. The reasons are money and opportunity. If a black person has access to, and money for a particular sport, he can and will become proficient at it. Black athletes excel mostly in track, basketball, football, baseball, and boxing. This is due to having the opportunity to participate in these sports.

In Harlem where I grew up, there was no opportunity to play golf, tennis or archery. These facilities don't exist in the ghetto. There was one swimming pool and one bowling alley in Harlem during the time I grew up there. I never could afford to go bowling so I never learned. During the hot months the swimming pool, which was the size of a football field, was so crowded that you were lucky to find a spot in the water to stand. Swimming was impossible.

On the other hand, the opportunities for the other sports were unlimited and inexpensive. Every game involved running. Football and basketball required only the ball and a place to play. Baseball was played with a tennis ball and a broom with the sweeping portion cut off. This is known as stickball. I became good at all of these sports because they were available to me, not because I was born with some inborn superiority for athletics.

As a matter of fact, it is a racist statement to insist that black people are possessed with "natural" rhythms or athletic capacities. It is a short step from black people being closer to animals or sub-human. It is a short leap from black people being good dancers to their being too lazy to work, and therefore spending all of their time dancing.

Another form of communicating ideas that has not gone out of style is the political speech, although it is having its troubles. In recent years long, empty orations at national party conventions have benumbed television watchers, and both parties are concerned. College students and citizens who are not politicians full time often need to speak their beliefs or proposals before groups. Sometimes they need to write the speeches out, and then often they slide into Engfish. It's the I've-got-to-be-impressive hangup again.

When Malcolm X first began speaking publicly after he had given himself a college education by reading in prison, he occasionally spoke Engfish out of insecurity. But as he gained confidence in his own powers, he called up his natural voices and got the Alternating Current flowing, using at times the vocabulary of his new book learning. He was one of those who helped black persons lift their heads; that took powerful speaking, for the heads had been bowed for centuries. Here is an excerpt from a speech he gave to thirty-seven teenagers from McComb, Mississippi, on December 31, 1964. It is colloquial in style and was probably spoken off the cuff, not written ahead of time; but it is still a model for *writing* ideas. More and more in the 1970's published writing in America is going to sound like talk.

One of the first things I think young people, especially now-adays, should learn is how to see for yourself and listen for yourself and think for yourself. Then you can come to an intelligent decision for yourself. If you form the habit of going by what you hear others say about someone, or going by what others think about someone, instead of searching that thing out for yourself and seeing for yourself, you will be walking west when you think you're going east . . . . This is one of the things that our people are beginning to learn today—that it is very important to think out a situation for yourself. If you don't do it, you'll always be maneuvered into a situation where you are never fighting actual enemies, where you will find yourself fighting your own self.

I think our people in this country are the best examples of that. Many of us want to be nonviolent and we talk very loudly, you know, about being nonviolent. Here in Harlem, where there are probably more black people concentrated than any place in the world, some talk that nonviolent talk too. But we find they aren't nonviolent with each other. You can go out to Harlem Hospital, where there are more black patients than any hospital in the world, and seem them going in there all cut up and shot up and busted up where they got violent with each other.

My experience has been that in many instances where you find Negroes talking about nonviolence they are not nonviolent with each other, and they're not loving with each other, or forgiving with each other. Usually when they say they're nonviolent, they mean they're nonviolent with somebody else. I think you understand what I mean. They are nonviolent with the enemy. A person can come to your home, and if he's white and wants to heap some kind of brutality on you, you're nonviolent; or he can come to take your father and put a rope around his neck, and you're nonviolent. But if another Negro just stomps his foot, you'll rumble with him in a minute. Which shows you that there's an inconsistency there.

I myself would go for nonviolence if it was consistent, if everybody was going to be nonviolent all the time. I'd say, okay, let's get with it, we'll all be nonviolent. But I don't go along with any kind of nonviolence unless everybody's going to be nonviolent. If they make the Ku Klux Klan nonviolent, I'll be nonviolent. If they make the White Citizens Council nonviolent, I'll be nonviolent. But as long as you've got somebody else not being nonviolent, I don't want anybody coming to me talking any nonviolent talk. I don't think it is fair to tell our people to be nonviolent unless someone is out there making the Klan and the Citizens Council and these other groups also be nonviolent.

Now, I'm not criticizing those here who are nonviolent. I think everybody should do it the way they feel best, and I congratulate anybody who can be nonviolent in the face of all that kind of action in that part of the world. I don't think that in 1965 you will find the upcoming generation of our people, especially those who have been doing some thinking, who will go along with any form of nonviolence unless nonviolence is going to be practiced all the way around.

If the leaders of the nonviolent movement can go into the white community and teach nonviolence, good. I'd go along with that. But as long as I see them teaching nonviolence only in the black community, we can't go along with that. We believe in equality, and equality means that you have to put the same thing over here that you put over there. And if black people alone are going to be the ones who are nonviolent, then it's not fair. We throw ourselves off guard. In fact we disarm ourselves and make ourselves defenseless . . . .

Malcolm X was in the habit of examining the accepted beliefs of everyone. That is a habit much like anticipating an opponent. Malcolm listened to people say righteously they were nonviolent and he went through that comment to his truth about it. He anticipated that listeners would say, "You are preaching violence," and he answered, "Now I'm not criticizing those here who are nonviolent. I think everybody should do it the way they feel is best . . ."

And he employs the Alternating Current, using elevated words like *nonviolence, inconsistency, situation, generation,* and *maneuvered* along with kitchen language: "But if another Negro just stomps his foot, you'll rumble with him in a minute." In the whole speech, kitchen language dominates.

As the chapter on Creating Form suggested, a sense of form may be helpful to you in writing. But there is nothing sacred about forms. Maybe you should tell a story in order to get across an idea, or tell a story and then tack a few essay paragraphs on it in which you reflect upon the experience because your reader may not get all the subtleties without help from you. The writing situation should partly determine your form. Here is a story in which the writer gives his thoughts about what is happening to him as well as describes the happenings.

FREEDOM FIGHTER

Remember how it was, those first couple days? Cars buried up to the aerial, drunks careering down the middle of West Michigan Avenue, the seal on the Mall with just its black little tail sticking out of the snow, Kalamazoo at Your Service flashing over WKZO (Please help, can someone get through with a snowmobile to Vicksburg?) . . . Kalamazoo was unreal. Traffic was going at one one-hundredth normal but I think the whole town had poured out into the streets, they were *walking,* as if this were some European city. If a car did venture out onto one of the main streets, by God it had to wait. The side streets were totally buried, fit for toboggans and skiers. For the last weekend in January, anyway, the pedestrian was king.

I know I had a heady, magnificent feeling of power, like I could kick a stalled truck, and be sure it wouldn't turn on me. Probably a lot of people felt this exhilaration, this liberation, classes called, nothing can happen! This may have been responsible, in part, for what did happen.

Holly and I were walking back from Eddie's, up Cedar Street approaching the stately backside of the East Campus, when we heard the sounds of people shouting, and the hopeless whirring of a tire on packed down snow. A Mustang was trying to make its way over unplowed Davis Street. Several people had got out to push, and when we reached the Davis Street corner the car was slowly moving. The occupants of the car, all Negroes, were yelling back at two white guys who were walking ahead of us. I don't know who started it. At first I thought it was a joke, It must be, on a night like this. But the shouts sounded bitter, stupid, and racial—nigger, black, white bastards! Suddenly the car stopped, the door swung open. Somebody jumped out. One of the whites was pinned in the snow. "What did you say?"

I stood there and watched as the whole car emptied. My mind was spinning. I couldn't believe it. I might be wrong, but I think there were eight people in it. The girls huddled by the car, looking terrified, and yelled "Stop!" I just stood there and watched. I saw one of the white guys get up and run like hell down Davis, leaving his friend alone. I probably would have stood there all night, watching a blur of snow and faces, seeing nothing, but Holly said "Koehler! What're you waiting for?"

I walked uncertainly toward the fighting. I don't really remember what happened. This white guy was being beaten up by two Negroes. There were only two malicious ones. The rest were trying to break it up. I don't know a thing about fighting, I don't think I've been in a fight since I was ten. I put my arms around a pair of brawny shoulders and tried to pull someone off. His face was streaked with blood. "He chipped my tooth, dammit, let me go!" Then someone hit me in the side of the face and I was lying on the ground, and my face hurts again, just a little, when I think about it. Someone tried to kick me in the groin but I moved and I felt a shoe graze lightly across my thigh. I got up and wanted to run but the fight was still going on. The white was struggling in the snow, someone was trying to choke him, and I think tears of pain were forming in his eyes. His face was bleeding. I wanted to shout "Hey! Let's all love each other!" I saw someone wind up and swing and hit me again, and I saw his face, with hatred directed solely at me. I stood at the outside of the group, watching, dazed. Others started running up to help.

Suddenly it was all over. The white got away and
scurried up the hill, toward U High. Someone asked me if
I was okay. I remembered that my hat had fallen off. One
of the Negroes picked it up and was holding it. I walked
up to him and said "That's mine." He turned and looked
at me and handed it to me as though the wind had blown
it off, and perhaps I should be more careful next time.
Davis Street was jammed with cars and headlights now,
and everyone was getting back inside. It was all over.

We started home. I told Holly that my ear was ringing
a little, that was all. And there was a pretty good knot on
the side of my head. She handed me a chunk of snow, and
I held it against my face, to keep the swelling down.

BOB KOEHLER

> *The truth is rarely pure and never
> simple.*
>
> OSCAR WILDE

WRITING NINETEEN: Write an idea paper in which you give yourself space to tell a lot of little stories, or a column for your campus
newspaper. Don't write just out of your mind, but also out of your
feelings, and choose what has chosen you, grabbed you hard by the
shoulder the way Tom Randolph and Malcolm X and Bob Koehler
were grabbed.

[George Bernard Shaw often sent his early drafts of his plays to his friend Ellen Terry, the actress, for criticism. Once she said she feared to suggest changes on his manuscript. He wrote back:]

"Oh, bother the MSS., mark them as much as you like: what else are they for? Mark everything that strikes you. I may consider a thing fortynine times; but if you consider it, it will be considered 50 times; and a line 50 times considered is 2 per cent better than a line 49 times considered. And it is the final 2 per cent that makes the difference between excellence and mediocrity."

chapter 18
sharpening

REHEATING a piece of writing after it has cooled, tempering it, and sharpening it is enjoyable—if you know how. Otherwise it may turn out worse, brittle or misshapen. In years of experience with editors and other readers who criticize his writing, a professional comes to identify some of the common weaknesses in all writing, and he looks for them when he sits down to improve his first or second draft of a piece of writing.

He looks for the excessive use of the verb *is* (and all forms of *to be*) of *it*, of adjectives, adverbs and passive verbs.

The verb *is* links other words, or proclaims something exists; it does not say much on its own. Writing dominated by *is* also suffers from too many nouns and adjectives, which the verb connects. It lacks the force and liveliness of writing filled with verbs that communicate specific action, like *careen, screech, tickle, swallow,* etc.

Too many uses of the word *is* drive a writer to stuffing his sentences with the words *it* and *there*. A writer who speaks honestly and wants his reader to know something that has counted for him seldom lets his sentences get sick in these ways; but he has gone to school, been asked to write Engfish. He cannot help being susceptible to these diseases. Here's a paragraph of free writing by a healthy writer:

> He doesn't have legs. Not ones that feel or move. It's been that way almost four years now. Wheels. I was scared to talk at first, felt like a kid asking what it is that everyone's talking about. But we did. We used to goof around and tell dirty jokes. I always felt a little fake. Dan and I took him to the bathroom every day. Had to be done in a special way. Were there once. Dan asked a question. I don't remember. I answered, "What do you think I am, a cripple?" That's what I said. I didn't look at anyone, just the wall. For about half an hour, I felt very whole, but my stomach was tin foil. They were quiet, both of them. Quiet as being alone. I wished someone would cut off my arms.

In that passage, *is* and *it* do not dominate. The word *there* appears only once, and denoting a place, not wasting space as it often does when used merely as a handle in front of the word *is*: "There is a need for change." The adjectives and adverbs that appear pull their weight. In several sentences the writer avoids using adjectives to describe his feelings, and instead employs a telling fact or metaphor: "I didn't look at anyone, just the wall," "I wished someone would cut off my arms." In this way he avoided the weakness of commonplace adjectives. He did not write: "I felt just awful," or "I was never so embarrassed in all my life."

In the above passage the only danger words that perhaps need replacing are *It's been* in the first line and *it is* in the third. Sentence number three might read better if it said: "*He's* been that way almost four years now." And the fifth if it did not contain the bracketed words: ". . . felt like a kid asking what [it is] everyone's talking about." But on the whole, this is a sharply written passage.

To show Is-ness and It-ache at their worst, here is another passage on the same subject.

> One of the worst feelings in the world is when you are being stared at. It makes you feel like your slip is showing or your pants are ripped. They mean no harm; it's just their way of being curious. It makes it hard for someone who is physically different. It is a shame that these people have to be unknowing.

Both writers apparently hated to see persons "physically different" made fun of. The second writer was an Engfisher who couldn't free himself to put down powerful facts. So he presented his sick sentences. If you are writing with a high degree of honesty, you will never find your words as ill as his when you sit down to write a second or third draft. But all writers at times put down sickly expressions. In the passage above, circle the uses of the verb *to be*; check them; and underline the adjectives. You will see how little meaning the words communicate. The passage is not worth sharpening. With its wasted words cut, it still does not compel the reader:

> Being stared at makes you feel like your slip is showing or your pants are ripped. The starers are just curious, they mean no harm. They don't realize how much they hurt someone who is physically different.

In any sort of writing, the excessive use of *it* piles up other unnecessary words in a sentence.

Original. By a recent poll it was revealed . . .

Revision. A recent poll revealed . . .

It has a way of picking up bad company. *It seems* are two words that frequently do bad things together.

Original. It seems that of the both groups, the boys are more conscious than the girls about subtleties of dress.

Revision. The boys are more conscious than girls about subtleties of dress.

Often writers say *seems* when no seeming is involved whatever, but rather clear and certain feeling or fact.

Note how cutting the uses of the verbs *would be* and *wasn't* (forms of *is*) allows the following sentence to be reduced from 34 to 23 words:

Original. Today an act like this would be considered a tragedy in a boy's life if he wasn't allowed at least a couple of hours to himself for the care and parting of his hair.

Revision. Today a boy denied a couple of hours to himself for the care and parting of his hair would consider himself tragically mistreated.

A helpful strategy in replacing *is* in a sentence consists of finding another verb which carries more meaning and allows you to drop a number of other unnecessary words.

When you notice a lot of adjectives and nouns and pronouns popping up in your sentences, you will probably find they were created
by the excessive use of *is* or other forms of *to be*.

Original. It was the style for the girls in that school to wear hair
ribbons.

Revision: The girls in that school wore hair ribbons.

One way to transfuse blood into a sentence anemic with Is-ness—
substitute a metaphorical verb for *is*.

Original. The poor subservient freshman is an inferior because he is
not a leader in organizations, says the Student Association president.

Revision: The poor freshman wags his tail as an inferior. He is never
a leader in organizations, says the Student Association president.

Shakespeare was a master of the metaphorical verb. In *Macbeth*
he made Malcolm say:

This tyrant whose sole name *blisters* our tongues,
Was once thought honest.

Suppose Shakespeare had written with Is-ness:

This tyrant whose sole name *is* a blister on our tongues,
Was once thought honest.

Again, one use of the verb *to be* is enough in the statement.

REVISING SEVEN: In one of your past longer pieces of writing circle
every use of the forms of the verb *to be*. Consider which need to be
eliminated and revise the sentences in which they appear. Remember
that Is-ness stands for a *weak* use of a form of *to be*. No writer can
write many sentences in a row without usefully employing *is*.

REVISING EIGHT: Check another of the long writings you have
already done. Look for the weaknesses mentioned in this chapter,
eliminate them, and make your paper both more concise and concrete.
In your writing you should be hunting for uses of *it* and *there*
which do not carry solid meaning but act merely as convenient handles
for introducing other expressions. For example:

Original. In some churches there are large choir stalls that partially
surround the minister.

Revision. In some churches large choir stalls partially surround the
minister.

But sometimes these words operate well as handles. They are hard to replace in these two sentences:

> It is cold out tonight.
> There are only four houses on the other side of the street on our block.

Too often, vague uses of *it* and *there* lead a writer to wasting other words as well:

Original. It is the task of the school to train all the students.

Such an It-ache as that may be cured by making a noun the subject of the sentence. At the same time, an editor would probably change the possessive construction "of the school" to "school's," a more informal but vigorous expression:

Revision. The school's task is to train all the students.
A sentence does not ache from a healthy use of *it* or *there*. For example:

> The ball rolled and rolled until it hit the fence.
> "He's sitting over there," said the witness, pointing.

In these sentences *it* represents the ball and *there* tells a place. These are different uses from those involved in *It is* and *There are*.
Dullness also results from the excessive use of passive verbs.

Passive. It was brought to our attention by the manager that we had not sent out the invoice.

Active. The manager told us we had not sent out the invoice.

Passive. The play was a performance that was observed by George with amazing indifference.

Active. George observed the play with amazing indifference.

Passive verbs suggest that nobody is doing anything. Just sitting around being acted upon.

Passive. The object that was stepped on by me was a ladybug with lavender spots.

Active. I stepped on a ladybug with lavender spots.

Passive. The scheme was conceived by John at four in the morning.

Active. John conceived the scheme at four in the morning.

Dullness may also be imparted to sentences by excessive use of the verbs

make	go	get
have	move	come

They are not full of specific meaning. Circle each use of them in your writing and question it: can the verb be replaced with a more particular and meaningful one? For example, *making* might be supplanted by

constructing	gluing	joining	stringing
building	piling	digging	sticking

and many other verbs. Even these are fairly general; for example, a writer might say "I *cemented* two stones together" rather than "I stuck two stones together." Choosing more precise and vigorous verbs puts life into writing because life is particular, not general.

Like Is-ness, the shoddy use of *make, have, go, move, get,* and *come* leads to a frightening waste of words:

Original. This land *has* the appearance of being arid.

Revision. This land looks arid.

These verbs frequently seed sentences with unnecessary nouns.

Original. He finally *came to* his decision. He would run.

Revision. He finally decided he would run.

You should remember that these suggested revisions are made out of context. The last revision above saves three words from the original sentences, but if the author's purpose was to slow down the reader and delay the divulging of the decision, he might better use the original version, which carries a different rhythm.

Beginning writers often insist on establishing the ownership of an object with the verb *have* before they let the owner use the object. Good way to clog the story.

Original. He *had* a bicycle. He rode it to work every morning.

Revision. He rode his bicycle to work every morning.

The principle involved in sharpening is to fill words with precise meaning or get rid of them. Beginning writers splatter adjectives and adverbs like buckshot. Consider this passage:

> **I summoned up courage and *boldly* set forth through the pathway. Suddenly loomed in sight five male patients sit-**

ting outside only a few feet from me. Too late to turn back, I consoled myself with the idea that an attendant was probably *unobtrusively* hidden from view but there, nevertheless, for protection.

Then the thought dawned on me that I was in the wrong and didn't deserve protection because I was trespassing— there were blockades which I had ignored, set up in front of the pathway. The patients, perhaps sensing my *nervous* anticipation, *possibly* evident in my *faltering* steps and *nervous* eye movements, said "hello" to me.

My *natural* reaction to this situation bothers me. In Psych class we consider mental patients just "sick people." I don't want to be guilty of sharing the *common* feelings of the *general* public.

Here in line 1, *boldly* is unnecessary with "summoned up courage" and "set forth," both expressions which imply boldness. In line 5, *unobtrusively* is unnecessary. Seldom does anyone hide obtrusively. In lines 10 and 11, *perhaps* is an honest word but the other italicized words overdo the notion of sensing nervousness. A sharp cutting is needed.

Original. The patients, perhaps sensing my nervous anticipation, possibly evident in my faltering steps and nervous eye movements, said "hello" to me.

Revision. Perhaps sensing my anticipation in my faltering steps and nervous eye movements, the patients said "hello" to me.

In line 13, *natural* is not an accurate word for what the writer wants to say. *Instant* or *stereotyped* would make more sense. In line 15, *common* is unnecessary. *Sharing* and *general* say enough by themselves.

Remembering the *repeat-and-vary* principle, the good writer avoids ruts. He does not allow himself to supply for every verb an adverb and for every noun an adjective until the pattern becomes monotonous and the words flabby. He avoids or changes dead patterns like these:

He slowly walked up the stairs, nonchalantly pushed on the door, and casually entered the room.

At the picnic were sticky-fingered children, rosy-cheeked mommas, and large-stomached fathers.

When he finishes his first or second draft, a good writer tests the adjectives and adverbs: are they pulling their weight? Do the other words around them render them unnecessary? See how freshly and powerfully Shakespeare uses an adverb in giving Regan, King Lear's daughter, these words about her father:

> 'Tis the infirmity of his age: yet he hath ever but *slenderly* known himself.

A fundamental in using adverbs and adjectives is not to let one of them smother the effect of another strong word. Don't let your straight man steal the attention from the comic. If you write

> She was *unusually* hideous.

you have lessened the force of *hideous* by making the reader attend to the weak word *unusually*. If you write

> It was a tremendously tall skyscraper.

you have lessened the force of *tall*. In fact, both *tremendously* and *tall* are tired and should be replaced with words that fix the height of the skyscraper in actual or metaphorical scale.

> I stood a hundred feet away and yet my neck ached from looking up to the top of the building.

This chapter has talked about weak uses of certain words. All of them may be used adequately or strongly by a skillful writer. Note in this beautifully phrased passage from "Self-Reliance" that Emerson uses many strong verbs but also forms of *to be*. He plants four adjectives within the space of seven words. He finishes with a sentence that carries the normally vague and weak verb *go*.

> Travelling is a fool's paradise. Our first journeys discover to us the indifference of places. At home I dream that at Naples, at Rome, I can be intoxicated with beauty and lose my sadness. I pack my trunk, embrace my friends, embark on the sea and at last wake up in Naples, and there beside me is the stern fact, the sad self, unrelenting, identical, that I fled from. I seek the Vatican and the palaces. I affect to be intoxicated with sights and suggestions, but I am not intoxicated. My giant goes with me wherever I go.

The power of this passage comes from its ideas as well as from its expression. Emerson is true to his thoughts and feelings, and there-

fore his words carry surprise. The words that precede or follow
ordinarily weak verbs like *to be* or *goes* are full of meaning—*intoxi-
cated, giant, fool's paradise.*

Sharpening writing is not as black and white a matter as this
chapter suggests. Many of the changes dictated here are debatable,
and only a person considering the total context of a word or phrase
can see whether or not it should be retained. Find ways of probing
your sentences so that you see alternative ways of stating them. *Is,
there,* and *it* frequently are wasted and breed other unnecessary
words. But they are good words in their place. You will find writers
as brilliant as Bernard Shaw using *it is* when the words are not
absolutely necessary, as in the quotation at the head of this chapter:

> And it is the final 2 per cent that makes the difference
> between excellence and mediocrity.

This *it* doesn't ache much. It could be eliminated and the sentence
written

> And the final 2 per cent makes the difference between
> excellence and mediocrity.

but the words *it is* in this passage act as emphasizers. They slow down
the reader and make sure he gives attention to *2 per cent.*

The moral of this chapter is not to do away with all uses of the
cited words, but to learn where to look for possible weak spots in
your sentences. The writer of this book originally wrote the first
sentence of the paragraph above in this way:

> Sharpening writing is not as black and white a matter as
> this chapter makes it appear.

Spotting the *it* in the sentence, and thinking about removing it, he
saw that he could drop three words, *makes, it,* and *appear,* and substitute only the word *suggests.*

REVISING NINE: Look over two of your past free writings and
attempt to eliminate from them weak passive verbs, empty verbs like
make and *have,* the overuse of adjectives, and the unnecessary use of
intensifying words like *tremendously* and *great big.*

When the college professor is asked to write an article for a
learned journal, he too often shifts into Pedantic and says:

> Unquestionably the textbook has played a very important
> role in the development of American schools—and I believe
> it will continue to play an important role.

You may have the urge here to say, "So have spitballs." The professor goes on:

> The need for textbooks has been established through many experiments. It is not necessary to consider these experiments but, in general, they have shown that when instruction without textbooks has been tried by schools, the virtually unanimous result has been to go back to the use of textbooks. I believe too, that there is considerable evidence to indicate that the textbook has been, and is, a major factor in guiding teachers' instruction and in determining the curriculum. And I don't think that either role for the textbook is necessarily bad.

The professor begins his statement with the weasel word *unquestionably*. The very point he is going to try to make in the paragraph he calls unquestionable before he starts. From then on he throws (*lobs* would be a better word; nothing has force in this paragraph) a bunch of dull generalizations in his reader's face. Something has played a *role* in the *development* of something. How many times have you heard that vague line? What role? An *important* role. What does that mean? What kind and rate of development? How did the schools develop as a result of the textbook? What a mishmash of educational language: "need established . . . many experiments . . . virtually unanimous result . . . considerable evidence . . . major factor." These are Weasel Words. They don't say anything for sure yet they keep insisting they are certain and unquestionable. The professor talks about impressive experiments but never mentions one. He doesn't think it is "necessary to consider these experiments" yet he employs them as the only evidence for his argument. Note his last sentence:

> And I don't think that either role for the textbook is necessarily bad.

That's the only possibly exciting sentence in the paragraph. Someone has apparently said that using a textbook to guide teachers' instruction or determine the curriculum is bad. Who said that? Why? The writer needs to say, but he isn't fixing to say anything for sure. He won't give the reader anything he can examine and be sure about. He's just talking through his weasel nose.

Every writer talks weaselry at times. This language is hard to see because it is so common.

> It was *sort of* a flop.
> He was *kind of* a hero to me.

That, *incidentally,* is four fouls.

Going through the weeds there was *almost* like walking in a swamp.

His father, *by the way,* is a crook.

> *"I've got a sort of idea but I don't sup-*
> *pose it's a very good one."*
> Winnie the Pooh (by A. A. Milne)

In hurried conversation such weaselries should be forgiven, but not in writing, where the author has a chance to revise and tighten. The weakness of *sort of* and *kind of* is that they do not tell the reader whether the writer really thought "it" was a "flop" or "he" was a "hero." If the writer wanted to communicate that the play was not completely a flop but a failure only in the first act, he should have said so. If he wanted to say that "he" was a hero in one way but not in another, he should have told in what way. Otherwise, he should have simply said: "It was a flop" and "He was a hero to me." Usually *sort of* and *kind of* take the punch out of the words they precede. They lessen rather than increase meaning. If you scatter them throughout your writing, your reader will eventually suspect you don't mean anything you say. Note these weasel words:

The *final* conclusions of the workshop.

There is a *limited amount* of seating space.

Throwing mud in her face wasn't *too* nice.

Falling down the stairs isn't *exactly* fun.

But being in that wreck was an *especially* devastating experience.

Mary was a *remarkably* lovely queen.

Other words frequently used in weasel fashion are *relative, particular,* and *various.*

This is a *relatively* minor matter and need not concern us long here.

If the reader doesn't know relative to what, he can't extract much meaning from *relatively.*

This is a *particularly* fine example of social organization.

Fine already tells the reader the example is above ordinary. *Particularly* steals attention from *fine.*

> In his travels around the world, the captain has encoun-
> tered many diseases in *various* countries and *various* envi-
> ronments.

This is straight cornmeal mush. Most readers would like it better
fried crisp and served with hot syrup. If the writer wants to make his
point with power, he should say "about two thousand diseases in
fifty-six countries and in environments ranging from ice floes to
tropical rain forests."

Most academic writing is loaded with weasel words and phrases;
for scholars are taught to be cautious, to qualify. But there are
times to be cautious and times to be bold. Watch this pedantic phrase
weasel its ways into an otherwise straightforward sentence:

> Last week the world was contained in a blue plastic egg
> filled with jelly beans and a set of rabbit teeth—*at least it
> was* for five-year-old Jack.

The author doesn't really mean to hint that anyone else's world
beside Jack's was filled with that bunch of jelly beans and set of
rabbit teeth, but she heard a weasel squeal somewhere and echoes
it in her sentence.

As I write this chapter warning others of weaseling, I remember
that when I was writing another text, an editor pointed out that
almost always when I used the words *in fact,* I followed them with
an unsupported personal opinion. Frequently writers try to make
up for weak opinions by introducing them with one of the following
expressions:

indeed	surely	honestly
obviously	certainly	frankly
of course	needless to say	sincerely

The most dishonest man I ever knew constantly prefaced his remarks
with the expression, "I would be less than candid if I did not say—."

Writers are often dishonest with themselves: they speak apolo-
getically, defensively, pompously, or condescendingly when they do
not feel apologetic, defensive, pompous, or condescending. A teacher
who once submitted a poem to an editor of a magazine, hoping for
publication, referred to her manuscript in her covering letter as "This
bit of fluff, modeled after 'The Children's Hour.' " Her comment
sounds like the introductory remarks many persons make before they
speak in a group meeting: "Now I don't claim to be an expert in this
subject and what I have to say probably isn't worth much . . ." Then

they make a fifteen-minute speech. One is tempted to say to the teacher: "If you think your manuscript is fluff, don't send it to the magazine"; and to the apologetic speaker: "If you don't think you are qualified to speak, don't speak. Or if you are qualified, don't waste our time telling us you aren't."

> *"What do you know about this business?" the King said to Alice.*
>
> *"Nothing," said Alice.*
>
> *"Nothing* whatever?" *persisted the King.*
>
> *"Nothing whatever," said Alice.*
>
> *"That's very important," the King said, turning to the jury. They were just beginning to write this down on their slates, when the White Rabbit interrupted: "Un*important, *your Majesty means, of course," he said, in a very respectful tone, but frowning and making faces at him, as he spoke.*
>
> *"Un*important, *of course, I meant," the King hastily said, and went on to himself in an undertone, "important—unimportant — unimportant — important —" as if he were trying which word sounded best.*
>
> *Some of the jury wrote it down "important," and some "unimportant." Alice could see this, as she was near enough to look over their slates; "but it doesn't matter a bit," she thought to herself.*
>
> LEWIS CARROLL

. . . childhood word-play, adolescent slang and double-talk, often derivative, but natural and exciting. In general the schools have made it their business to kill this kind of playful interest, and they have had the backing of society in this effort . . . most professionals with highly developed skills are fond of playing with those skills.

W. NELSON FRANCIS

chapter 19

words speaking to words

WORD PLAY

EVERYTHING is peaches and cream. Like something the cat dragged in. Like hunting for a needle in a haystack. Things have gone all to pot. Great oaks from little acorns grow, and a stitch in time saves nine.

A college student looking at a list like that wrote: "Everything is clichés and Pream." That's word play. *Pream* rhymes with cream, *clichés* reminds one of the sound of *peaches*. Pream is a powdered substitute for cream. Another student said he felt like someone who had dragged in the cat. And a number played with the word *pot*.

A cliché is a much-used expression. At what point it becomes overused and offensive is difficult to say, for some listeners expect more freshness than others. A case can be made for clichés. Their familiarity reassures and soothes, say their defenders. Surely one cannot rid all his conversation of them. Proverbial sayings are also old and yet cherished all over the world. In the United States we say,

He who laughs last laughs best.

In Liberia people say,

You are leaning on a dry bamboo.

Mosquito says: If you want a man to understand you, speak in his ears.

We generally take the drowning child out of the water before slapping it.

You will enjoy reading Liberian proverbs more than American because they are new to you.

Naturally, conversational clichés are easier to take than written clichés, for they are gone on the wind; but the man or woman who suffuses his talk with them misuses his friends.

WRITING TWENTY: Think of other dull word combinations like *grave responsibility, definite contrast, grim tragedy, bitter truth.* Play with them until you come up with ten new combinations or twists that you think work.

Doing that, one student wrote; "It's both a pressure and a privilege to be here." Another wrote: "Home is where the garbage is," and "Love Is a Many-Splintered Thing," and "I want a girl just like the girl that turned down dear old Dad."

The secret of productive word play is simple: Let yourself go. All great persons—artists, scientists, engineers, architects, cooks, designers —fool around. If their play produces something usable, they use it. Maybe a new kind of soup. If not, they feel no pain or guilt. You cannot feel guilty about play and become a creative person. In this game you must be loose with language. Sinful. Show no respect for the tried and blue. Expect a lot of misfires, like bad firecrackers. The girl who wrote the story about the bus driver delivering schoolchildren (printed in Chapter 8) ended with a masterful play on the saying that man has feet of clay, meaning he is subject to error and weakness.

I watched the bus drive away on wheels of clay.

The word player is not so much playing chess as just playing around. He may decide to put the play to practical use, but he does not need to any more than he needs to publish his first three bad drafts of a piece of writing. The more you play with words, the more often you will find playful statements crossing over into serious expression. E. E. Cummings, an American poet, constantly sawed up his words and tacked pieces on them. He looked at the word *mankind* and decided to write it *manunkind*. Then he used that new word in the first line of a bitter poem about the evils man has committed in the name of progress. It begins:

> pity this busy monster,manunkind

This was not simply a trick by Mr. Cummings. For years he had written against war and man's cruelty to man.

Play with titles of articles or books, with titles for your own writings. First study newspaper and magazine article titles. Note the puns, the newly created words. Here are some examples:

(a) *How to Cheat on Personality Tests,* by William H. Whyte, Jr.
(b) *A Problem of Design: How to Kill People,* by George Nelson
(c) *Arms and the Boy,* by Wilfred Owen

"Arms and the Boy," a title of a poem, plays on the first line of Virgil's *Aeneid*, which begins: "Arms and the man I sing . . ." The poet Wilfred Owen is suggesting that the reader should remember that boys rather than men are often killed in war.

(d) *The Beast in Me and Other Animals,* by James Thurber
(e) *Bed of Neuroses,* by Wolcott Gibbs
(f) *Golf Is a Four Letter Word,* by Richard Armour

The word play in all these titles is pointed. It makes a reader think twice and see significance. When Sidney Cox, a writing teacher at Dartmouth College, published a book of reflections and musings about writing—not a program of specifics for learning to write, he called it *Indirections: for Those Who Want to Write*. He was playing on the word *Directions*.

> . . . the light of magic suggestiveness
> may be brought to play for an evanescent
> instant over the commonplace surface of
> words: of the old, old words, worn thin,
> defaced by ages of careless usage.
>
> JOSEPH CONRAD

Try to write the truth in your language and at the same time let your words speak to each other. One day a student playing with words wrote:

November, and the cornfields are brown and broken and
they rattle in the freshening wind. Meanwhile across the
cornflakes heavy voices grumble the usual. A word of meaning drowns in a sea of crunch.

When he handed this paragraph to a teacher, he appended this
comment:

I was just playing with words and sounds and pictures.
Somehow it reminds me of T. S. Eliot's coffee spoons [in
"The Love Song of J. Alfred Prufrock"]. Know what? I'll
bet if the thing were printed, someone would analyze it.

Here the writer is dishonest. The passage is more than meaningless
sounds and pictures. In his play he must have had in mind tension
between the fresh wind in the cornfields and the stale breakfast
table conversation. It is a delightful and valid statement which makes
its point in a sidelong manner. If incorporated into a larger context,
it might become the most powerful paragraph of a paper. What a
writer says unconsciously may carry more meaning than what he plans
meticulously.

WRITING TWENTY-ONE: Try playing with words as you do a
shotgun writing. After Eric and his grandmother had discussed a
number of extinct prehistoric animals, Eric asked, "Can those dino-
saurs ever get unstinct?" A girl watching a class fall silent when a tape
recorder was brought into the room said, "Most people turn off when
the tape recorder turns on." Start writing about something and consider words that oppose it *in meaning.* And in *form,* as Eric did. When
you think of writing that someone's remark "left little room for doubt,"
you might say, "left only a small closet for doubt." Or to reverse the
idea—"left a large attic for doubt." Write for fifteen minutes. Try to
speak a truth that counts for you, however large or small. You don't
need to force the play. The best play occurs when the player gets outside himself and becomes hooked by the game. While he is trying to
beat out a bunt he doesn't say to himself, "I will enjoy the game." He
legs it to first as fast as he can.

Note how the words in the following paragraph speak to each other:

On Sundays the machine usually behaves better in accepting coins. Several times it has fooled me with its ready-to-
serve manner. I walk down the eight flights from third
floor, put in my change, push the Coke button and am

answered by the delightful sound of a falling cup and a nice long rebellious belch from the machine: I get 10¢ worth of Coke cup and air.

WRITING TWENTY-TWO: There are kind, constructive, and happy families who never engage in word play. The author of this book was brought up by a mother never playful with language. Not until I was thirty did I realize word play was easy. I thought it an esoteric game like *jai-alai*. In my early days I would never have seen possibilities for word play in the names of the players on the basketball roster of Ohio University, 1969, which I give here from the printed program I picked up at a game one night.

Battle, Steve	Portsmouth, O.
Canine, John	Hazel Park, Mich.
Coon, Larry	Athens, O.
Courtright, Grant	Stoutsville, O.
Glancy, John	Dahlgren, Va.
Groff, Dave	Mansfield, O.
Hunter, Larry	Athens, O.
Kowall, Ken	Parma Heights, O.
Love, Craig	Franklin, Mich.
McDivitt, Greg	Windham, O.
McKee, Gerald	Dayton, O.
Milhollan, Jack	Washington, Pa.
Miller, Mike,	Middletown, O.
Parker, Doug	Columbus, O.
Pirillo, Guy	Urichsville, O.
Wolf, Gary	Columbus, O.

Play with the names that speak to each other. Make several different statements or poems with them. You can do anything you want—tell a story, make an explanation, give a description of a place or institution, or take a trip through this country or another, using some of these names. It is an exercise like shooting baskets. Probably won't result in anything publishable or count in the conference standings. But it may help you see materials for writing—the signs or comments or names that are all around you—as seeds, fertilizer, soil, for growing things. If the basketball names do not excite you, find another list in your life somewhere and work with it.

METAPHOR

Metaphor, the statement of one thing in terms of another, is related to word play. A college girl writes in her journal:

> After having three dates during the weekend, one of my
> roommates spent several hours baking cookies for her Army
> boy friend. A girl from down the hall came in and said,
> "Those cookies are half Bisquick and half guilt."

This habit of seeing likeness between things apparently different is
one we all command at times. A fifth-grade child says:

> A tree in spring is a double-barreled shotgun exploding.

As a writer you need not waste time trying to decide whether or not
what you are writing is a metaphor, simile, or fabulous reality. The
point is whether or not you are getting your words to speak to each
other. For example, the following sign,

HILLTOP MARATHON
ROAD AND WRECKER SERVICE
Located on E. Main Hill
DON DARLING AND JOHN LOVETT
OWNERS

contains words that speak to each other and create what might be called
a fabulous reality, but a skillful writer might make them work for
larger purposes, in an extended context. The professional writer stores
material like that in his mind or records it in his journal, then pulls
it out when the occasion is ripe. The sign above shows Darling and
Lovett are engaged in helping persons in trouble. They ask money for
the services. A writer who was talking about persons who appear kindly
but act only to make money might say they remind him of a sign he
once saw . . .

Strangely, a skillful writer with metaphors seldom commands them
to appear. He collects visual and auditory impressions and waits for
them to form into metaphors while he is writing. He draws them from
his close knowledge, intimate experience. He does not calculate or
manufacture them. Watch this metaphor rise out of the materials:

> Formica-topped desks never scratch. I can't bur or mar
> them. Number 248 cubicle that I have been assigned holds
> compact, practical drawers and desk firmly bolted to a
> wall, unmoveable, without handles. I never knew how
> much handles on a drawer meant to me until I was de-
> prived of them. I actually thought at first that I like
> formica tops. But my fingers don't like the formica. It's
> not grooved and soft like a battered old oak desk.
> Nothing in my room cares about me.

This is the metaphorical habit—to see likenesses and differences in un-expected but valid comparisons. College students frequently speak this way when they don't think they need to come up with Engfish. During a campus controversy over the desirability of removing credit for physical education courses or dropping them altogether, a boy wrote:

> **Supporters of our PE program at Western should be hung in a locker.**

A girl wrote in her journal:

> **What's my mind doing now? Nothing of importance. It feels like I've got a bathing cap on one size too small.**

Another girl wrote:

> **We went to the basketball game tonight. That's kind of a funny sport that goes back and forth fast across the court like one of those balls connected by a rubber band to a paddle.**

WRITING TWENTY-THREE: Try writing two papers, each of twenty minutes or more in which you extend a metaphor so it affects the whole writing. Here's an example:

> **In small towns everything's just scattered around, like Augusta. There's a car without an engine or wheels rusting in a driveway. A dried-up antique gas pump stands on the sidewalk of the main street without a gas station around it. An abandoned building next to the restaurant is long and flat and the broken windows that ring the structure stare into one huge empty room. Impossible to figure out what it ever housed. I feel like I should pick things up in Augusta and straighten them out like I do in my living room, put the gas pump and car away in the junk drawer and sweep the old building under a rug.**
>
> **Order is easier to ignore.**

There are dangers also in metaphors. When you forget the dead and hidden ones in the language, you may compose foolish sentences. For example:

> Changing the course of a fast, deep river would normally be a lost cause, but this is one cause the North High family cannot afford to lose hold of.

This is a metaphor used by a student editor to ask others to help him reform the school newspaper. In it, he forgets what he is saying and asks the readers to keep hold of a river. He should remember that water is impossible to grasp.

Here is an excerpt from a paint company's directions for using artists' colors:

> Where very thin glazes are desired, Liquitex colors mixed with the Medium may be quickly and lightly rubbed over the surface with fingers and thumb in the manner of oil glazes. On the other hand, unwanted color or glaze may be wiped off.

The writer committed a blooper in using the phrase "On the other hand." He forgot its dead metaphor. Just before that he is talking about literal fingers and thumb. Like a thousand other phrases in everyday language, "on the other hand" was once a brilliant metaphor. Now men use it so unconsciously they need to be jogged with the vaudeville gag: "On the other hand—she had a wart."

WRITING TWENTY-FOUR: Write two 10- to 20-minute free writings in which you talk of things you love. Let yourself describe them in metaphor and simile that come from your deepest knowledge about objects or processes or occupations. Don't be satisfied with simple, brief metaphors: "His face was like a sunny day." Develop a metaphor, let its parts speak to each other and create new and continuing comparisons, as this beginning writer did:

> **When I think of barnacles I laugh because if they were attached to my bottom I'd feel important—like the Queen Mary. Maybe I ought to think like this when I take a bath and slide across the porcelain ocean at the end of a narrow day.**

> *Alice didn't dare to argue the point, but went on: "And I thought I'd try and find my way to the top of that hill—"*
>
> *"When you say 'hill,'" the Queen interrupted, "I could show you hills in comparison with which you'd call that a valley."*
>
> *"No, I shouldn't," said Alice, surprised into contradicting her at last: "a hill can't be a valley, you know. That would be nonsense—"*

The Red Queen shook her head. "You
may call it 'nonsense,' if you like," she
said, "but I've heard nonsense compared
with which that would be as sensible as
a dictionary!"

LEWIS CARROLL

EXPOSING THE ROOTS OF WORDS

Once you have caught the habit of making words speak to each
other, you will find yourself examining what each word says by itself,
who its parents were, and what it says when its original meanings are
reactivated. Then your language will not be soggy but fresh and
crackling. In *Walden* Henry Thoreau began writing a sentence,

> We meet at meals three times a day, and give each other a
> new taste

and he remembered the metaphor in the word *taste*. Because he did
not allow the word to become abstract in his mind, he was able to
finish the sentence in this way:

> of that old musty cheese that we are.

and on another page he said:

> If you have built castles in the air, your work need not be
> lost; that is where they should be. Now put the foundations
> under them.

William Hazlitt said:

> Miracles never cease, to be sure; but they are not to be had
> wholesale, or *to order*.

And so beginning writers can do when they allow themselves to think
about what their words are saying. In an education book a student
saw the question

> What is a good English teacher?

and she wrote underneath it:

> Who is a good English teacher?

With that little move she showed up the pedant who thinks he can
create good teachers by listing their qualities or making up a job
description. Steve Tod recorded what a mother said to her three-year-

old, "Mary Jane, get out of your Coke!" and showed he recognized that the verb was meant literally there.

To *belittle* is a word now almost always used figuratively. It takes on new power in this passage where the writer thought about its literal meaning and utilized it.

> I am an amateur mechanic I guess. I can fix the car or truck as a rule when something goes wrong. I put a whole new ignition system in the truck and two thermostats and a water pump—it was hot that day—and I change plugs, points, and oil, and I put a fuel pump on the old Studebaker and a carburetor, and I change tires and do body work and can start a car without pushing it or using jumpers by jacking it up in back, spinning the rear wheels, and popping the clutch in third gear. I guess I'm kind of a mechanic. I even completely rebuilt my cycle. It's still not all together yet, but I'll be out belittling hills with it by spring.

To put new meaning into old words or restore meaning now dead is to do a favor to your reader who would prefer going to sleep in a bed than in your writing. In this little unfinished journal entry a writer has started to consider seriously the word *woman*.

> Even my own mother doesn't know quite what woman is. Too often she tries to pass herself off as lady instead. Though—there are real ladies I admire. I want to be able to see the lady and the woman incorporated into one vital human being.

Such thinking about the meaning of words is not trivial. Customarily reformers and innovators and system builders breathe life into dead words. In 1947 the philosopher-psychologist Erich Fromm began to construct a new philosophy of the personality. He wrote:

> Responsibility and response have the same root, *respondere* = "to answer"; to be responsible means to be ready to respond.

and also:

> Respect is not fear and awe; it denotes, in accordance with the root of the word (*respicere* = to look at), the ability to see a person as he is, to be aware of his individuality and uniqueness. To respect a person is not possible without knowing him . . .

Sometimes a writer spins out a whole story without realizing that it is building up layer by layer a new or supercharged meaning for an old word. In the following story, a college senior uses five good-sized paragraphs to build her ironic meanings for the common terms *death* and *life*. Stories of the death of relatives are frequently sentimental, carrying more emotion than the action warrants, or insisting on a stereotyped response that does not fit the particular experience. Not so with this account.

She greeted me when I bent over. I thought she said, "My girl," but I wasn't sure. Her speech was almost unintelligible. She was half sitting, half lying in a huge bed and the fluorescent lighting that flooded the ward and turned the sheets and curtains a glowing, blazing white made her face and ugly pinkish yellow and robbed it all of the contouring shadows that might have humanized it. Her eyes were shut, her jaws slack, her whole face vacant and over-relaxed. Her wrists were tied to the sides of the bed. And IV needles had been pushed into her arm and secured by a piece of now blood-spotted gauze. The green tubes of the suction machine were held in her nostrils by a metal clip, and a criss-cross of adhesive tape.

Suddenly, an animal spasm went through her body. She half sat up. Her frame jerked and twisted. Her arms strained to reach and tear away the tubes. The identification band on her wrists—a blue plastic ring like a child's dime-store bracelet—shook up and down on her thin wrist. Her head went back, her mouth opened wide, and she gasped for air, her throat throbbing. I waited for her eyes to open —I waited for many minutes until I understood that she would never look at me again. Then I walked out . . .

I stood outside waiting for one of my elders to say, "Take these tubes out, and leave her alone." I thought "They'll never get their hands on me. I may have to walk into the woods to die in peace, but they'll never make my death an endurance contest." We waited an hour and then two. There was no place to sit down and nothing to do. Finally Aunt Millie, who was a registered nurse, and had begun to take over the situation said, "Why don't you folks go down to the lounge? I'll stay here and take care of her."

It was a reasonable suggestion only we had no place, no function outside her room. We drifted down to the lounge and sat with our coats thrown over the backs of our chairs and our eyes turned inwards. I flipped through a pile of magazines, trying to distract myself with a picture essay on Japanese women, menu suggestions in a Campbell's soup ad, and the other slick, glossy things one finds in *Life*.

Aunt Millie came up to the lounge around twelve o'clock and said, "I'll stay, if you'd like to go home now. I'll call." Aunt Millie hadn't been to see Grandma in a couple of years. We picked up our coats and shuffled out.

The house was cold when we got home. I went right upstairs and got into bed. It didn't seem like I'd lain there long before I heard the telephone ring. I went downstairs late the next morning and sat on the davenport. Mom came in and said, "Grandma died about two o'clock last night, Sarah." I looked up and said, "Thanks, Mom," but didn't feel anything. I didn't care. That death was only a biological fact, as pointless and trivial as the eight horrible hours of vegetative life they'd forced on her.

In that hard story that tamps down so much feeling, the author played seriously with the words *death* and *life*. Because she had the habit of putting down names of things making up her experience, she found herself writing the name of a magazine that also played upon her subject, and she used that name with double meaning. Playing with words may be a funny or solemn act. Either way the words can speak to each other and set up a dialogue that the reader can enjoy and learn from —a second communication beyond the direct one between writer and reader.

irony. 2 *a: the use of words to express
something other than and esp. the opposite of the literal meaning.*
*Webster's Seventh New
Collegiate Dictionary*

chapter 20
writing
indirectly

You DON'T HAVE to write in a straight
line that runs right at your reader. You can shoot words off on a
diagonal, a little off target, and expect the reader to see where the
bull's-eye really is. Making a point indirectly gives it surprise.

You may turn upside down what you say. Exaggerate. You may
say exactly the opposite of what you mean. Take up a serious subject
lightly or a trivial subject heavily. A funeral is no place for jokes, but
a writer can write humorously about funerals. Evelyn Waugh did and
called his novel *The Loved One,* a story about an ostentatious burying
park in California. Jonathan Swift wrote ironically about poverty
and called his essay "A Modest Proposal for preventing the Children
of Poor People from being a Burden to their Parents or the Country"
(by roasting them as food for the rich).

Here are some of the ways a writer speaks indirectly:

(a) *A writer may play dumb,* pretend to be holding one opinion
while tipping off the reader to his true, and often opposite, opinion.

In chapter seventeen of *Huckleberry Finn,* Samuel Clemens, talking through Huck, speaks so indirectly, yet with such a straight face,
that many readers don't see what he is saying in this description of the
Grangerford house and family:

> It was a mighty nice family, and a mighty nice house, too. I
> hadn't seen no house out in the country before that was so
> nice and had so much style. It didn't have an iron latch on

the front door, nor a wooden one with a buckskin string, but a brass knob to turn, the same as houses in a town. There warn't no bed in the parlor, not a sign of a bed; but heaps of parlors in towns has beds in them. There was a big fireplace that was bricked on the bottom, and the bricks was kept clean and red by pouring water on them and scrubbing them with another brick; sometimes they washed them over with red water-paint that they call Spanish-brown, same as they do in town. They had big brass dog-irons that could hold up a saw-log. There was a clock on the middle of the mantel-piece, with a picture of a town painted on the bottom half of the glass front, and a round place in the middle of it for the sun, and you could see the pendulum swing behind it. It was beautiful to hear that clock tick; and sometimes when one of these peddlers had been along and scoured her up and got her in good shape, she would start in and strike a hundred and fifty before she got tuckered out. They wouldn't took any money for her.

Well, there was a big outlandish parrot on each side of the clock, made out of something like chalk, and painted up gaudy. By one of the parrots was a cat made of crockery, and a crockery dog by the other; and when you pressed down on them they squeaked, but didn't open their mouths nor look different nor interested. They squeaked through underneath. There was a couple of big wild-turkey-wing fans spread out behind those things. On a table in the middle of the room was a kind of a lovely crockery basket that had apples and oranges and peaches and grapes piled up in it which was much redder and yellower and prettier than real ones is, but they warn't real because you could see where pieces had got chipped off and showed the white chalk or whatever it was, underneath.

This table had a cover made out of beautiful oil-cloth, with a red and blue spread-eagle painted on it, and a painted border all around. It come all the way from Philadelphia, they said. There was some books too, piled up perfectly exact, on each corner of the table. One was a big family Bible, full of pictures. One was "Pilgrim's Progress," about a man that left his family it didn't say why. I read considerable in it now and then. The statements was interesting, but tough. Another was "Friendship's Offering," full of beautiful stuff and poetry; but I didn't read the poetry.

Another was Henry Clay's Speeches, and another was Dr. Gunn's Family Medicine, which told you all about what to do if a body was sick or dead. There was a Hymn Book, and a lot of other books. And there was nice split-bottom chairs, and perfectly sound, too—not bagged down in the middle and busted, like an old basket.

They had pictures hung on the walls—mainly Washingtons and Lafayettes, and battles, and Highland Mary, and one called "Signing the Declaration." There was some that they called crayons, which one of the daughters which was dead made her own self when she was only fifteen years old. They was different from many pictures I ever see before; blacker, mostly, than is common. One was a woman in a slim black dress, belted small under the arm-pits, with bulges like a cabbage in the middle of the sleeves, and a large black scoop-shovel bonnet with a black veil, and white slim ankles crossed about with black tape, and very wee black slippers, like a chisel, and she was leaning pensive on a tombstone on her right elbow, under a weeping willow, and her other hand hanging down her side holding a white handkerchief and a reticule, and underneath the picture it said "Shall I Never See Thee More Alas." Another one was a young lady with her hair all combed up straight to the top of her head, and knotted there in front of a comb like a chair-back, and she was crying into a handkerchief and had a dead bird laying on its back in her other hand with its heels up, and underneath the picture it said "I Shall Never Hear Thy Sweet Chirrup More Alas." There was one where a young lady was at a window looking up at the moon, and tears running down her cheeks; and she had an open letter in one hand with black sealing-wax showing on one edge of it, and she was mashing a locket with a chain to it against her mouth, and underneath the picture it said "And Art Thou Gone Yes Thou Art Gone Alas." These was all nice pictures, I reckon, but I didn't somehow seem to take to them, because if ever I was down a little, they always give me the fan-tods. Everybody was sorry she died, because she had laid out a lot more of these pictures to do, and a body could see by what she had done what they had lost. But I reckoned, that with her disposition, she was having a better time in the graveyard. She was at work on what they said was her greatest picture when she took sick, and every day and every night it was her prayer to be allowed to live till she got it done, but she never got the chance. It was a picture of a young woman in a long white gown, standing on the rail of a bridge all ready to jump off, with her hair all down her back, and looking up to the moon, with the tears running down her face, and she had two arms folded across her breast, and two arms stretched out in front, and two more reaching up towards the moon—and the idea was, to see which pair would look best and then scratch out all the other arms; but, as I was saying, she died before she got her mind made up, and now they kept this picture over the head of the bed in her room, and every time her birthday come they hung flowers on it. Other times it was hid with a little curtain. The young woman in the picture had a kind of a nice sweet face, but there was so many arms it made her look too spidery, seemed to me.

This young girl kept a scrap-book when she was alive, and used to paste obituaries and accidents and cases of patient suffering in it out of the *Presbyterian Observer*, and write poetry after them out of her own head. It was very good poetry. This is what she wrote about a boy by the name of Stephen Dowling Bots that fell down a well and was drownded:

ODE TO STEPHEN DOWLING BOTS, DEC'D.

And did young Stephen sicken,
   And did young Stephen die?
And did the sad hearts thicken,
   And did the mourners cry?

No; such was not the fate of
   Young Stephen Dowling Bots;
Though sad hearts round him thickened,
   'Twas not from sickness' shots.

No whooping-cough did rack his frame,
   Nor measles drear, with spots;
Not these impaired the sacred name
   Of Stephen Dowling Bots.

Despised love struck not with woe
   That head of curly knots,
Nor stomach troubles laid him low,
   Young Stephen Dowling Bots.

O no. Then list with tearful eye,
   Whilst I his fate do tell.
His soul did from this cold world fly,
   By falling down a well.

They got him out and emptied him;
   Alas it was too late;
His spirit was gone for to sport aloft
   In the realms of the good and great.

If Emmeline Grangerford could make poetry like that before she was fourteen, there ain't no telling what she could a done by-and-by. Buck said she could rattle off poetry like nothing. She didn't ever have to stop to think. He said she would slap down a line, and if she couldn't find anything to rhyme with it she would just scratch it out and slap down another one, and go ahead. She warn't particular, she could write about anything you choose to give her to write about, just so it was sadful. Every time a man died, or a woman died, or a child died, she would be on hand with her "tribute" before he was cold. She called them tributes. The neighbors said it was the doctor first, then Emmeline, then the undertaker—the undertaker never got in ahead of Emmeline but once, and then she hung fire on a rhyme for the dead person's name, which was Whistler. She warn't ever the same, after that; she never complained, but she kind of pined away and did not live long.

What you have read is a mild satire of the décor of a house and a strong satire of a sentimental little girl who wrote bad poetry. Obviously Huck thinks the house beautiful, but Clemens suggests with small cues that he does not. He might admire artificial fruit, but when he has Huck mention "where pieces had got chipped off and showed the white chalk or whatever it was," you should begin to suspect his intentions in this writing. Think of the whole picture: the mantel a garish display of painted scene; crockery birds, dog, cat; and turkey wings. On the table an oil-cloth spread displaying a spread eagle— more wings. The books: standard family pieces, revealing no individuality of mind in their choice, all perfectly piled as if never used. The pictures on the wall patriotic and sentimental. The room is as gaudy as a souvenir shop at Niagara Falls, and Clemens wants the reader to know this at the same time he wants him to see that Huck Finn is completely inexperienced in judging such matters. The room goes perfectly with Emmeline Grangerford's poetry, which Twain hits more directly in hard satire.

Clemens' indirectness enables him to make three points at once. He scores the Grangerfords' lack of cultural independence, shows his hero limited in experience, and slyly criticizes the American middle-class for its use of pseudo art objects in its homes.

(b) *A writer may directly say he doesn't understand, when he does,* as this high school student did in a poem:

> I wonder if the mail has come
>   (Not that I really care.)
> Our quarrel was really very dumb.
> I wonder if the mail has come!
>   (I shouldn't have said that 'bout her hair.)
> Should I have written? Do I dare?
> I wonder if the mail has come.
>   (Not that I really care.)
>
>   KATHY CURRIER

(c) *A writer may take on another character's views,* perhaps his own when he was young, and pretend he doesn't know any more now than he did then, as did this girl in an account of her childhood:

TOMATOES

I was four when I had my first encounter with a tomato. We lived in Santa Barbara in a gray house separate from our neighbor by a garden of green and black stripes. The old man, Mr. Swift, fussed in his garden each dewy morning and worried his tomato plants into growing green and tall.

One early summer morning I was playing in the outskirts of the garden and happened to notice ladybugs crawling on Mr. Swift's prize plants. I didn't want them chewing up the fruits of my dear neighbor's labor so I decided to help him. I knew he would thank me when he found out I had gotten rid of the speckled pests for him. The only trouble was I was afraid to touch the bugs, so I had to break off each leaf that had an orange dot on it. I had gone through six rows when my mother called to me through the screened window that lunch was ready. Mr. Swift never knew that I tried to help him because I wasn't able to finish my job. A mysterious telephone call during lunch upset my mother and she spanked me right in the middle of a fried egg sandwich and wouldn't let me go outdoors the rest of the day.

It's a wonder that poor Mr. Swift's garden ever grew. One evening after supper my mother sent me out in the yard to break up a tea party that had been going all afternoon. Three of my dolls lay asleep on the ground around the orange crate tea table, and I feared they would be sick because it had turned very cold. I bundled them in my wagon and was pulling them to the back door when I noticed the garden.

Someone had played a mean trick on poor old Mr. Swift. Each of his tomato plants was hidden under a sawed-off milk carton. I knew they couldn't breathe inside there and would die if I didn't uncover them. It didn't take as long as getting rid of the bugs because I could just kick over each box with my foot. It was dark when I finished and got my dolls in the house. My mother scolded me for tracking in mud; I had been too late though, because next morning all the plants lay wilted on the ground. My neighbor didn't understand when I told him they died because they couldn't get their breath—he said, "The wind did it." I don't think he was a very smart farmer.

I don't know if Mr. Swift planted tomatoes again the next year because that winter we moved to Nebraska. We lived on the corner one block over and two blocks down from Grandma's house. In the spring Grandma gave me some seeds so I could plant a garden of my very own and learn responsibility. I decided I would have tomatoes because I already knew all about growing them. Besides, maybe I could send some to poor Mr. Swift. Daddy helped me. He spaded up the garden and planted the seeds, and then I watched them grow. My mother let me use my allowance to buy a sprinkling can from the dime store so I could water my garden. Daddy showed me which were the weeds and I tugged them out by the roots so they wouldn't choke my tomatoes. My garden grew and Daddy put a tall slender stake for each plant to climb. I watered my garden four times the first day and at least once a month after that. My garden grew as I played with the three boys next door, but I never got any tomatoes to send to my old neighbor. My mother told me that the odd blue flowers on my tomato plants were called four o'clocks, and I picked a bouquet for her.

CAROLINE SIEBLER

When you write indirectly, you must be consistent in style and viewpoint. You cannot use the Alternating Current without blowing the whole electric circuit. You must take a position or attitude or mood or role and stay in it throughout your writing. You are working on at least two levels. On the first, you must move authentically at all times. If your name is Alice and you are traveling through a Wonderland, you must believe in it all the time. You may have doubts and express amazement at what you see, but finally you must believe. And the Queens and Humpty Dumptys you encounter must be naïve and small-minded at all times on the first level, no matter how cleverly on the second level you manage to make them appear normal human beings.

In the story "Tomatoes," the author maintains the child's point of view beautifully except in a few spots, such as when she uses the word "outskirts" and the phrase "fruits of my dear neighbor's labor." Look for others. When you play another role than your own, you must stay in a voice that is right for that role.

> *Either stick to tradition or see that your inventions be consistent.*
>
> HORACE

(d) *A writer may make fun of pompous or pedantic persons or milksop and toadying persons by mimicking their language and pushing it to further excesses.* This exaggeration is often called burlesquing. For example:

IMPORTANT THINGS TO REMEMBER

Some things in this course will be more important than others. The most important thing to remember is that the War of the Tulips was fought before the Treaty of Pootrecht. Other important battles were the Alley Ambush of 1412 and the Small Slaughter of 1303. These are all important, but not as important as the date of the War of the Tulips.

(e) *A writer may blow up a trivial matter so large that it bursts.* For example:

The students who support the campaign to bring greasy and crumbly potato chips back to our cafeteria have completely rejected the traditions of Rich Central and are attempting to maliciously destroy the unity of our school

> . . . They are undoubtedly using innocent potato chips as a
> guise for their plot to overthrow the Cafeteria Honor
> Committee and instill chaos, disunity, and trash through-
> out the school . . .

This was the method Jonathan Swift used in *Gulliver's Travels,* a cutting satire of the way adult human beings conduct themselves in every
department of life. In one part of the book he blew men up and in
another he reduced them.

(f) *A writer may attack himself, or someone else he thinks needs
defending.*

To the Editor:

> Frank Forest ticks me off too. His office implies repre-
> sentation of all the students at Western, even though only
> six per cent voted for him. Doesn't he know he has to
> speak for ALL the students?
> What right does he have to be involved in any other
> organization besides Student Association? What right does
> he have in using any means possible to point out problems
> on the campus and in society? Who does he think he is—
> asking me to read the Kerner Commission Report, when I
> want to go out and hustle girls? Who is he to ask the
> Faculty why we must study Physical Geography while our
> cities burn? And even though he looks around his classes
> and sees more and more boredom and apathy, who does he
> think he is trying to correct it? Why does he keep bothering
> everybody? (He says because of wars, hate, racism, exploi-
> tation, authoritarian system); I say it's because of com-
> munist B.S.
> And if all this isn't enough, who gave him the idea that
> he could grow his hair long? Doesn't he know he's gotta
> look like the rest of us good students? Imagine, he thinks
> he can get away from our mold!
> As a responsible, mature student at Western, I will not
> let Frank Forest get away with this. I demand that he get
> his hair cut, not join any organization besides S.A. and the
> Chess club, not affiliate with those "dirty commies" and
> get back into the game.
> It is time the student body asks Forest to be like past
> presidents (let's see, what were their names?). After he gets

back into the game, think of the increased benefits for him and us. He can use his office as another glory to add to his record. We can continue getting drunk, going to boring irrelevant classes, living in dormitories (even until we're twenty), and when we send our kids to Kalamazoo Central [High School], we can thumb through our Physical Geography notes to find out what to do, or else call in the police. I can hardly wait.

(signed) Frank Forest

(g) *A writer may treat an act lightly that is ordinarily feared,* in order to reduce its power.

For example, Julie Beach, writing in a student newspaper, begins a column with these paragraphs:

> For those students who have not yet reached the grand old age of eligibility for a driver's license, here are a few helpful hints to get them through the ordeal.
>
> First of all, get plenty of sleep the night before the test is going to be taken. It helps one get a passing grade if the road signs can be read clearly.
>
> When walking out to the parking lot with the policeman, try to remember where the car is parked. It doesn't pay to put him into a grouchy mood by walking around the lot for half an hour.
>
> After getting into the car, remember to unlock the door on the passenger's side. If a tapping noise is heard, don't be alarmed. It is only the officer knocking on the window, trying to get in.
>
> The key should now be placed in the ignition, then turned. If for some unknown reason it won't turn, take it out and flip it over; it was probably in upside down . . .

(Reminder for persons working on tightening: in paragraph 2 the words "is going to be taken" could be omitted, and also the word "noise" in paragraph 4.)

(h) *A writer may turn upside down or outrageously distort the treatment of an event* in order to ridicule the straight, sober, or trite treatment it is usually given.

For example, sports writers frequently present a dull roundup of the year, in which they try to make every team's record look impressive. Steve Henson, sports editor for *The Torch* (newspaper of Rich Township High School Central Campus, Park Forest, Illinois, May

13, 1966), decided he had had enough of such trite stuff and wrote a spoof, part of which follows:

> . . . You all remember Central's football team, better known as Bill Barz. Smashing through the season nearly undefeated (well, you can't win 'em all) Barz and his teammates beat up everybody (if not on the field then out in the parking lot after the game). Cinderella Quanstrom put on his helmet and glass slippers and really turned in a great season. We can't forget guys like Denny Zumbahlen and Larry Morris, who averaged 38 tackles per game—31 of them after the whistle had blown.
>
> The Olympian Gridders were undefeated at home, using the advantage of the home field, the home refs, and Central's own Mr. Matheny running the scoreboard. It was simple—how else could you beat somebody 51–0? "Football Player of the Year" has to go to little 6'8", 295 lb. Bill Barz, to go along with his other awards of all-conference, all-area, all-suburban, all-state, and all-world . . .
>
> The varsity cagers were a great team, though, and exciting to watch. Hundreds of records were set during the season. Hot Dog Madderom averaged about 40 points per game and set a game high record when he tossed in 68 points against T. F. South. Randy hit on an amazing 22 field goals in that game in only 97 shots from the field. His best performance was in the Oklahoma game. Randy really scored and made several fine passes. Ed Younker tied the world record of falling asleep during a game (17 times) and Bob Moyer hit the most number of free-throws without a miss by a manager: 2 (also a world record). Bob Ewing grew the longest beard by a 6-foot forward in the entire South Suburban area . . .
>
> The Rich Central golf team has not been up to par this spring. Don Richmond, the "most consistent performer," really tore up the course at Olympia Fields last week, with a 67; in fact some fairways are still being repaired. He shot a Country Club record 58 last Saturday, with an eagle on the 5th hole, birdies on the 7th and 8th, and by forgetting to play the back nine . . .

One of Steve Henson's strategies in this column is to begin a statement in conventional manner and then end it with a kicker:

. . . who averaged 38 tackles per game—*31 of them after the whistle had blown.*

. . . He shot a Country Club record 58 last Saturday with an eagle on the 5th hole, birdies on the 7th and 8th, and *by forgetting to play the back nine.*

Another of his strategies is to present an actual fact and invent new facts which carry it to ridiculous heights:

. . . to go along with his other awards of all-conference, all-area, all-suburban, all-state, and *all-world.*

The truth is that Rich Central teams had a good season; for example, the baseball team won the District Championship and the football team lost only one game. But the indirect writer does not speak pure and whole fact. He risks being misunderstood. Mr. Henson's spoofing is consistent enough to make most readers aware of his intent, but even though he said, "we remind you to not believe everything you read" one student complained in a letter, saying,

You stated that *no* one ever went to *any* of the wrestling meets, and you did not even recognize the existence of a wrestling team.

This proves you have never gone to a wrestling meet; regular, or any of their district, sectional, or state meets : . . So shape up, and apologize for the unjust insult you tossed to our boys, or don't call yourself a fair sports editor.

Answering that letter, Mr. Henson said:

If you believed that I was not exaggerating when I said "nobody went to any of their meets" and that no wrestling team even existed, then you must have taken everything else in the column seriously too. You must have believed that I was not exaggerating when I said that Barz was 6'8" and 295 lb., or that Madderom scored 68 points against T. F. South, or that Zumbahlen and Morris tackled 31 men after the whistle, or that Ewing tossed the shot through the gym wall into the little theatre.

He shows by his answer that he realizes that indirect writing cannot alternate between straight and indirect expression. It must be consistent in its attitude.

At times all of us speak indirectly naturally and with ease. To a girl falsely modest about her pretty new dress, we say, "You look horrible,

Anne, absolutely rotten." In sarcasm we say to a person who has assigned us an unpleasant job, "Oh, this is lovely work—I wouldn't want to do anything else." A common line spoken by a soldier in World War II to another soldier digging a ditch was: "Whatya gripin' about? You're learnin' a trade." We mimic the way a teacher acts or talks. In dozens of ways, we speak with double tongue, knowing closely our audience and sensing how far we can go in indirection without losing them. As writers, we can learn to sustain and unify a piece of indirect communication which cuts and cuts down, astounds and delights, cajoles and teases.

WRITING TWENTY-FIVE: Write quickly a piece of indirect writing about something or someone you know well and feel strongly about. Whatever your degree of factualness or exaggeration, make your statement ring true. Do not attack or ridicule someone for something he did not do or say and cannot have done or said. All must be true, at least in the sense of being representative. Play with ideas, approaches, words. Then reconstruct, make consistent, tighten, sharpen, polish.

A short note about imaginative writing. Beginning writers often believe that really good writing, really impressive writing, must be made up rather than based on fact. Really. Look at that word. It's got *real* in it, like most good writing. Jonathan Swift wrote four stories of trips to fabulous lands where his Gulliver met giant and tiny men, people who lived in the sky, talking horses; but all the time Swift was writing about England, that real land, like America or China, where stupid and self-centered little men and big men go clumping around talking large and talking small and looking bad to anyone who can see them clearly, really. Lewis Carroll took his reader with Alice through the looking glass to places where egotistic and pompous queens and Tweedle brothers were certain of all sorts of foolishness. Lewis Carroll was also talking about England. And so really that most wise men in the United States and other countries think he is describing them. The best imaginative writing is based on the real.

> *"Of course you know your A B C?"*
> said the Red Queen.
> *"To be sure I do,"* said Alice.
> *"So do I,"* the White Queen whispered; *"we'll often say it over together, dear. And I'll tell you a secret—I can read words of one letter! Isn't* that *grand? However, don't be discouraged. You'll come to it in time."*
>
> LEWIS CARROLL

chapter 21

para-
phrasing

HENRY THOREAU was right to say that we should wear old clothes for major enterprises. We should confront our severest tests feeling most ourselves, with patches at elbow and knee that remind us of work already done and years already lived. And so with words, we should own them by use. They should sound right to us because we have heard them in our own mouths.

And yet the day will come when we attend the President's ball or our own wedding and we cannot wear old clothes. Then we need to have practiced wearing a stiff collar or it will redden our neck and stiffen our behavior. And so with words, if we do not practice using words stiff to us, we will never make them supple and comfortable in our mouths.

The dilemma: how to enlarge our vocabularies so as to write more accurately and precisely and yet avoid speaking a phony language.

One way is to increase our reading vocabulary—to look up new words in dictionaries and fix their meanings so securely they become as familiar to us as friends' faces. Then to use them strategically in our writing, but sparingly. We are apt to use new words clumsily, so they do not quite fit the grooves in which we place them, so they bring to our readers' faces smiles of amusement rather than admiration.

We must learn all the ways of a word before introducing it to others as ours. We can do this by studying good writers closely, *paraphrasing* their words into our words while trying to retain their meanings— all shades and connotations—exactly.

Often teachers say they never knew a subject until they began to teach it. Often writers say they never knew what another writer was saying until they tried to put it in their own words. Paraphrasing is difficult. You must thoroughly understand a writer before you can translate him into other words. And your words must not only make as much sense as his—and the same sense—but they must be written in American-English idiom, the way we Americans put such words together.

Here are several lines from Walter Lippmann's *Public Opinion,* a book written in 1922, still the most penetrating statement ever made on the subject of stereotyping. Mr. Lippmann wrote:

LIPPMANN I

There is, of course, some connection between the scene outside and the mind through which we watch it, just as there are some long-haired men and short-haired women in radical gatherings. But to the hurried observer a slight connection is enough. If there are two bobbed heads and four beards in the audience, it will be a bobbed and bearded audience to the reporter who knows beforehand that such gatherings are composed of people with these tastes in the management of their hair.

PARAPHRASE I

There is obviously some relation between the exterior situation and the mind with which we observe it, just as there are some black-jacketed men and tight-slacked women at drag raceways. But to the hasty perceiver a small relationship is sufficient. If there are two black jackets and four pairs of tight slacks in the crowd, it will be a black-jacketed and tight-slacked group to the reporter who believes ahead of time that such crowds are made up of persons who dress this way.

This paraphrase is valid. Its new phrases remain faithful to Lippmann's ideas. It uses specific examples of its own which reveal that the paraphraser understands the point of Lippmann's examples. And its phrasing remains true to American-English idiom, except in the somewhat ridiculous hyphenated word involving the opposite notions of tight and slack.

One cannot make a a good paraphrase by automatically substituting a dictionary synonym for each word in the original text. He must understand that text and the precise meaning in that context of each word the author has used. Like a good translator of a foreign language, he must take the thought into his mind and speak it forth again in natural, idiomatic phrases. A trained reader can easily see when a paraphraser is just substituting words rather than understanding and translating. For example, here is another statement by Lippmann:

LIPPMANN II

In all these instances we must note particularly one common factor. It is the insertion between man and his environment of a pseudo-environment.

A student attempting to paraphrase those sentences wrote:

PARAPHRASE II

In every case we must underly one general fact. It's the entering of a false behavior of humans in their society.

He is not using American-English idiomatically. Americans do not say that a person "underlies a fact." The next sentence in the paraphrase is totally unidiomatic. It does not make sense at all. Who is entering a false behavior? Is a behavior ever entered? The paraphraser has not even seen the principal relationship of the elements in Lippmann's second sentence. On one side is man and on the other his environment. Between them is a pseudo or false environment.

man	false	environment
	environment	

At one time the paraphrase substituted the word *behavior* for *environment* and at another time *society* for *environment*. Society may be man's environment at times, but behavior never. The weakness of *society* as a synonym for *environment* is that it is not all-inclusive. Other things, such as air, land, and water, may also be man's environment. A sounder word for *environment* would be *surroundings*, which could include both man and nature. If the paraphraser could not come up with as apt a synonym as *surroundings* for *environment*, he would have done better simply to repeat the word *environment*. In para-

phrasing one cannot always find a precise and accurate substitute word
—yet precision and accuracy are the first requirements.

PARAPHRASING ONE: Write a paraphrase of the following passage
by Paul Goodman:

> Consider a likely useful job. A youth who is alert and will-
> ing but not "verbally intelligent"—perhaps he has quit high
> school at the eleventh grade (the median), as soon as he
> legally could—chooses for auto mechanic. That's a good
> job, familiar to him, he often watched them as a kid. It's
> careful and dirty at the same time. In a small garage it's
> sociable; one can talk to the customers (girls). You please
> people in trouble by fixing their cars, and a man is proud
> to see rolling out on its own the car that limped in behind
> the tow truck. The pay is as good as the next fellow's, who
> is respected.
>
> So our young man takes this first-rate job. But what when
> he then learns that the cars have a built-in obsolescence,
> that the manufacturers do not want them to be repaired or
> repairable? They have lobbied a law that requires them
> to provide spare parts for only five years (it used to be ten).
> Repairing the new cars is often a matter of cosmetics, not
> mechanics; and the repairs are pointlessly expensive—a tail
> fin might cost $150. The insurance rates therefore double
> and treble on old and new cars both. Gone are the days of
> keeping the jalopies in good shape, the artist-work, of a
> proud mechanic. But everybody is paying for foolishness,
> for in fact the new models are only trivially superior; the
> whole thing is a sell.

In paraphrasing this passage, use words in a manner that belongs
to you and other Americans you know. Don't paraphrase the first
sentence by saying, "Now bring to your own attention a possibly
efficacious livelihood possessing utility." Your voice may differ from
other Americans of your age, but you would probably do better to
begin, "Think about a possibly valuable employment." If *employment* sticks in your pen, repeat *job*. Take up the challenge: try to
restate all statements but if all other words you find distort Mr.
Goodman's meaning, repeat his word. When you finish the first draft
of your paraphrase, read it aloud—the surest way to discover whether
or not you are writing in the American idiom. And expect that you
will need a second draft for sandpapering the edges. Read your paraphrase to others who have tried the same task.

PARAPHRASING TWO: Write a paraphrase of the following passage by Walter Lippmann.

STEREOTYPES

The subtlest and most pervasive of all influences are those which create and maintain the repertory of stereotypes. We are told about the world before we see it. We imagine most things before we experience them. And those preconceptions, unless education has made us acutely aware, govern deeply the whole process of perception. They mark out certain objects as familiar or strange, emphasizing the difference, so that the slightly familiar is seen as very familiar, and the somewhat strange as sharply alien. They are aroused by small signs, which may vary from a true index to a vague analogy. Aroused, they flood fresh vision with older images, and project into the world what has been resurrected in memory. Were there no practical uniformities in the environment, there would be no economy and only error in the human habit of accepting foresight for sight. But there are uniformities sufficiently accurate, and the need of economizing attention is so inevitable, that the abandonment of all stereotypes for a wholly innocent approach to experience would impoverish human life.

What matters is the character of the stereotypes, and the gullibility with which we employ them. And these in the end depend upon those inclusive patterns which constitute our philosophy of life. If in that philosophy we assume that the world is codified according to a code which we possess, we are likely to make our reports of what is going on describe a world run by our code. But if our philosophy tells us that each man is only a small part of the world, that his intelligence catches at best only phases and aspects in a coarse net of ideas, then, when we use our stereotypes, we tend to know that they are only stereotypes, to hold them lightly, to modify them gladly. We tend, also, to realize more and more clearly when our ideas started, where they started, how they came to us, why we accepted them. All useful history is antiseptic in this fashion. It enables us to know what fairy tale, what school book, what tradition, what novel, play, picture, phrase, planted one preconception in this mind, another in that mind.

The purpose of this exercise is to sharpen your understanding and command of words, to present to you words new and old to you that carry new shades of meaning. You must get your clues as to the meaning of each word from the context in which it appears. What is Lippmann's main point? How does that point weigh upon his words to bend or press them toward one of their possible meanings rather than another? You must use a good dictionary constantly and never be content with the first meaning of a word you encounter until you have looked further. Study all possible meanings and try to guess which one Lippmann intends here. For example, in another place in his book Lippmann says:

> The alternative to the use of fictions is direct exposure to the ebb and flow of sensation. This is not a real alternative, for however refreshing it is to see at times with a perfectly innocent eye, innocence itself is not wisdom, though a source and corrective of wisdom.

Considering what you have read so far in these excerpts from *Public Opinion*, which of the following words do you think most accurately paraphrases *innocent* here?

honest	fresh	unprejudiced	naive
harmless	moral	clear-eyed	guiltless

None of these words expresses precisely what Lippmann means by *innocent* here. No dictionary can give every possible meaning which an accurate writer may build up for a word. Probably the words *unprejudiced* and *fresh* are nearest to Lippmann's meaning of *innocent* here. *Unprejudiced* in the sense that the eye and the mind attached to it were not overly influenced by what they perceived in the past, but were approaching a new experience relatively freshly, ready to see the object before them as well as to see it in terms of past views of somewhat similar objects.

From this example, you can see that there are no limits to the depths of subtlety you may descend to in paraphrasing a keen and sensitive writer's sentences.

PARAPHRASING THREE: Choose a passage of one to two hundred words which challenges you to new perceptions. Copy it down and then paraphrase it. If possible, persuade another person to paraphrase it and compare your version with his.

> *It is not all books that are as dull as their readers.*
>
> HENRY THOREAU

There is another writing skill, akin to paraphrasing, which is needed in many pursuits today—summarizing. Committee meetings need to be reported on, minutes kept, projects reported to the boss. Someone else didn't go to the Student Association meeting and you have to tell him about the wild speech the new president made.

To make a good summary, a person must understand what he's summarizing and control the techniques of compression. A good model to look at is the encyclopedia entry written by an expert.

Here is such a summary about a historical figure. You may think it is fairly long, that it tells considerably more than you ever knew about Davy Crockett. But James D. Hart, the writer of *The Oxford Companion to American Literature* (1965), from which this biography is taken, had available to him a number of full-length biographies of Crockett in book form, probably two to four hundred pages long, and many articles. So this entry in his reference book is a highly distilled summary.

CROCKETT, DAVY (David) (1786-1836), born in Tennessee, spent a shiftless youth until his political career began (*c.* 1816) with his appointment as justice of the peace. He boasted that none of his decisions was ever reversed, because of his dependence on 'natural-born sense instead of law learning.' After being twice elected to the state legislature, he accepted a humorous proposal that he run for Congress, and to his surprise was elected, serving from 1827 to 1831, and again from 1833 to 1835. Because of his opposition to Jackson, the Whigs adopted him as a convenient tool through whom to draw the backwoods democracy to its standard. Davy was soon turned by skilful politicians into a frontier hero, whose picturesque eccentricities, backwoods humor, tall tales, shrewd native intelligence, and lusty pioneer spirit were all aggrandized. Whig journalists were soon at work, and in short order turned out such books, attributed to Davy, as *Sketches and Eccentricities of Col. David Crockett* (1833), *An Account of Col. Crockett's Tour to the North and Down East* (1835), *The Life of Martin Van Buren* (1835), and *Col. Crockett's Exploits and Adventures in Texas* (1836). With the exception of the last, which is posthumous, he may have had a hand in all these works, and he gladly claimed the *Tour* and life of Van Buren. Swallowing the Whig bait, he enjoyed his sudden rise to fame, and was glad to aid in propagating the myth, which, however, removed him from office, since his constituents would not tolerate his desertion of Democratic principles. Piqued, he left Tennessee to participate in the war for Texan independence, and a few months later died in the heroic defense of the Alamo, adding a final dramatic chapter to his career. *A Narrative of the Life of David Crockett, of the State of Tennessee* (1834) passes as his autobiography, although the claim has often been disputed. In any case the book has the robust manner attributed to Crockett, and contains fine examples of the farce and exaggeration of the tall tale.

This report includes a great number of specific facts—dates, offices held, political parties, names of books—encompassing a lifetime, and yet told in less than 350 words. Although James D. Hart, the editor, was writing a reference book, he did not present simply a collection of facts about Davy Crockett. He wrote the article with an angle: Here is Davy Crockett, who became an American hero celebrated in folk song and story. How did that happen? Did his life merit the myth that has arisen about him?

Remembering his audience of educated Americans, Mr. Hart did not begin the article by saying Crockett is a famous backwoods hero. He expected his audience to know that, and he got right down to telling how Crockett became famous. He omitted many facts about Crockett's life, partly because he had to save words (he was writing an 888-page reference work which names and describes thousands of persons, books, newspapers, and places), and partly because he did not want to divert the reader with facts not critical to his angle.

Mr. Hart did not think he was "letting the facts speak for themselves." He knew that all facts take on meaning because of their setting. He made his judgment about Crockett and chose facts which bore upon it. He presented Crockett as a man who rode luck to fame, allowed himself to be used by politicians, permitted his name to be connected to books that were in large measure not written by him, and deserved his fame as a skillful teller of tall tales.

> *Even the reporting of pure physical research findings, to cite an extreme example, is not unbiased. It is biased in favor of revealing the findings. In recent years the practical import and responsibility of such a bias has been felt deeply by*

atomic scientists. The question is not
whether a communication is biased. The
question is: toward what value system is
the communication biased?

GERHART WIEBE

To write this report, Mr. Hart had to know a great deal about
Davy Crockett. If he had known less, he would not have been able
to find so many facts which touched his angle. Like all good pieces
of writing, this report sounds authoritative partly because it implies
the writer knew more facts than he employed—the iceberg structure
as Hemingway called it.

For Mr. Hart, writing the encyclopedia entry was summarizing his
reading and thinking about Davy Crockett, easier than reporting a
meeting or a project involving a large number of persons, but presenting the same basic challenges: to capture the essential lines of
development, cause, effect, telling facts, the beliefs, consequences,
value of all the acts and words involved. Now suppose that Mr. Hart's
biography of Crockett is too long for another writer's purposes, and
he must summarize it. He must not only choose what he thinks are
the salient facts, but he must convey the subtle judgments of Crockett
that Mr. Hart speaks between his lines. Here is an attempt at such a
summary plainly retaining part of Mr. Hart's phraseology.

. . . born in Tennessee, spent a shiftless youth until 1816
when he became justice of the peace, then state legislator,
and national Congressman (1827-31, 1833-35). Opposed
Andrew Jackson, was made into frontier hero by Whig
journalists, who turned out such books attributed to Davy as
Sketches and Eccentricities of Col. David Crockett (1833).
He enjoyed propagating the myth. *A Narrative of the Life
of David Crockett* (1834) passes as his autobiography and
contains fine examples of farce and the tall tale. His constituents would not tolerate his deserting Democratic principles and he was voted out of office, whereupon he went to
Texas and died in the heroic defense of the Alamo.

Summary writing is excellent training for a writer: It forces him to
learn how to avoid wasting words. The principles involved in summarizing written or spoken material are essentially the same as for
other kinds of writing: look for oppositions that produce tension or
controversy. Quote persons as you quote a book or play or movie in
writing a critical review—enough to give the sound of the person and

the body of his argument and no more. State the generalizations with force, and if possible, zest. Your words can speak to each other in a committee report as well as in a satire.

WRITING TWENTY-SIX: Summarize something you have a desire or need to hold on to or use—the proceedings of a meeting, a chapter in a book, a speech you heard or read.

chapter 22
the
order
of
words

A CHILD OF SIX speaks as if he knew his meaning depends a great deal on word order. He wouldn't think of saying:

Of wouldn't he think saying.

And he wouldn't mess up the agreement signals in this sentence by using a word that signals twoness when it needs to signal oneness:

Johnny and Bill has his own bike.

And he wouldn't say:

It was nice of they.

because in the American grammatical system words like *he, she,* or *they* preceded by prepositions signal their relationship by changing to the object form (*him, her,* or *them*). Kids know this by the time they're six or eight. But sometimes they run into an adult—maybe a teacher—who is so worried about someone saying,

> You and me should go to the show.

that they say,

> She did not give it *to* you and *I*

when their unconscious and normal feeling for the signal would make them say,

> She did not give it *to* you and *me.*

J. D. Salinger made his hero Holden Caulfield, in *The Catcher in the Rye,* talk in this highly self-conscious ungrammatical way:

> I think I probably woke he and his wife up . . .

When Eudora Welty said that beginning and professional writers have the same troubles—not being serious or truthful—she might have added that they both have the same troubles with grammar. Most editors find little that is grammatically weak about the writing they edit, and when they do, the weaknesses are usually confined to a few troubles to be expected in the writing of anyone using the American grammatical system. Frequently they involve (1) confusing word order, (2) lack of clear signal by pronouns, and (3) verbs that do not signal which nouns they belong to.

In reading over the first draft of your writing, look first for these possible weak spots.

Word order signals meaning:

Original. When green I love the woods most of all.

Is that when I am green (sick at the stomach) (Young, like a green plant?), or when the woods are green? If the latter, the sentence should read:

Revision. I love the woods when green most of all.

or

Revision. I love the green woods most of all.

Thoreau opened Chapter Two of *Walden* with this sentence:

Original. At a certain season of our life we are accustomed to consider every spot as the possible site of a house.

His grammar would have been slightly confusing had he written:

Misrevision. We are accustomed to consider every spot at a certain season of our life as the possible site of a house.

Now *spot* and *season* are too close to each other. The phrase *at a certain season* should be close to *accustomed.*

In your writing, place next to each other those words which belong together in meaning. In the following sentence, the words in italics and in small capitals belong together in meaning but are separated from each other in position:

> This task, which George found highly agonizing, *grew* under the heat of the afternoon sun *soon* to be *unbearable,* and he QUIT working at it steadily EVENTUALLY.

When the words are rearranged (and a Whichery removed), the sentence is improved:

Revision. Under the heat of the afternoon sun, this agonizing task soon grew unbearable and George eventually quit working at it steadily.

The new order makes more sense, but it reveals the sloppy thought on the part of the writer. If the task "soon" grew unbearable, then why did George wait until "eventually" (whatever that means) to stop working at it? Either the "soon" or the "eventually" should be eliminated. Better yet, the writer might tell the reader what he means by "soon" or "eventually." How many hours or minutes?

Not every sentence changes its meaning with a change of word order. For example:

Original. Our minds thus grow in spots . . .
Revision. Thus our minds grow in spots . . .
Revision. Thus grow our minds in spots . . .
Revision. In spots thus grow our minds . . .

American-English grammar does not do all its signaling of meaning by word order.

REVISING TEN: Examine your last two long pieces of writing for blunders and weaknesses in word order. Write down on a separate sheet of paper your weak sentences and your revision of them. Reading aloud will help you in this task.

All writers and speakers occasionally let one of the segments of their sentence dangle out on a limb where it can fall off the tree. The most distinguished example is probably a sentence in Thomas Jefferson's First Inaugural Address:

> About to enter, fellow citizens, on the exercise of duties which comprehend everything dear and valuable to you, it is proper that you should understand what I deem the essential principles of our government, and consequently those which ought to shape its administration.

What is "about to enter" is Jefferson, not "you," who are fellow citizens, or "it," which here is one of those vague words which can't enter anything. A dangling construction fails to make clear who is doing what.

> While walking back from my English class, a squirrel came up and stepped on my foot.

Squirrels returning from English classes will upset anyone.

More examples of dangling constructions:

> Not finishing dinner until 8:30, another problem was in the making.
>
> By subtly mentioning to one set of parents that it would be nice if we could all be together, they usually take the hint and invite others.

But enough of these sinful errors. The good writer masters grammar in order to control his words, and meaning is his target. In a given paragraph, he may use an expression that is technically a dangling construction but nevertheless communicates his meaning clearly. For example, here is the masterful English writer William Hazlitt beginning the third paragraph of his essay on Sir James Mackintosh:

> To consider him in the last point of view first. As a political partisan, he is rather the lecturer than the advocate.

The first sentence does not show clearly who is doing the considering, and the whole group of words is not really a sentence at all. But it works, and an editor would be a fool to change it.

The commonest word-order change made in manuscripts by editors is to bring together subjects and verbs which have been thoroughly separated.

Original. *Professor Rending,* in approaching his subject, stumbled in circles, like a drunk.

Revision. In approaching his subject, *Professor Rending* stumbled in circles, like a drunk.

The method here is to pull out the segment of a sentence which is properly introductory, such as

When he was altogether prepared,

from the sentence in which it occurs:

President Wilson, when he was altogether prepared, presented his plan to the League of Nations.

and put it at the beginning.

Revision. When he was altogether prepared, President Wilson presented his plan to the League of Nations.

Often, such rearrangement allows the writer to eliminate a wasted expression such as a Whooery:

Original. Queen Gertrude is a weak person, who is, in spite of her faults, held in high regard by the three men in her life.

Revised. In spite of her faults, Queen Gertrude is held in high regard by the three men in her life.

All writers slip occasionally in making clear the reference between pronouns and their antecedents and the agreement between subject and verb. Therefore editors routinely check for these slips and find them frequently:

Sol and his buddy Georgie, who is his uncle's favorite baseball player, often *tries* to eat more than he can hold.

Revised. Sol and his buddy Georgie—his uncle's favorite baseball player—often *try* to eat more than they can hold.

The haggling and the bickering and the many hours of long drawn-out close reading I had to do when I was tired— it was all too much for me.

Revised. The haggling and the bickering and the many hours of long drawn-out close reading I had to do when I was so tired were all too much for me.

Note that most slips in pronoun reference and noun-verb agreement occur in long sentences which interrupt themselves with qualifications and side-trips. Editors examine such sentences closely, expecting meaning may have slid into a ditch.

Commonly professional writers use *which* and *that* to refer to the the word immediately preceding:

I like HAMBURGERS *which* are well done but not dry.

But increasingly these days, they are using *which* or *that* to refer to a whole action described in a number of preceding words:

> Renny approves of making changes now, which is all right with me.

You will do well to stay with the conservative practice of including a clear referent word immediately preceding *which* or *that* as in HAM-BURGERS *which*. If you ignore this practice and create a sentence that cannot be misunderstood by your reader, let it stand; but the odds are against you. Note that if the example contained three more words,

> Renny approves of making changes now in the plan, which is all right with me.

the reader couldn't be sure whether what is "all right with me" is the whole plan or the changes. The reader's understandable interpretation of the sentence is probably that *which* refers to *plan*, the word immediately preceding it.

These little matters of reference and agreement are the higgledy-piggledy of grammar. More crucial matters exist. When you think of word order—the way words come together in phrases and clauses (pieces, hunks, segments, absolutes, whatever you call them at the moment)—think of how you may control it to bring your writing alive.

Try telescoping three or four sentences into one, so that the first reaches out and grabs part of those that follow. Here are three sentences too closely related to stand separately:

Original. Immediately Juliet sees the only solution to her problem. That solution is suicide. This is a highly illogical choice.

You can tack on to the first sentence the essential elements of the second and third sentences:

Revision. Immediately Juliet sees the only solution to her problem— suicide, a highly illogical choice.

Such tacking-on must be done with care. If the sentences preceding those above have suggested that the author is judging Juliet's behavior, this revision may be clear. But if not, the reader might take the sentence to say that Juliet sees suicide as a highly illogical choice, a meaning which would jar against the notion embodied in "only solution."

Study the Tack-On sentences of good writers. You will see they frequently write down a subject and verb (and sometimes an object of the verb) and then simply add nouns or prepositional phrases, or phrases beginning with verb forms ending in *-ing* or *-ed*:

(a) *It would become a sorcery,*
            a magic.

ARCHIBALD MAC LEISH

(b) *There is a pulpit at the head of the hall,*
        occupied by a handsome gray-haired judge
            with a faculty of appearing pleasant and impartial
                to the disinterested spectator,
                            and
                        prejudiced and frosty
                    to the last degree
                to the prisoner at the bar.

MARK TWAIN

(c) *Each of us lives and works on a small part of the earth's surface,*
                moves in a small circle,
                        and
        of these acquaintances
                knows only a few intimately.

WALTER LIPPMANN

(d) *There were several ladies on board,*
        quite remarkably beautiful or good-looking,
        most of them, alas,
                    now dead.

IVAN TURGENEV

(e) *Let us arrange the contents of the heap into a line,* with
        the works that convey pure information at one end, and
        the works that create pure atmosphere at the other end, and
        the works that do both in their intermediate positions,
            the whole line being graded so that we pass from
                one attitude to another.

E. M. FORSTER

Occasionally an author uses the Tack-On method at the beginning of his sentence:

(f) Approaching Concord, doing forty, doing forty-five, doing fifty,
        the steering wheel held snug in my palms,
        the highway held grimly in my vision,
        the crown of the road now serving me (on the righthand curves),
                    now defeating me (on the lefthand curves),
        I began to rouse myself from the stupefaction which
            a day's motor journey induces.

E. B. WHITE

Most beginning writers need to nudge themselves into Tacking-On more often but the habit comes naturally to many persons. These statements were written by high school students not coached to Tack-On:

It is the great American tradition to shed your
anxieties and slothfully recline at the rim of a pond,
        resting and
        letting your unattended pole slip in the motionless wet.

While playing tennis I feel a sense
of freedom,
of being able to release the pent-up emotions from
           hours, days.

Man, who could have been so useful, is now dead,
not physically,
but emotionally and mentally.

Another way of exploiting the force of word-order in American-English is to place a word in an unusual or dominant position in the sentence.

> *[Ask] How many words out of their usual place, and whether this alteration makes the statement in any way more interesting or more energetic.*
>
> EZRA POUND

In many sentences the position of most weight for a word is the end. Frequently you can punch a word by putting it last in a sentence.

I went up to get a friend to go to class with. While waiting for her to get ready, I glanced around the dorm room. There were clothes, hairdryers, curlers, pressers, strewn all around the six-girl room. On the desk sat a book entitled *Social Disorganization*.

Note how the power of the statement would be lessened had the last sentence been written:

A book entitled *Social Disorganization* sat on the desk.

Of Sir Walter Scott, William Hazlitt wrote:

The old world is to him a crowded map; the new one a dull, hateful blank.

Had he placed his words in normal order, he would have written less forcefully:

The old world is a crowded map to him; the new one a dull, hateful blank.

Hazlitt's version forces the essential words to the end of each word group, where they gather power and achieve parallelism. To move a word out of normal position is to surprise the reader.

Normal Order. He was a lost man.
Unusual Order. He was a man lost.

A writer must develop an ear for normal word order and respect that order. If he continually scrambles it, he will confuse his reader rather than surprise him. The principle involved here is the old one mentioned in Chapter 11: repeat and vary. Vary the normal pattern, but sparingly. And don't forget to create a pattern of expectation in the first place.

REVISING ELEVEN: Take two of your past writings, one free writing and one a planned longer work, and go over each word and sentence to see where you can change word order and improve the clarity or force of your statements. Write in the changes on the original so you and others can see what difference they make in the writing.

chapter 23

observing conventions

FROM THE AGE OF FIVE onward most Americans know and practice the social conventions of their region and economic class. They say "thank you" and "you're welcome" and they eat with or without napkins or finger bowls or whatever is proper to the persons they associate with. Their ego is involved. They want to be liked, to feel right in the social circle they choose for themselves.

But most Americans don't know the publishing conventions of the educated world. They have been taught commas and semicolons as they have been taught "please" and "May I introduce my brother—" but each year in school they learn them for a test and forget them the following day. Why? Because they never expect to have their writing published, or even dittoed and passed around the class. Their ego is not involved.

But the torture of being required each year to learn again what they never learned and aren't going to remember once again this year is slow and unbearable. *Semicolon* becomes a dirty word. Like Mrs. Malaprop, they confuse *apostrophe* with *parenthesis* and *hypothesis* and *apotheosis*.

What should they do if they're sixteen or sixty and haven't learned the American conventional system for aiding readers in understanding the meaning of printed rather than spoken sentences? About the only chance they have is to study sentences in print and deduce for themselves the system. If they look to a textbook for rules, they will forget them again quickly and painfully.

If you're in this unhappy group of persons laden with guilt about commas and italics, begin observing. Construct generalizations which explain why certain mechanical conventions of print are used in the right-hand column of sentences below. For your convenience the left-hand column presents sentences naked and innocent of most punctuation or other signaling devices. Look at them first. Make your guess at what they need in the way of signals. Then study the signals printed in the right-hand column, which follow the normal conventions of writing published in most magazines or books. Note that they do not follow newspaper conventions, which are different from those of books.

DIALOGUE

Well, if we went to Raleigh we could get Mr. Isaacs Christmas candy. Before she could answer Mamas footsteps passed in the hall overhead so she said Don't you reckon we ought to stay closer-by than Raleigh? He turned to her. Look—are you sticking with me or not? She looked and said Yes. Let's go then. She scraped their dishes and left them in the sink and said I'll get my coat. Where from. My room. All right but come straight back.	"Well, if we went to Raleigh, we could get Mr. Isaac's Christmas candy." Before she could answer, Mama's footsteps passed in the hall overhead so she said, "Don't you reckon we ought to stay closer-by than Raleigh?" He turned to her. "Look—are you sticking with me or not?" She looked and said "Yes." "Let's go then." She scraped their dishes and left them in the sink and said, "I'll get my coat." "Where from?" "My room." "All right, but come straight back."

REYNOLDS PRICE

SEMICOLONS, COMMAS, PERIODS, DASHES, COLONS

Learn these marks in this order if you want to master punctuation quickly. The semicolon has only four or five major uses, the comma dozens. If you know a semicolon is not called for, you can bet wisely that what you need is a comma.

UNPUNCTUATED	CONVENTIONALLY PUNCTUATED
1. Well I agree you could say the atom bomb doesn't go boom	Well, I agree. You could say the atom bomb doesn't go boom;

it just obliterates a few hundred thousand people.

2. The world needs a little loosening of discipline and the schools need a little tightening of self-discipline.

3. He was no good for he had fallen apart at both the seams and the cuffs.

4. Renny a boy without guts was my enemy but Pedro a boy without guts was my friend.

5. I like Jackson Michigan Michigan City Indiana and Indianapolis Indiana.

6. It was a large city however I walked its streets without fear.

7. She was however a girl one could get along beautifully without.

8. Those days when Grandpa was a boy are long gone now the snows are deep and my Jaguar won't start.

9. In the last analysis Bertram doesn't measure up to the job.

10. Although a writer can lie about facts he should never lie about feelings.

11. When the moon comes over the woodshed behind the university library it feels out of place because Robert Frost is not there.

it just obliterates a few hundred thousand people.
(or):
　Well, I agree you could say the atom bomb doesn't go boom. It just obliterates a few hundred thousand people.

　The world needs a little loosening of discipline, and the schools need a little tightening of self-discipline.

　He was no good, for he had fallen apart at both the seams and the cuffs.

　Renny, a boy without guts, was my enemy; but Pedro, a boy without guts, was my friend.

　I like Jackson, Michigan; Michigan City, Indiana; and Indianapolis, Indiana.

　It was a large city; however I walked its streets without fear.
(or):
　It was a large city; however, I walked its streets without fear.

　She was, however, a girl one could get along beautifully without.

　Those days when Grandpa was a boy are long gone; now the snows are deep and my Jaguar won't start.

　In the last analysis, Bertram doesn't measure up to the job.
(or):
　In the last analysis Bertram doesn't measure up to the job.

　Although a writer can lie about facts, he should never lie about feelings.

　When the moon comes over the woodshed behind the university library, it feels out of place because Robert Frost is not there.

What a sight it is, to see Writers committed together by the eares, for Cere-monies, Syllables, Points, Colons, Com-

ma's, Hyphens, and the like? fighting,
as for their fires, and their Altars; and
angry that none are frightened at their
noyses, and loud brayings under their
asses skins?

BEN JONSON

12. I liked working there in the city next to the subway with its rattle its earth jar its grimy dirt that settled in the whorls of the ear and transferred itself from my sweating neck to my white collar by nine each morning.

I liked working there in the city next to the subway with its rattle, its earth jar, its grimy dirt that settled in the whorls of the ear and transferred itself from my sweating neck to my white collar by nine each morning. (or):
I like working there in the city next to the subway—with its rattle, its earth jar . . .

13. She is sweet notwithstanding her sour tongue and pretty as cottage cheese.

She is sweet, notwithstanding her sour tongue, and pretty as cottage cheese.

14. I always found Archie that sad bag of a man worth his weight in tin.

I always found Archie—that sad bag of a man—worth his weight in tin.

15. We walked across the square a place deserted by everyone but the familiar urchins who were dipping their feet in the fountain as if it were a cold day in February.

We walked across the square—a place deserted by everyone but the familiar urchins, who were dipping their feet in the fountain—as if it were a cold day in February.

16. She was a beautiful plump hen of a woman whose legs were properly pipe-stems ending with gigantic feet and I loved her clucking and pecking her squawking and fluttering.

She was a beautiful plump hen of a woman whose legs were properly pipe-stems ending with gigantic feet; and I loved her clucking and pecking, her squawking and fluttering.

17. The Alsatians were losing the Martian war quickly they had no missiles or orbiting vehicles.

The Alsatians were losing the Martian war quickly; they had no missiles or orbiting vehicles. (or):
The Alsatians were losing the Martian war quickly: they had no missiles or orbiting vehicles.

18. The General Velocipedes car was a beauty stinking heater buckling back wheels and valves that needed regrinding after a turn around the block.

The General Velocipedes car was a beauty: stinking heater, buckling back wheels, and valves that needed regrinding after a turn around the block.

SIGNALS FOR EMPHASIS

Conventionally, book and magazine writers and editors emphasize words with italics and quotation marks. When they use a word as an example of a word rather than as a regular part of a sentence, they usually put it in italics, which are indicated in handwriting or typescript by a single underline. (A double underline indicates small capitals; triple underline, capitals.)

19. The use of and is more difficult than most beginning writers realize.	The use of *and* is more difficult than most beginning writers realize.
20. Phrases like in terms of and with respect to can kill off an otherwise good speech.	Phrases like "in terms of" and "with respect to" can kill off an otherwise good speech.

More often than not, the words *say, call, refer to as* are followed by quoted words.

21. Those are what Mr. Wick calls "critical elements."

Frightened by Mrs. Clutched, their old third-grade teacher, many beginning writers use quotation marks around any word that would seem unusual in the sterile air of Mrs. Clutched's classroom. They say:

We had a "bunch" of good pitchers on our team and they used to "bug" each other constantly.

Nothing looks more square to an experienced editor or reader than this overuse of quotation marks. It implies either that the writer is a phony and won't admit that the words he's quoting belong in his vocabulary, or that the words *bunch* and *bug* are absolutely new to his readers in the use he has put them to. If they are slang, he should decide whether or not he wants to employ slang. If it is inappropriate to the subject and situation, he should not use it. If it is customarily set in italics—and there you can see the principle behind italics and quotation marks: to help the reader when he needs help, to inform him of what he is not apt to see on his own when he is reading in a healthy state of perception—then he should use italics or quotation marks.

NUMERALS

Unless numerals are being used in an article or book constantly, the professional writer conventionally writes in words those numbers that can be written in two words or one, and all others in numerals. He never begins a sentence with a numeral; for without an opening capital letter, a sentence looks as if it is part of the preceding sentence.

22. We counted twenty-four eggs within one hundred feet but there were 142 in the whole area.

If a sentence requires a number like 136 (written in numerals because it cannot be written in two words) and several other numbers, they are all written in numerals, for the sake of consistency:

23. ALWAYS: Three thousand and eighty-four men were ready; they each had 136 ounces of food, 32 feet of rope, 2 cans of suppressed napalm, and 12 rounds of ammunition.

NEVER: In the cages were rabbits in groups of 4, 3, and 6. 7 of them were kept in the barn in a larger enclosure, and 413 in all the buildings combined.

TITLES

Quotation marks are not used around words that appear above a piece of writing as its title. That would be like writing,

My name is "John."

Exception: When the title consists of, or in part of, words borrowed from another source, those borrowed words may be enclosed in quotation marks. Even then, if the borrowed word or phrase is well-known, it need not be quoted:

To Be or Not to Be a Ham

Writers citing names of other published works are careful to follow a consistent signaling system. Usually they *italicize* (or *underline*) names of whole works—a novel, history, encyclopedia, anthology, play, magazine, newspaper. They *put in quotation marks* smaller parts of those whole works: a chapter, article, poem, newspaper report (its title is its headline).

24. Jerry Kobrins Why Gleason Got the Headlines is another star-centered article in TV Guide but Up at Yale by Neil Hickey seriously looks at what college students are writing that could raise the level of television drama.

Jerry Kobrin's "Why Gleason Got the Headlines" is another star-centered article in *TV Guide,* but "Up at Yale" by Neil Hickey seriously looks at what college students are writing that could raise the level of television drama.

25. The Old which is the first chapter of Renfrew's latest book The Gnu and the Auld is a masterpiece of humor.

"The Old," which is the first chapter of Renfrew's latest book, *The Gnu and the Auld,* is a masterpiece of humor.

SIGNALING POSSESSION

The apostrophe to signal possession is the hardest conventional sign to remember because it is slowly fading away in use. In formal names printed in capital letters, it is no longer used:

VETERANS ADMINISTRATION

In the days before dictionaries began to establish conventions firmly (Dr. Samuel Johnson's *Dictionary* of 1755 solidified spelling and other writing conventions in England, and Noah Webster's *Dictionary* of 1828 did the same in America), writers often used the apostrophe to indicate plurals, as did Ben Jonson in 1640 in the line quoted in this chapter:

> . . . Points, Colons, Comma's

(Capital letters were conventionally used in England and American then for most major nouns in a sentence), and in Chaucer's day (1400), possession was signaled by an *-es* ending on words:

> As dide Demociones doghter deere . . .
> That lordes doghtres han in governaunce . . .

Chaucer used no apostrophes for possession, although here the daughters in both lines belong to the fathers mentioned. Writing about two hundred years later, Shakespeare commonly used an *-s* ending to signal possession, but still without an apostrophe:

> It was a Lordings daughter, the fairest one of three . . .
> A womans nay doth stand for nought . . .

Conventions in publishing change like conventions in ladies' dresses but not as fast. At the moment, most printed books and magazines in the United States are employing the apostrophe to signal possession, even though it is no more necessary in most instances than in Shakespeare's day.

26. I got my moneys worth when all the ladies cakes were left in my car. | I got my money's worth when all the ladies' cakes were left in my car.

27. A womans nay doth stand for nought. | A woman's nay doth stand for nought.

28. Jamess trouble was not the Worthingtons trouble. | James's trouble was not the Worthingtons' trouble.

SCHOLARLY WRITING

Two common miswritings in scholarly work are the abbreviation for *page* or *pages* and the signal for paragraph indention.

WRONG: pg (pgs)   RIGHT: p. (pp.)

℗   ¶

Pg. may be some lazy person's abbreviation for *pig*, but it is not the conventional abbreviation for *page*. Understandably persons make the sign of a double-stemmed capital P to indicate *paragraph*, but the proper sign has nothing to do with the letter P. It is a sign used in illuminated manuscripts before 1440, then without such long stems, and still in use today.

Footnotes are a pain to writers, readers, editors, and printers; but some scholarly tasks require them so that scholar-readers may trace easily the steps through which a writer made his case. Like all conventions, footnotes are being constantly changed in form, usually in the direction of simplicity.

In footnotes, *Ibid.* means "the same as above." The following set of footnotes reveals a standard pattern. Why do some *Ibid.* entries include page numbers and some not?

1 Fred M. Oliver, *Love Problems of High School* (New York, 1939), pp. 33-34.
2 *Ibid.*
3 *Ibid.*, p. 101.
4 Karl Heimson, "The Courting Pattern," *New Ways in Education* (Englewood Cliffs, Texas, 1956), p. 555.
5 Oliver, p. 101.
6 Heimson, p. 420.
7 *Ibid.*, pp. 419-425.
8 William G. Looney and James Brass Smith, editors, *Thinking and Talking* (New York, 1965), p. 13.
9 George Walker, "Sex," *The Teacher's Magazine,* vol. 14 (June, 1967), pp. 13-14.

Text of paper employing above footnotes:

Fred M. Oliver, psychologist at Nendy High School, Oak Pond, New York, cites the informal conversation of students. Jane, a senior, says "I'm mad for you, John," meaning in the new dialect of her group that she has decided to take John's part in his quarrel with his girl friend Susan.[1] This new game, played at several high schools in the area,[2] represents a clever playing with words—taking old slang or in-group expressions and giving them their literal rather than traditional meaning. "Cool it" to these students means to open the windows or turn down the thermostat.[3]

Conventional students in a Kansas high school do just the opposite. They develop a new language for love and dating which consists of giving new double meanings to the commonest expressions, like "Wash the linoleum" or "Is it cold out?"[4]

Oliver[5] and Heimson,[6] however, both state explicitly that they admire high school students' ability to invent new language. Heimson presents six pages of new expressions created by students in a high school of only one-hundred students.[7] Thirteen out of the twenty-five articles in a recent anthology on language center on the speech of American teenagers.[8] Parallels with these American developments have been found in Hungary by George Walker.[9]

This passage is footnoted in conventional form, but it is ridiculously overfootnoted. The reader couldn't stand that many footnotes in that short a space. The writer of these paragraphs is so overwhelmed by his sources that he has lost command of his own expression and line of development. If you are required to use footnotes, reserve them for documenting ideas or facts either so unusual and controversial or so detailed that they need to be credited to a writer. Footnote what readers are likely to want to check further.

A list of books, which occurs at the end of a paper, an article, a chapter, or a book, usually contains fuller information about the books: the publisher, number of volumes in a set, etc. In footnotes, names of authors are arranged in normal order: first name first. In a bibliography, they are arranged last name first, so that the order of the books in the list will be useful, easy to consult because arranged by authors' last names alphabetically:

BIBLIOGRAPHY

1. Heimson, Karl. "The Courting Pattern," *New Ways in Education* (Englewood Cliffs, Texas, Pinetree Press, 1956), 158 pp.

The "158 pp." indicates that the volume contains 158 numbered pages, a way to show the reader how extensive the book is.

BIBLIOGRAPHY

2. Looney, William G. and James Brass Smith, editors, *Thinking and Talking* (New York, Mouth Press, 1965), 450 pp.
3. Oliver, Fred M. *Love Problems of High School* (New York, Kissinger Co., 1939), 413 pp.

In short papers documenting notes make more sense at the end of the paper than as footnotes at the foot of each page. Footnotes are hard to type at the bottom of the page—the writer can't gauge how much room he needs. And they are hard to set in type—the printer can't gauge the room either, and he must shift to smaller type as well. An intelligent alternative to footnotes used frequently in scientific publications employs parenthetical references: (2: 33-34), which means that the book referred to is number 2 in the bibliography and the references are to pages 33 and 34 in it. Part of the above text would then be written this way, referring to the piece of bibliography given above, which would be printed at the end of the paper or article. The paper would contain no footnotes:

> This new game, played at several high schools in the area (2: 33-34), represents a clever playing with words—taking old slang or in-group expressions and giving them their literal rather than traditional meaning. "Cool it" to these students means to open the window or turn down the thermostat (3: 101):

The wise writer and editor adopt a pattern of documentation of sources that fits the purposes of the writer and, as much as possible, of the reader. If the place of publication and publisher are not apt to be significant to the reader, the writer omits them from footnotes and supplies them only in bibliography. Almost always he gives page references and dates of publication because they are useful to the reader in locating material and in assessing the up-to-dateness of assertions and facts. All conventions need the help of common sense: the man who speaks outside in February with his head bare in order to observe a convention may find others soon observing his funeral.

Here are a few more models of conventional footnotes: For a book:

1 George M. George. *The Georgeness of the World* (New York, George Book Company, 1918), pp. 33-34.

For a magazine:

2 Margaret Mead, "Trends in Personal Life," *The New Republic* (September 23, 1946), 115: 348.

For a newspaper article:

3 "College Dating Changes Pattern," *The New York Recorder*, June 2, 1952, p. 13.
4 George Kriver, "Bronx Hospital Planned," *The Bronx Bomber*, June 3, 1967, p. 1.

For a government document:

5 *Dating Problems in Urban High Schools*, United States Health Service Publication 1090 (Washington, 1953), p. 7.

For an encyclopedia:

6 "Harvard University," *The Encyclopedia Britannica*, 14th edition.

For an excerpt from a book not read in the original but seen reproduced in part in another book:

7 Francis E. Merrill, *Courtship and Marriage* (New York, 1949), in Edwin R. Clapp and others, eds., *The College Quad* (New York, 1951), p. 74.

For a personal interview or conversation arranged by the author:

8 Interview with John Rogers, Dean of Men, Northside High School, Chicago, Illinois, April 4, 1967.

BORROWING WORDS

Conventionally the professional writer commands his words and those of others, but he never implies he owns the words of others. He inserts borrowed words naturally into his own sentences.

Wasting Borrowed Words:

His dearest relative described him as "He was a great guy, full of fun, but gentle."

Commanding Borrowed Words:

His dearest relative described him as "a great guy, full of fun, but gentle."

The professional writer does not refer to a statement he is quoting as a *quote*, for he is doing the quoting, not the author. He calls the statement a *statement,* an *assertion,* an *argument,* etc. He remembers that quotes do not speak, only persons.

For example, one quote states: "The Undersecretary rejected the budget proposals of the whole Council."

For example, an unidentified London *Times* reporter states that "The Undersecretary rejected the budget proposals of the whole Council."

The professional writer remembers that in conversation he must say "I quote" but in writing he indicates this act by quotation marks.

War Magazine says, and I quote, "Wretches strew the beaches in a lovely pattern."

War Magazine says, "Wretches strew the beaches in a lovely pattern."

If you respect your writing, learn the craft and learn the conventional systems of signaling meaning to the reader. But do not use these signals as a substitute for the order and clarity you must achieve with words. If you want the reader to become excited, you must write excitingly. You cannot force excitement by putting three exclamation marks at the end of your sentence! ! !

List of Sources

List of Sources

Page

1 Henry David Thoreau, *Journals*, July 14, 1852.

2 Ralph Waldo Emerson, "Nature," *The Complete Essay and Other Writings*, edited by Brooks Atkinson (New York, The Modern Library, 1950), p. 17.

3 Quoted in Clara M. Siggins, "Then It Got Buggles," *College Composition and Communication* (February, 1962), 6. 56.

3 Friedrich Nietzsche, *Beyond Good and Evil* (Chicago, Regnery, Gateway Edition, 1955), p. 77.

5 Gene Baro, "News and the Newsman," *The Reporter* (September 21, 1967), p. 50.

5 Eudora Welty, *Delta Wedding* (New York, New American Library, Signet Edition, 1963) p. 220.

5 Eudora Welty, quoted by Reynolds Price, "A Kind of Valedictory," *The Archive*, Duke University (April, 1955), p. 2.

6 Samuel Johnson, source unknown.

8 Samuel Butler, *Works* (London, Jonathan Cape, 1923–26), XVIII, 210.

12 Wallace Stevens, "Adagia," *Opus Posthumous* (New York, Alfred A. Knopf, 1957), p. 158.

15 Donald Hall, "A Clear and Simple Style," *The New York Times Book Review* (May 7, 1967), p. 30.

16 E. M. Forster, *Aspects of the Novel* (New York, Harcourt, Brace, 1927) p. 197.

16 Henry Moore, "The Painter's Object," *The Creative Process*, edited by Brewster Ghiselin (New York, New American Library, Mentor Edition, 1955), p. 77.

18 Alfred Kazin, "The Language of Pundits," *Atlantic Monthly* (July 1961), pp. 73–74.

19 Wallace Stevens, "Adagia," *Opus Posthumous* (New York, Alfred A. Knopf, 1957), p. 162.

22 John Ciardi, "Work Habits of Writers," *On Writing, by Writers*, edited by William W. West (Boston, Ginn, 1966), p. 153.

24 Sidney Cox, *Indirections* (New York, Viking, Compass Books, 1962), p. 130.

25 William Hazlitt, "On the Familiar Style," *The Hazlitt Sampler* (New York, Fawcett World Library, 1961), p. 228.

25 Benjamin Franklin, quoted in Carl Becker, *The Declaration of Independence* (New York, Alfred A. Knopf, Vintage Books, 1958), pp. 208–209.

27 Wallace Stevens, "Adagia," *Opus Posthumous* (New York, Alfred A. Knopf, 1957), p. 169.

31 Samuel Butler, *The Note-Books* (London, Jonathan Cape, 1926), p. 97.

32 Henry David Thoreau, *Walden and Other Writings* (New York, The Modern Library, 1937), p. 88.

33 Lewis Carroll, *Through the Looking Glass* (New York, Random House, 1946), p. 36.

33 Norman Podhoretz, *Making It* (New York, Random House, 1967), p. 106.

Page

38 Henry David Thoreau, *Walden and Other Writings* (New York, The Modern Library, 1937), p. 86.

39 Bernard Shaw, *John Bull's Other Island* (New York, Harper & Brothers, 1942), p. 209.

41 Jack London, *People of the Abyss* (New York, Harcourt, Brace, 1946), p. 213.

42 Ralph Waldo Emerson, "Thoreau," *Lectures and Biographies* (Boston, Houghton Mifflin, 1893), p. 362.

43 Lynnette Madama, "Double Solitaire," *The Western Review* (Western Michigan University, October 25, 1966), p. 5.

45 Thomas Henry Huxley, To Charles Kingsley, September 23, 1860, in Leonard Huxley, *Life and Letters of Huxley* (New York, D. Appleton, 1901), I, 235.

49 Michihiko, Hachiya, *Hiroshima Diary* (Chapel Hill, University of North Carolina Press, 1955), pp. 11, 91–92.

50 Mario Roveda, "Through the Gates," *Unduressed* (Western Michigan University, April 7, 1968), p. 2.

53 Darcy Cudlip, "First Car," *Ibid.*

56 Sidney Cox, *Indirections* (New York, Viking, 1962), p. 131.

62 Frank O'Connor interviewed by Anthony Whittier, *Writers at Work: The Paris Review Interviews,* First Series (New York, Viking, 1959), p. 169.

62 Kathleen Bolinger, "Linus's Blanket," *Unduressed* (Western Michigan University, December 16, 1968), p. 5.

65 Samuel Butler, *The Note-Books* (London, Jonathan Cape, 1926), p. 106.

66 George Bernard Shaw, "Who I Am, and What I Think," *Selected Non-Dramatic Writings,* edited by Dan H. Laurence (Boston, Houghton Mifflin, 1965), p. 449.

69 T. S. Eliot interviewed by Donald Hall, *Writers at Work: The Paris Review Interviews,* Second Series (New York, Viking, 1965), p. 96.

70 Marianne Moore interviewed by Donald Hall, *Ibid.,* p. 82.

71 William Hazlitt, "On Paradox and Common-place," *Table Talk* (London, J. M. Dent, 1952), p. 146.

72 William Hazlitt, "On the Ignorance of the Learned," *Ibid.,* pp. 70–71.

74 John Stuart Mill, *On Liberty* [1859] (New York, Appleton-Century-Crofts, 1947), p. 36.

77 William Shakespeare, *The Merchant of Venice,* III, i.

79 Richard Thurman, "Not Another Word," *The New Yorker* (May 25, 1957), pp. 37–44.

97 William Wordsworth, "The Prelude," *Complete Poetical Works* (Boston Houghton Mifflin, 1904), p. 1956.

97 Mark Twain, *Huckleberry Finn* (New York, Houghton Mifflin, 1958), pp. 3–4.

98 J. D. Salinger, *The Catcher in the Rye* (New York, New American Library, 1953), p. 144.

99 Sidney Cox, *Indirections* (New York, Viking, 1962), p. 6.

99 Joy Pepper, "Blinded," *Unduressed* (Western Michigan University, April 14, 1969).

Page

103 Karen Bosine, "We Were Getting Along," *Ibid.,* p. 12.

106 Truman Capote interviewed by Pati Hill, *Writers at Work: The Paris Review Interviews,* First Series (New York, Viking, 1959), pp. 294–295, 296–297.

114 Dr. Seuss, *Horton Hatches the Egg* (New York, Random House, 1940), n. p.

120 Ralph Waldo Emerson, "The American Scholar," *The Complete Essays and Other Writings,* edited by Brooks Atkinson (New York, The Modern Library, 1950), p. 47.

121 James Baldwin, *The Fire Next Time* (New York, Dell, 1964), pp. 14–15.

121 N. H. and S. K. Mager, editors, *The Pocket Household Encyclopedia* (New York, Pocket Books, 1953), p. 168.

121 Irma S. Rombauer and Marion Rombauer Becker, *The Joy of Cooking* (Indianapolis, Bobbs-Merrill, 1953), p. 313.

122 Henry David Thoreau, source unknown.

124 Dave O'Connor, "Barbaric?" *Unduressed* (Western Michigan Unversity, April 14, 1969), p. 2.

129 Henry David Thoreau, *Journals,* April 22, 1851.

130 Henry David Thoreau, *Journals,* October 4, 1851.

134 Sidney Cox, *Indirections* (New York, Viking, 1962), p. 132.

135 Oscar Wilde, *A Woman of No Importance,* quoted in *The Wit and Humor of Oscar Wilde,* edited by Alvin Redman (New York, Dover, 1952), p. 33.

138 William Carlos Williams, "The Dance," *The Collected Later Poems* (New York, New Directions, 1950), p. 11; and "Poem," *The Collected Earlier Poems* (1951), p. 340.

140 Wallace, Stevens, "Adagia," *Opus Posthumous* (New York, Alfred A. Knopf, 1957), p. 176.

140 Norman Podhoretz, *Making It* (New York, Random House, 1967), pp. 139–142.

142 Mary McCarthy interviewed by Elisabeth Niebuhr, *Writers at Work: The Paris Review Interviews,* Second Series (New York, Viking, 1965), p. 302.

146 American Humane Association, Denver, Colorado, undated pamphlet.

147 Frederick Douglass, *Life and Times of Frederick Douglass* (New York, Collier Books, 1962), 484–485.

149 Donald Hall, "A Clear and Simple Style," *The New York Times Book Review* (May 7, 1967), p. 30.

150 E. B. White, "Letter to the East," *The New Yorker* (February 18, 1956), p. 72.

150 William Hazlitt, "On Shakespeare and Ben Jonson," *The Hazlitt Sampler* (Greenwich, Connecticut, Fawcett Publications, 1961), p. 16.

152 Erich Fromm, *Man for Himself* (New York, Rinehart, 1947), p. 105.

156 Barnett Newman, "For Impassioned Criticism," *Art News* (Summer, 1963), p. 58.

160 Ken Macrorie, "Almost a Proper Integrity," *North American Review* (Summer, 1964), p. 75.

Page

161 Ken Macrorie, "Arriving and Departing," *The Reporter* (September 13, 1962), p. 52.

162 Ray Bradbury, "Seeds of Three Stories," *On Writing, by Writers*, edited by William W. West (Boston, Ginn, 1966), p. 49.

163 Kenneth Clark, "The Value of Art in an Expanding World," *Hudson Review* (Spring, 1966), p. 23.

163 Samuel Butler, quoted in Henry Festing Jones, *Samuel Butler* (London, Macmillan, 1920), II, 294–295.

165 Ezra Pound, *ABC of Reading* (New York, New Directions, 1960), p. 62.

167 James Thurber interviewed by George Plimpton and Max Steele, *Writers at Work: The Paris Review Interviews*, First Series (New York, Viking, 1959), p. 87.

168 Eudora Weltz, "Must the Novelist Crusade?" *Atlantic Monthly* (October, 1965), p. 106.

170 Wallace Stevens, "Adagia," *Opus Posthumous* (New York, Alfred A. Knopf, 1957), p. 170.

171 Robert Lipsyte, *The New York Times* (August 5, 1966).

176 William Hazlitt, "On the Ignorance of the Learned," *Table Talk* (London, J. M. Dent, 1952), p. 71.

179 Barry Guitar, "Reviewpoint," *The Western Review* (Western Michigan University, March 21, 1966), p. 3.

180 Ernest Hemingway interviewed by George Plimpton, *Writers at Work: The Paris Review Interviews*, Second Series (New York, Viking, 1965), p. 235.

181 Tom Randolph, "Natural Athletes, Natural Rhythm," *Western Herald* (Western Michigan University, April 9, 1969), p. 2.

184 Malcolm X, *Malcolm X Speaks*, edited by George Breitman (New York, Grove Press, 1965), pp. 137–139.

186 Bob Koehler, "Freedom Fighter," *The Western Review* (Western Michigan University, February 21, 1967), p. 1.

188 Oscar Wilde, *The Importance of Being Earnest, The Plays of Oscar Wilde* (New York, The Modern Library, n.d.), p. 54.

189 Bernard Shaw, in *Ellen Terry and Bernard Shaw: A Correspondence*, edited by Christopher St. John (New York, The Fountain Press, 1931), pp. 113–114.

196 Ralph Waldo Emerson, "Self-Reliance," *The Complete Essays and Other Writings*, edited by Brooks Atkinson (New York, The Modern Library, 1950), p. 165.

199 A. A. Milne, *The House at Pooh Corner* (New York, E. P. Dutton, 1928), p. 96.

201 Lewis Carroll, *Alice in Wonderland* (New York, Random House, 1946), pp. 140–141.

202 W. Nelson Francis, "Pressure from Below," *College Composition and Communication* (October, 1964), pp. 147–148.

204 E. E. Cummings, "XIV," *Poems, 1923-1954* (New York, Harcourt, Brace and World, 1954), p. 397.

204 Joseph Conrad, preface to *The Nigger of the "Narcissus"* in *Three Great Tales* (New York, Alfred A. Knopf, Vintage Books, n.d.), p. ix.

Page

208 Nancy Hunter, "In Small Towns," *Unduressed* (Western Michigan University, April 14, 1969), p. 1.

209 Lewis Carroll, *Through the Looking Glass* (New York, Random House, 1946), p. 29.

210 Henry David Thoreau, *Walden and Other Writings* (New York, The Modern Library, 1937), pp. 123, 288.

210 William Hazlitt, *The Spirit of the Age* (London, Oxford University Press, 1935), p. 13.

211 Erich Fromm, *Man for Himself* (New York,Rinehart, 1947), pp. 99, 101.

214 Mark Twain, *Huckleberry Finn* (New York, Houghton Mifflin, 1958), pp. 85–88.

219 Kathy Currier, "Triolet," *Aurora 66*, Portage Northern High School, Portage, Michigan, p. 23.

221 Horace, *The Art of Poetry* in *The Complete Works*, edited by Casper J. Kraemer, Jr. (New York, The Modern Library, 1936), p. 401.

222 Frank Forest, *Western Herald* (Western Michigan University, October 21, 1968), p. 2.

223 Julie Beach, "Driving's a Dilemma," *The Lakeview Crystal* (Lakeview High School, Battle Creek, Michigan, February 4, 1966), p. 4.

227 Lewis Carroll, *Through the Looking Glass* (New York, Random House, 1946), pp. 143–144.

228 Walter Lippmann, *Public Opinion* (New York, Macmillan, 1922), p. 87.

229 Walter Lippmann, *Ibid.,* 16.

230 Paul Goodman, *Growing Up Absurd* (New York, Random House, 1960), pp. 19–20.

231 Walter Lippmann, *Public Opinion* (New York, Macmillan, 1922), pp. 89–91.

232 Henry David Thoreau, *Walden and Other Writings* (New York, The Modern Library, 1937), p. 97.

233 James D. Hart, *The Oxford Companion to American Literature* (London, Oxford University Press, 1965).

234 Gerhart Wiebe, "Mass Communications," in Eugene and Ruth Hartley, *Fundamentals of Social Psychology* (New York, Alfred A. Knopf, 1952), p. 179.

237 Gabor Peterdi, *Printmaking* (New York, Macmillan, 1959), p. xxii.

238 J. D. Salinger, *Catcher in the Rye* (New York, New American Library, 1953), p. 157.

240 William Hazlitt, *The Spirit of the Age* (London, Oxford University Press, 1904), pp. 130–131.

243 Archibald MacLeish, "Poetry and the Press," in *Thought and Statement,* edited by William G. Leary and James Steel Smith (New York, Harcourt, Brace, 1960), p. 481.

243 Mark Twain, "The Evidence in the Case," *Ibid.,* p. 373.

243 Walter Lippmann, "Stereotypes," *Ibid.,* p. 221.

243 Ivan Turgenev, "A Fire at Sea," *Ibid.,* p. 25.

243 E. M. Forster, "Anonymity, An Inquiry," *Ibid.,* pp. 440–441.

243 E. B. White, "Walden," *Ibid.,* p. 39.

Page

244 Ezra Pound, *The ABC of Reading* (New York, New Directions, 1960), p. 64.

244 William Hazlitt, *The Spirit of the Age* (London, Oxford University Press, 1904), p. 76.

246 George Eliot, *Middlemarch* (New York, Houghton Mifflin, 1956), p. 52.

247 Reynolds Price, *A Long and Happy Life* (New York, Avon Books, 1960), p. 121.

248 Ben Jonson, *Timber, or Discoveries,* in English Prose, 1600–1660, edited by Victor Harris and Itrat Husain (New York, Holt, Rinehart, and Winston, 1965), p. 330.

Index

Index